The TV Wine Guy

The TV Wine Guy

Taking the snobbery out of wine . . .
one bottle at a time

Alan Aylward Jonathan Welsh James Bruce

WINDING
STAIR
PRESS

The TV Wine Guy
Text copyright © 2002 by Forevergreen Television and Film Productions Inc.

Cataloguing in Publication Data is available.

ISBN 1-55366-244-X

Winding Stair Press
An imprint of Stewart House Publishing Inc.
290 North Queen Street, #210
Toronto, Ontario
Canada M9C 5K4
1-866-574-6873
www.stewarthousepub.com

Credits
Every effort has been made to trace the ownership of the illustrations in this Title. The Authors will gladly receive any information that will enable them to rectify any error or omission in a future reprint.

Photographs have been supplied by the individual wineries unless otherwise credited below.

John Nadeau's photo, used throughout in "Notes from the Cellar", courtesy of John Nadeau.
Michael Dubrule: Pages 2, 21, 22 (top), 23(top), 30(bottom), 43(top), 46, 53(bottom), 152, 182, 185, 187, 200, 201.
Steven Elphick: Pages 94, 97, 112, 139, 146, 147, 150(top), 178, 183, 195, 196, 199.
Jose Crespo: Front cover. Pages: 91, 100, 102, 104, 106, 109.
Moira Saganski: Pages 137.
Archie Hood: Page 141(top).
Karen Reid, RGD: Page 141(bottom diagram).
Wine Council Of Ontario: Pages 3, 4, 6-7(map), 20, 22(bottom), 23(bottom).
Niagara Parks Commission: Pages 12(top), 42, 43(bottom), 47(top).
Kurtz Orchards: Page 44(top).
Niagara Peninsula Conservation Authority: Pages 126, 127.
Wine Country Cooking School: Page 150(bottom).
LIV Restaurant: Page 151.
Good Earth Cooking School: Pages 153, 154, 155.
The McMichael Gallery: Pages 176, 177.

Photographs on pages 24, 25, 31, 88, 89, 90 used by permission of the St. Catharines Museum.
Photograph on page 59 used by permission of the Mackenzie Heritage Printery Museum.
Photographs on pages 60, 61 used by permission of the Laura Secord Homestead.
Photographs on pages 108, 110, 111 used by permission of the Jordan Historical Museum.

This book is available at special discounts for bulk purchases by groups or organizations for sales promotions, premiums, fundraising and educational purposes. For details, contact: Stewart House Publishing Inc., Special Sales Department, 195 Allstate Parkway, Markham, Ontario L3R 4T8. Toll free 1-866-474-3478.

1 2 3 4 5 6   07 06 05 04 03 02

Printed in Canada

Contents

Acknowledgments

We'd like to take this opportunity to thank and express our gratitude to the many people at the wineries; the vintners and grape growers; the people at the Wine Council of Ontario and the Vintners Quality Alliance; and the owners, chefs, and staff at the hotels, restaurants, and inns who have provided their gracious hospitality, support, contributions, and encouragement throughout the production of the TV series and the compilation of this book. From the proprietors to the support staff, they offered their kindness, and we want to share our gratitude.

First and foremost we would like to extend a special thanks to Jim MacDonald, former president of CH-TV (formerly ONtv) in Hamilton and later president of the Canadian WIC TV network, who seeded and nurtured our television adventure from a wacky idea to a flight of 130 shows.

And to Donald Ziraldo, founder of Inniskillin Wines, Ontario's most noted wine ambassador, for his written contribution and his unwavering friendship.

Our special thanks, appreciation, and recognition are extended to photographer Steven Elphick, who has created the photographic backbone to this book.

For their kind written contributions to the book we'd especially like to thank:

Michael Olson, chef professor extraordinaire at the School of Hospitality and Tourism, Niagara College;

Maria Moesnner, resident sommelier for Inniskillin Estate Wines;

Martin Malivoire, vintner and proprietor, Malivoire Estate Wines, and his right hand, Elena Gayley-Pride;

John Nadeau, proprietor of The Wine Establishment in Toronto;

And Andrew Brandt, Chair of the LCBO, for his kind words.

We would also like to note the generous support of the following people:

Al Gilchrist, president of Nokia Canada, for "keeping us connected";

Tony Flus of Hertz in St. Catharines, for "keeping us moving";

Debi Pratt of Inniskillin Wines, for "keeping us informed";

Michael Dubrule, whose photographic flattery is always appreciated;

Arden Phair, curator of the St. Catharines Museum on the Welland Canal at Lock 3; and also to Suzanne Melville;

April Petrie of the Niagara Parks Commission;

Christine Hayward of the Ball's Falls Historical Park under the auspices of the Niagara Peninsula Conservation Authority;

Robert Benson of the Shaw Festival company, along with Odette Yazbeck of the Publicity Department;

Helen M. Booth, curator of the Jordan Historical Museum in the hamlet of Jordan;

Anne Just of Kurtz Orchards on the Niagara Parkway;

Connie Febraro and Steven Weir from the McMichael Collection in Kleinburg;

Alison Fryer of the Cookbook Store in Toronto;

Nicolette Novak, doyenne of the Good Earth Cooking School in Beamsville;

Sabeeya Ament and Lillian Tepera, of Nokia;

Sue Forcier, with the Mayor's Office in Niagara Falls;

The Niagara College Culinary Institute's Vincenza Smith, J. Mark Hand, Albert Cypryk, and the gentle giant Jim MacLean;

And Albert Zappitelli of the Sheraton Fallsview Hotel.

A special thank you goes to Arden Phair, Helen Booth, April Petrie, and Christine Hayward for permission to draw freely from their many writings.

And last but not least to our families:

Jonathan's wife, Heather Smith, whose patience is a bedrock—and without whose guidance Jonathan would be lost—and Hilary, Owen, and Julia, whose shiny faces keep him alive.

Alan's wife, Anneke Nijenhuis, whose quiet intelligence and unwavering encouragement are a refreshing tonic to a weary traveler; and Amy and Aaron, two of the neatest kids on the planet.

Jim's friends and loved ones, including four fabulous children—Jamie, Charlton, Ann, and Rob—seven grandchildren, and Pegi, whose patience and support have made dreams possible.

Notes from the Authors

Our offering will not join the wine canon. It doesn't cite definitions, rules, regulations, or dos and don'ts about wine and how it should be appreciated. There are several exceptionally detailed dictionaries, bibles, guides, and even novellas on the subject if you seek to worship at the altar. While wine critics can provide some helpful clues, maps, and indicators, they too rely on their own unique palates to make their subjective assessments. They are as valuable as you make them out to be.

Without apologies we forgo the pomp, ceremony, and biased opinions that connoisseurs, critics, and wine snobs have bestowed upon the appreciation of wine. To them it has become an obsessive infatuation punctuated with definitive terms and unforgiving rituals. You can shelve any notion that after reading this book your newly hatched wine wisdom will place you above your neighbor. If you are interested in wine as a part of life's adventure, enjoying it only requires an open mind. The best part is that you have only yourself to satisfy.

"Appellation" signifies a designated wine region governed by rules and regulations. The system of appellation control was introduced by the French in 1935 as a means of protecting quality-conscious wine producers from unethical practitioners.

This wine biographical touring cookbook is a hybrid compendium of stories, legends, and information about wines, winemakers, chefs, wineries, personalities, vintners, history, culture, art, and travel. It is a "salt and pepper" salute to the world of discovery, where wine is a cordial ambassador and travel companion on your pilgrimage. It celebrates the fellowship that comes about when wine is appreciated as one element in the pursuit of all that life has to offer. It's a fascinating journey. And we've come to realize that there doesn't seem to be a final destination.

Wine is an unpredictable living beverage as old as civilization itself. Good wine, delicious food, companionship, and opportunities to learn through traveling contribute to a wonderful blend of pleasures, each element providing something to the whole experience and memory bank. Like a well-prepared meal where the spices, flavorings, textures, and aromas create that overall sense of pleasure, wine can be one of the ambient factors in the quest for balance.

Good wine is the wine you like. Although we've endured our share of obsessive conversations about wine, we've also met hundreds of winemakers, chefs, vintners, and growers who taught us to beware of the subjectivity that others might try to impose on you. We've learned to trust our own palates and broaden our experiences by trying different wines with different foods. The stories, recipes, side trips, events, and people you'll read about in this book are drawn from our on- and off-air adventures. And to further help you on the tour, we've asked John Nadeau, president of The Wine Establishment in Toronto, some questions about storing and serving wine. His answers are scattered throughout the book in sections called "Notes from the Cellar". All of these pieces are interconnected with the pleasure principles of enjoying life to the fullest.

NOTES FROM THE CELLAR

What better person to give wine appreciation tips than John P. Nadeau, president of The Wine Establishment in Toronto? Under John's direction, The Wine Establishment has built a worldwide reputation among wine lovers as Canada's top retail outlet specializing in commercial, residential, and custom-designed wine storage and cellaring systems. With a mandate to improve the "experience of wine" for its clients, the company has grown into a key distribution center for exquisite wine accessories such as crystal stemware and decanters and is also a leader in wine education.

This tour is dedicated to a young and dynamic "new world" wine region: Ontario. From the corridor of the Niagara Peninsula through the fruit orchards of southwestern Ontario to the pristine beauty of Pelee Island and Lake Erie North Shore, Ontario's wine industry is constantly growing, changing, defining, and redefining itself. Touring the wineries and restaurants, historical landmarks, and other sites offers a wonderful *à la carte* experience that has something to offer everyone. The gifted winemakers, vintners, growers, and chefs who collectively represent a united nations of styles and tastes have helped us come to understand that while Ontario is already producing world-class wines, the future looks even brighter. We hope you will discover this for yourself.

In these pages we hope you'll come to appreciate that like everything else in life, the moment you think you've mastered wine, it surprises you. That's the magic of wine. Nothing can be taken for granted. Every bottle is as unique as a human fingerprint and every year has something unique to offer. In wine there are few absolute answers. Most of the fun's in the questions and the search.

Finally, while it's wonderful to find *that* wine that pleases you most, there is always another out there waiting for you to come across it. In these pages, we encourage you to trust your own palate and to constantly try new wines and foods. Every label and every vintage has something to offer. We hope you'll join our efforts to *take the snobbery out of wine...one bottle at a time*, and enjoy every sip you take along the way.

Cheers!

Alan Aylward, Jonathan Welsh, James Bruce

Words from a Vintner

Vintner, Donald Ziraldo

A revolution has erupted in the Canadian wine industry, mirroring the explosive success of other new-world wine regions such as California and New Zealand. The province of Ontario, Canada's eastern wine region, possesses three designated viticulture wine regions: the Niagara Peninsula (the Golden Horseshoe), Lake Erie North Shore, and Pelee Island. Canada's appellation of origin control system—the Vintners Quality Alliance, or VQA—like those of France and Italy, ensures that our wines meet stringent quality standards, for both viticulture and enology/winemaking. The VQA label is your assurance that you will be pleased with what flows from the bottle.

Alongside the success has come growing recognition and valuable information delivered in a lighthearted manner in fun books such as this offering, designed to "take the snobbery out of wine…one bottle at a time." Education and knowledge are important aspects of the wine journey. Jonathan and Alan's TV series and, from it, this book certainly help make the consumer feel less intimidated by the wine experience.

There is much to learn about wine and wine growing: from the variable influence of climate and soil, the importance of oak aging, and the complexities of the fermentation process; to all the nuances that are perceived while tasting the final product, including how wines marry with food. It can be an intimidating journey but it should always be a journey of discovery.

Ontario is a wonderful four-season destination filled with a multitude of attractions, and a companionable way to discover the region is through wine and food.

If you ask me why I established Inniskillin Wines and have spent the last twenty-eight years in Canada's wine industry, I could give you an array of reasons. I've always been intrigued by all aspects of winemaking, from the growing of the vines, through the fermenting of the fresh juice, right up to the tasting of the final product. The many pleasures also include the opportunity to work alongside creative people such as Jonathan and Alan, who share my passion for wine and wish to share it with you. But there is magic afoot, make no mistake about it. Here's just one little secret I'll gladly share with you.

The French have a term to describe the magic that permeates the vineyard: It is "terroir." This encompasses certain parts of the world—wine regions—where Mother Nature has forged the perfect partnership among topography, climate, and soil that allows wine grapes to flourish and thrive. Each region also carries an identity that imparts to the wine grapes a distinctive character all their own. It is surprising to see the differences even within one region. You can experiment by discovering the unique flavors of different single vineyard varietals such as Chardonnay (produced from a single vineyard site) even within the Niagara appellation. Taste for yourself. See if you can distinguish the various fingerprints. There's no mystery to it. You can discover the magic of "terroir."

*The French term **terroir** is universally used by winemakers to distinguish one grape-growing location from another, and includes natural elements such as climate, soil type, drainage, winds, and humidity.*

Another piece of Canadian magic is icewine, Canada's frosty gift to the wine lover and our country's proud standard-bearer around the globe. The magic of icewine is outlined and illustrated in detail in these pages.

This book is a simple journey marked by a celebration of myriad makers of wine in Canada. It is a journey along Ontario's pleasant wine routes. It is a welcome opportunity for you to develop an affinity for the land that offers its bounty in such a unique way. You will meet the people behind the labels and, by doing so, truly experience the magic of wine.

It is this simple magic that has Canadian wines flourishing. It has become my personal commitment to help ensure that this magic is kept alive to be shared by all who value the community of wine and food. We are proud producers of quality wine, we've been showered with international prestigious awards, and our products grace the tables of the world. Come join our community and ensure that the land's bounty is preserved and nurtured for generations to come. It's a legacy for all.

Think globally, drink locally!

Donald Ziraldo
President and Co-Founder
Inniskillin Wines

Words from The Chair

LCBO Chairman,
Andrew S. Brandt

As the Chair and Chief Executive Officer of the Liquor Control Board of Ontario for the past ten years, I have witnessed a revolution in the wine world. Back in the '70s, many people's concept of a good bottle of domestic wine was a sweet sparkler with a plastic cork. Their import of choice? A squat bottle of Chianti wrapped in straw.

How times have changed! Interest in wine has expanded significantly in the past decade, and as wine lovers have become more educated, the demand for quality information about wine has grown as well.

Regretfully, much of the excellent material available today is directed at the sophisticated, already well-informed consumer of wine. While these materials are excellent for either those with a passion for the minutia or insomniacs, it is difficult to find a wine writer who writes for the newcomer.

By asking questions of the experts and getting down to basics, Jonathan Welsh, Alan Aylward and Jim Bruce have written a book that teaches and instructs us from the ground up. They don't get caught up in the snobbery or pretentiousness of the wine world; instead, they treat the subject with the irreverence it deserves.

Every wine region in the world has its own unique blend of weather and soils. This distinct climate, or **terroir** *as the French call it, expresses itself in the character of the grapes grown and wines produced.*

Wine is a drink to be consumed with friends and enjoyed. For you and me, a tiresome discourse on acidity, extract, and tannic structure is not required in order to enjoy a good bottle of wine.

In his TV series, Jonathan's interview style is that of an accomplished actor. He lets the subjects feel that he is astonished and amazed by the answers he gets to his probing questions. His eyes light up in fascination even when he hears information that is surely not new to him.

On a professional level, Jonathan has a particular passion for Canadian wine, and few people have contributed more to the promotion and knowledge of Canadian wine. His televised "New World Wine Tour" series has covered just about every inch of the new world, and he has the mud on his shoes to prove it. Traveling around Canada with the flair and exuberance of a teenager with his first driver's license, Jonathan talks to the movers and shakers of the industry—from the folks who grow the grapes, to the winemakers, writers, chefs, and everyday consumers.

Wine is a matter of personal taste to Jonathan. His and your likes and dislikes—not those of the winemaker, the wine critic, or myself for that matter—are paramount to him.

As you travel along the road with this intense, driven, enthusiastic wine lover, you will expose yourself to a down-to-earth, frank exposé of wine, from the grapes in the field to the wine in the bottle. I am certain you will find this book insightful and instructive.

Cheers!

Andrew S. Brandt
Chair and CEO
Liquor Control Board of Ontario

VQA: Vintners Quality Alliance

 Every wine-growing country in the world has a set of standards for its finest wines. A set of regulations and laws specify which grapes may be grown, where and how the wines must be made, and the standards the wineries must meet. In Canada, this is called the Vintners Quality Alliance (VQA).

Like the DOC designation in Italy, the AOC in France, and the QMP in Germany, the VQA identification in Canada is the consumer's guarantee that the wine has been produced to the finest standards. Wines bearing the VQA medallion must have met stringent production and appellation standards and been approved by a VQA grading panel. Canada has three distinct wine growing regions, and they are located in the provinces of British Columbia, Nova Scotia, and Ontario.

In Ontario, Niagara is one of three designated viticultural areas, which have traditionally produced the finest and most distinctive wines. The other two are Pelee Island and Lake Erie North Shore.

Vintners Quality Alliance Ontario is authorized by law to set and enforce standards for the production of wines in the province. Through a distinctive designation on each bottle, consumers can easily identify those wines of superior quality and their viticultural area of origin. In Ontario, all VQA wines must be made from 100% Ontario grapes.

The first record of wine labeling dates back to the Egyptians who, almost 4,000 years ago, marked their wine containers with details about their vineyards, harvest dates, and even the name of the winemakers.

Let the Journey Begin!

Jonathan Welsh, our intrepid host, in the vineyard

"Who took the cork out of my lunch?"
—W.C. Fields

No Cork-Dorks or Wine Snobs Please

When Jonathan and I first discussed the production of a TV series on wine we instinctively knew we had to demystify the subject. One of the barriers to enjoying wine, for so many people, is the enigmatic prose and imperious descriptors that critics use in evaluating wines (see how easy this is to do!). Describing the taste of wine is part of the fun but descriptors like "wet dog," "essence of lava," "scent of rose hips," and "aromas of ash and tobacco" are, to say the least, getting in the way of learning about wine.

How could we make it more accessible and less intimidating to the average person? We weren't out to reach the converted wine elite. They spend a lot of money on status wines and have the means to gaze triumphantly into the ether while sipping a Grand Cru from St. Emilion or Pauillac. A simple polling of family, friends, and acquaintances told us that most people would rather have dinner with the winemaker as opposed to a critic. If anyone could help us understand this magic elixir it would be the people who make it.

From these simple statistical measures we readily adopted the slogan, "Taking the snobbery out of wine… one bottle at a time." Throughout the first 130 half-hour episodes you won't find a wine critic, and during production if anyone attempted to flaunt their pretensions, Jonathan was quick to unrobe them with his humorous quips and irreverent demeanor.

At one of the tables in our series a guest winemaker was taking great pains to explain the various nuances in an older Riesling, including a desirable scent of gasoline fumes. Jonathan nodded in agreement with every descriptor the winemaker cited. After several colorful terms had been used, Jonathan added some of his own eloquent interpretations, including the aromas of "wet diaper" and "petroleum jelly." The winemaker, whose first language was not English, agreed with Jonathan's observations and probably didn't pick up on the witty comeback.

Wine critics, like film or literary critics, certainly serve a useful function for, and a responsibility to, their clients. We never dismiss the value a critic can offer the consumer or the winemaker. On the other hand, we have seen how some people accept with "blind trust" the poetic waxing of critics. They quote their favorite critic's review, award points, and believe that they have elevated themselves into the highly restricted club of wine connoisseurs. Thanks to the winemakers, vintners, and growers that we've met, we have learned that this is epicurean hogwash!

Virtually every winemaker, vintner, viticulturist, and chef we've ever met has reinforced the importance of the individual palate in judging any wine, or any food for that matter. Like fingerprints, no two palates are alike. In fact, a single wine can have a remarkably diverse taste sensation for any number of people. Not only does each person taste a wine differently, they may also perceive the same wine differently depending on an array of other circumstances, such as the time of day, the last aroma they noted, the spirit of the conversation at the table, their like or dislike of the ambience in the restaurant, or their own disposition that particular day.

A case in point. While filming a comparative tasting of several different wines, everyone in the crew was enraptured by the fascinating winemaker's candor and passion. He had a charming and disarming way of weaving wonderful stories around each wine that he offered us for tasting, and he was enamored with our enthusiastic interest in wine. Like sharing a secret with long-lost comrades-in-arms he leaned forward and whispered that he had something "special" in the cellar he'd like to share with us. It wouldn't be bottled for release for another six to eight months, and it was a Pinot Noir that would knock the socks off any competition.

Designated as a prized wine, it would be released under a "Family Reserve" label. We were impressed by

"There are only two things you need to know about wine. Either you like it or you don't."
—Allan Schmidt, winemaker

Vineyards grace the Niagara Escarpment

his description and already salivating at the opportunity to taste this very special vintage. It was everything he said it was and more. Our director of photography, Bob, was our official Pinot Noir judge and confirmed what we had all sensed. This Pinot was history in the making. We knew we had to have it. For the first time on location each of us actually wrote personal checks to reserve our own case of this remarkable Pinot Noir. (And we were accustomed to never having to pay for anything while on location!)

When the wine finally arrived, phones started buzzing between cast and crew. It was unanimous: The wine was next to awful and, considering the hefty price tag, extremely disappointing. A couple of months after the trauma had subsided, we tasted a second bottle. It wasn't as great as when we tasted it right from the barrel while under the spell of the winemaker's charms, but it also wasn't as bad as when we had tasted our own first bottle. Lessons learned. Wine is a beverage that is subject to the time, place, occasion, and company you share it with, and paying more doesn't necessarily ensure greater pleasure.

Winemakers believe that wine is grown in the vineyard!

Highly fertile soils, especially those rich in nitrogen, are not considered ideal for wine grapes as they encourage too much growth, which can diminish the depth of flavor qualities in finished wine.

We've heard of tests where the people responsible for constructing the descriptors for wine on menus couldn't, under blind tasting of the same wines, match the descriptor back to the original wine they wrote about. A wonderful gentleman we met on one of our journeys had his own way with wine critics. The late, highly respected actor Barry Morse, best known for his role in the popular TV series "The Fugitive," told us of a mischievous prank he once pulled on some wine critics when he was the host of a British TV chat show back in the early days of television. Doubting their "remarkable palate" claims, he invited three respected critics onto his show. He relished the anxiety on their faces when his assistants arrived with blindfolds and several decanters filled with various wines. This was a live telecast before a studio audience, so we can imagine how distressing the situation was for his unsuspecting guests.

To the delight of the host and his audience, the three blindfolded wine critics fared poorly on virtually every level of assessing the wines put before them. Not only were they unable to identify regions, age, and the presence of oak, tannins, berries, and other fundamental flavor profiles, but also, in the most embarrassing scenario, two of the three mistook a white wine for a red. We cite this as a story that serves to reinforce the most important aspect of your quest to discover wine. Trust your own palate.

Perhaps this is also the reason that wine is one of the most illusive, mystifying, and fascinating beverages in the world. Wine has been made for thousands of years, written about in the Bible, and revered by ancient civilizations, kings and commoners alike. Wine is a good-natured monitor of history, culture, artistic expression, civilization, conversation, marriage, celebration, promotion, sorrow, and myriad other circumstances and events. It is meant to be enjoyed in moderation and as a convivial meal companion. If you ever wanted to have the ultimate ambassador at your dining table, wine would certainly rank as one of the most accommodating, approachable delegates.

The term "light" may be used to indicate a wine with light body weight, a wine that's young, fruity, and drinkable, or a wine that's relatively low in alcohol content.

Wine enthusiasts and novices spend their lives exploring wines that range from awful to mediocre to remarkable, knowing that the perfect wine they seek is the one that they haven't had yet. Every year supplies a different vintage, every region offers a parade of varieties or blends, every producer develops a unique style, every barrel produces a distinct grain and toasting, every bottle provides a different nuance, and every glass conjures up a shade of difference.

Wine appreciation and wine discovery is a never-ending quest, but above all else, wine can be the confidante, the intimate, trusted adviser, companion, and accomplice that every pioneer deserves on their journey to discover the very best that life has to offer.

So here we go. We have discovered from our voyage into the world of wine that the best-laid plans usually run astray. We have learned that the journey is usually more fun and informative than reaching the destination. Each person, stop, and indulgence along the way offers taste adventures that help each of us gravitate to what we prefer. We hope our experiences and the travel stories laced throughout this book will complement the trials and tribulations unique to your personal quest. And we hope you'll always remember that—since wine does contain alcohol—moderation is the rule, not the exception.

Cheers! À votre santé! ¡Salud y pesetas! Prost!

Alan Aylward

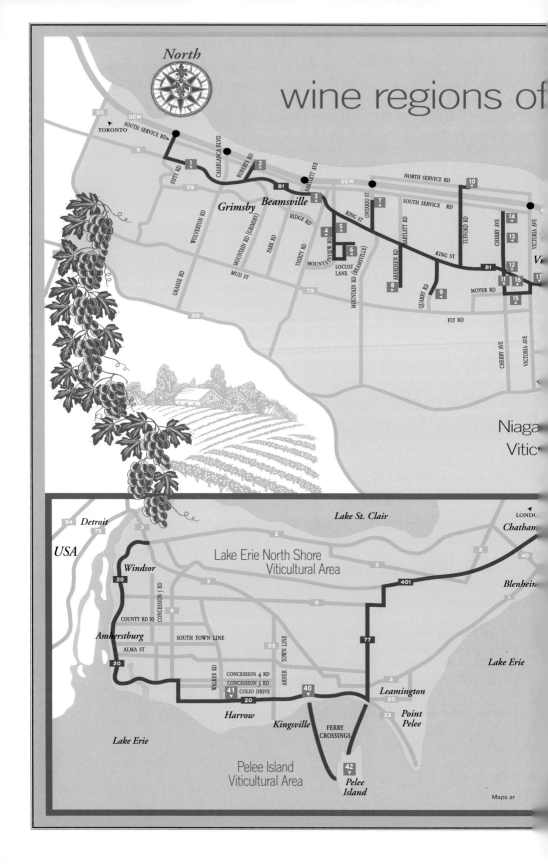

wine regions of

North

TORONTO

SOUTH SERVICE RD.
QEW
20

FIFTY RD
CASABLANCA BLVD
ROBERTS RD
8
79
1
2

Grimsby   *Beamsville*

WOLVERTON RD
MOUNTAIN RD (GRIMSBY)
PARK RD
RIDGE RD
THIRTY RD
MOUNTAINVIEW RD
MOUNTAIN RD (BEAMSVILLE)

BARTLETT AVE
QEW
81
3
KING ST
ONTARIO ST
7
NORTH SERVICE RD
SOUTH SERVICE   RD
TUFFORD RD
CHERRY AVE
VICTORIA AVE
10

14
13
12
15

GRASSIE RD
MUD ST
73
20

4
5
LOCUST
LANE
6
ABERDEEN RD
BARTLETT RD
KING ST
81
11 16
MOYER RD

8
QUARRY RD
9
FLY RD

CHERRY AVE
VICTORIA AVE

Niaga

Vitic

V

USA
94
75
Detroit
3

Windsor
20
CONCESSION 5 RD

COUNTY RD 10
9

Amherstburg
SOUTH TOWN LINE
ALMA ST
20

Lake St. Clair
LOND
Chatham

Lake Erie North Shore
Viticultural Area
2
2
3
8
401
77

2
40

Blenhei

WALKER RD
ARNER TOWN LINE
CONCESSION 4 RD
CONCESSION 3 RD
41 COLIO DRIVE
23
20
40

Harrow
Kingsville   FERRY
CROSSINGS

3
20
Leamington
33   *Point
Pelee*
Lake Erie

Lake Erie

Pelee Island
Viticultural Area
42
*Pelee
Island*

Maps ar

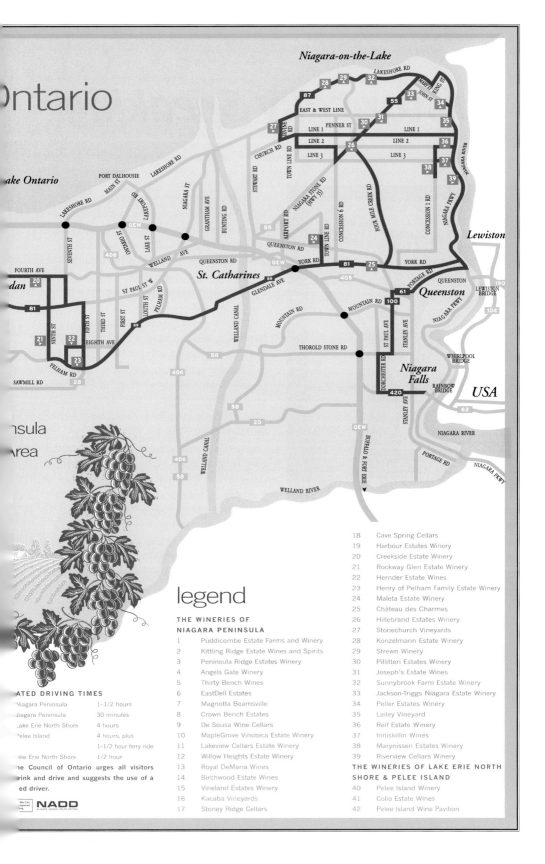

Ontario

Niagara-on-the-Lake

Lake Ontario

PORT DALHOUSIE

Lewiston

St. Catharines

Queenston

LEWISTON BRIDGE

WHIRLPOOL BRIDGE

USA

Niagara Falls

RAINBOW BRIDGE

NIAGARA RIVER

WELLAND RIVER

nsula
Area

...he Council of Ontario urges all visitors
...rink and drive and suggests the use of a
...ed driver.

We Can't Stopped...

NADD

Historically Speaking

Promoting early Ontario wines in the "olden days"

Ontario's wine history is preceded by a world wine history dating back thousands of years. Considering the fact that wild vines have inhabited the earth for millions of years, it's surprising that it took humans so long to discover the joys of wine. Some scholars suggest that wine may have been available as long ago as 8,000 B.C. Biblical writings suggest that Noah may have been the first grower of grapes for the specific purpose of making wine.

Throughout history wine has had its most notable relationships with royalty and religious orders. Only recently has wine become a beverage that can be enjoyed by commoners such as us. This may be a blessing because historians also note that up until a couple of hundred years ago, wine wasn't necessarily a pleasant-tasting experience, at least not by today's standards. In ancient history wine may have been popular for its side effects as opposed to its gastronomic delights. The concept of moderation probably evolved with the advent of the wheel.

Egyptian high society had already been enjoying the side effects of wine for centuries when they began trading with their Eastern neighbors. The Greeks were very fond of their wine and, like the Egyptians, they made many references to the pleasure of wine and how it had to be a gift from the gods. With little concern for moderation, in those days those who overindulged probably met several gods firsthand.

The Roman Empire is most credited with spreading wine throughout Europe. As the Romans conquered new lands and peoples, they ensured that vines were planted and wine was made. Spreading the "good word," so to speak!

Much of wine history is entwined with monasteries and the sacramental use of wine. Christian monasteries preserved winemaking skills and knowledge after the collapse of the Roman Empire. As the churches and cathedrals spread and grew wealthier, the making and consuming of wine was increasingly seen as a luxury and a much-needed solace from the trials and tribulations of the times. The wine of the common folk left much to be desired. The church controlled the making of finer wines and, while little was known about the health aspects of wine, it is probably fair to suggest that some form of moderate wine consumption helped prolong otherwise very short lives.

We've often heard about Europeans having wine on the dinner table and serving small portions diluted with water to children. We've been led to believe that this is done to rear children in the appreciation of wine as a fine, wholesome daily beverage to be enjoyed with food. However, a wine museum curator in Bordeaux suggests that wine was actually added to the polluted drinking water as a disinfectant, not as a gesture of liberal values! More support for the health benefits of wine.

It appears that the Benedictine monks were the most famous for cultivating and producing some of Europe's most splendid wines during the Dark Ages. It also appears that they were well-known drunkards who spent much of their time in an intoxicated stupor. Perhaps that was why a Benedictine monk by the name of St. Bernard left the order to start the Cistercian order. The new order's membership grew quickly but the practice of overindulgence apparently didn't elude the Cistercians.

Down through the ages, wine has accompanied civilization. While wine has been revered by snobs throughout its history, it may have been the British who elevated wine hubris to its most eloquent heights. We had a chance to reflect on this possibility while filming on location in Bordeaux.

A British family on holiday arrived for lunch at an outdoor café in Pauillac and offered some unusual wine parlance. They were driving a black Mercedes with a relatively large trailer in tow. The parents and three young children, ranging in age from about four to twelve, sat next to us. We couldn't help but overhear their conversation. The mother was more attentive to the children while the father seemed pensive. We had tried to strike up a

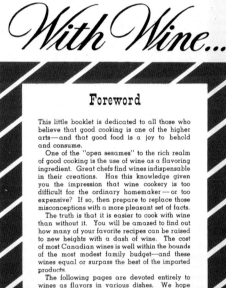

With Wine...

Foreword

This little booklet is dedicated to all those who believe that good cooking is one of the higher arts—and that good food is a joy to behold and consume.

One of the "open sesames" to the rich realm of good cooking is the use of wine as a flavoring ingredient. Great chefs find wines indispensable in their creations. Has this knowledge given you the impression that wine cookery is too difficult for the ordinary homemaker — or too expensive? If so, then prepare to replace those misconceptions with a more pleasant set of facts.

The truth is that it is easier to cook with wine than without it. You will be amazed to find out how many of your favorite recipes can be raised to new heights with a dash of wine. The cost of most Canadian wines is well within the bounds of the most modest family budget—and these wines equal or surpass the best of the imported products.

The following pages are devoted entirely to wines as flavors in various dishes. We hope you will try the recipes, because we know you will be tempted to use them again and again

Most winemakers consider wine a food stuff

While wine and other fermented beverages have been made for millennia, it wasn't until 1857 that Louis Pasteur discovered that fermentation—the conversion of sugar or starch into alcohol—was caused by yeast.

conversation with them but the father wasn't particularly interested and the mother, albeit somewhat friendlier, had her hands full with the kids and taking care of their lunch order. Dad was studying a wine-buying guide.

The youngest girl spoke in a most articulate and adorable British accent.

Girl: Are we going to Chateau Pomerol today, Daddy?

The eldest son piped in, using the same blunt tone his preoccupied father had used earlier.

Boy: Don't be ridiculous, Lucy. We were at Chateau Pomerol yesterday. Today we're going to Chateau Cordeillon Bage and Margaux.

This was the family summer holiday! The trailer was slowly being filled with daddy's favorite Bordeaux wines. Three weeks in Bordeaux hunting wines from chateau to chateau, wife and kids in tow.

It appears that the British are one of the largest per capita importers of fine wine throughout the world. During the Middle Ages, the British love of wine certainly proved instrumental in the development of the bustling Bordeaux wine exporting business. The British had a long history of fighting with the French over the vineyards, which eventually came to an end with the killing of General Talbot during a final battle of the Hundred Years' War in Castillion.

But what about Ontario's rise to stature in this wine-crazy evolution? There are some who suggest that Viking explorers found grapevines when they landed in Newfoundland in about A.D. 1000; thus the naming of the new land as "Vineland," "the land of vines."

Indigenous peoples of Ontario were said to have fermented grapes for ceremonial purposes at the foot of Niagara Falls. By the mid-1500s French explorers and the Jesuit missionaries who followed were noted to have recognized and established some order of Eastern Canada winemaking using local Labrusca and Concord grapes.

While there has been some history of vine tending throughout the 1600s and 1700s, it seems that the most serious Ontario commercial wine endeavors started with the arrival of a retired German officer named Johann Schiller. Johann also made wine in his earlier days in Germany. Settling in the Credit River area of Mississauga

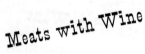

Meats with Wine

CANADIAN BACON WITH SHERRY

1 pound Canadian bacon, thinly sliced; 1½ cups (approximately) Canadian Sherry.

Place bacon in frying pan, cover with sherry, and let it stand at least ½ hour. Then simmer, covered, over very slow fire until Sherry practically disappears, 20–25 minutes. Excellent with waffles. Serves 4–6.

Serve with Canadian Claret

LAMB CHOPS IN WINE

8 lamb chops; 2 tablespoons butter; 1 cup button onions; 4 medium-sized carrots, cut julienne; ½ cup Canadian dry white wine; 2 cups sliced mushrooms; salt and pepper.

Brown chops, onions, and carrots in butter. Add wine, mushrooms, and seasonings, cover, and simmer slowly for 30 minutes. Serves 4.

Serve with Canadian Claret

Wine and food are akin to "love and marriage"

Catawba is a deep pink–skinned grape varietal cross between Labrusca and vinifera, most noted in the eastern United States, and was first identified in North Carolina in 1802.

on land granted to him for his British military service, he cultivated vines and made wine for himself and to sell to his neighbors. While not the first to make wine in Canada, he may have been the first to cover his costs if not turn a small profit.

Several years after Schiller's death, some of his property was sold off. It was Count Justin M. de Courtenay who furthered the Ontario winemaking process, and in 1867 he received exceptional reviews for his house wine in Paris at a major exposition. Around this time, some American businessmen had purchased land for vineyards on Pelee Island, Canada's southernmost property in Lake Erie. Some of America's busiest wineries were located in Sandusky, Ohio, and the plantings of Catawba grapes on Pelee Island became a reliable quality grape source.

By the late 1890s the Erie North Shore area of Essex County was the largest single wine-growing region in Canada. Of the forty-odd wineries across the country, 85% of them were located in Ontario. The Concord grape (developed in the town of Concord around the mid-1800s) was the backbone of Canadian wines for almost a century and then became the predominant grape used to produce the well-known sugary pop wines that boasted a duck on the label. While not well regarded by fine-wine lovers, the "duck" wines were popular and profitable well into the 1970s.

In the mid-1970s serious winemakers and vintners began a movement for the production of higher-quality wines with the more revered European vine stocks and some of the more highly regarded hybrid crossings. Throughout this book, you'll find biographies of several of the important vintners and winemakers who worked towards this end.

The most important aspect of all of this is to realize that in a relatively short period of time Ontario winemakers have elevated wine standards remarkably. You can taste the improvement yourself and take some solace in noting the lengthy prestigious lists of international awards that adorn winemakers' retail shops and brochures.

Sauces with Wine

SAUCE COLBERT

1 cup hot water; 1 tablespoon beef extract; 2 tablespoons melted butter; juice of 1 lemon; 1 teaspoon minced tarragon or parsley; 2 tablespoons Canadian Sherry; salt and pepper.

Dissolve beef extract in hot water in double boiler. Add butter gradually, beating constantly with wire whisk. Add lemon juice, Sherry, and minced tarragon or parsley. Approximately 1¼ cups sauce.

SPAGHETTI SAUCE

1 pound ground beef; 3 tablespoons butter; 1 can condensed tomato soup; ½ cup chili sauce; 1 large onion sliced; 1 teaspoon powdered garlic; 1 teaspoon poultry dressing; ¼ cup vinegar; ⅛ teaspoon cayenne; salt; 1 cup water; 1 cup Canadian Sherry.

Brown ground beef in butter. Add all other ingredients and simmer, covered, 3 to 4 hours, adding more water if necessary. Approximately 4 cups sauce.

Or is it wine in the sauces?

The primary natural acid in grapes is tartaric acid, followed by malic acid. This acidity is an important element in the balance of a wine's taste structure, and critical to the aging ability of wine.

Niagara Peninsula

Niagara Falls seen from overhead

The Niagara Escarpment

Only about a one-hour drive from the city of Toronto is the beginning of a twenty-five-mile (forty-kilometer) stretch—between the charming towns of Grimsby and Niagara-on-the-Lake—which is home to many of Ontario's finest wineries.

Similar conditions exist here to other great wine-producing regions of the world—including Burgundy, Loire Valley, and Oregon. The ideal mix of soil and minerals, the moderating effect of Lake Ontario, and the sheltering effect of the Niagara Escarpment, all offer a perfect microclimate for growing the classic wine grapes of Europe.

From the rich, flat land in the Niagara-on-the-Lake area to the limestone earth at the base of the Niagara Escarpment—450 million years old and a World Biosphere Reserve—vitis vinifera vineyards provide the area's winemakers with the opportunity to produce a great variety of unique and outstanding wines.

A number of beautiful towns and villages add to the rich experience of the region. They offer superb restaurants, world-class theater, more than 100 parks and recreation areas, historic sites and magnificent estates, challenging golf courses, shops, and drives along splendid routes. Winston Churchill once described the Niagara Parkway as one of the prettiest Sunday drives in the world.

The majestic Niagara River wends its way north to empty into Lake Ontario

Inniskillin

FAST FACTS

R.R. #1
Niagara-on-the-Lake, Ontario
L0S 1J0
Tel: 905-468-2187; 888-466-4754
Fax: 905-468-5355
E-mail: inniskil@inniskillin.com
Web: www.inniskillin.com;
www.icewine.com

Inniskillin has come a long way since the first winery was housed in an old packing shed at Donald Ziraldo's family nursery.

Now about one and a quarter miles (two kilometers) away from its original setting, Inniskillin's vineyard is called the Brae Burn Estate. "Brae Burn" is of Gaelic origin and translates as "hill stream," referring to the nearby Niagara Escarpment and the Niagara River. The historic Brae Burn barn, which was constructed in the mid-1920s, houses the winery boutique. The barn is an adapted reproduction of a design by famous architect Frank Lloyd Wright. (See "Anatomy of a Winery," www.winerack.com/anatomy, by Donald Ziraldo.)

Visiting Inniskillin is a total wine experience, providing one of the most informative self-guided tour programs in North America. The tour features twenty stations depicting and explaining every phase of grape growing and winemaking, from the vineyard to the tasting room.

Inniskillin owns approximately 130 acres in two vineyards, Brae Burn and Montague. The balance of grapes comes from a select group of dedicated growers including Klose, Seeger, Schuele, and Culp vineyards.

Inniskillin continually streamlines its product line to concentrate on specific vitis vinifera varietals, meeting the strict standards of the VQA. Varietals include Chardonnay, Riesling, Pinot Grigio, Pinot Noir, Cabernet Franc, Cabernet Sauvignon, and Merlot. The tiering of the varietals and their particular styles have been harvested to achieve Black, Pearl, Silver, Gold, and Travigne labels.

Over the years, winemaker Karl Kaiser has expanded his icewine portfolio. Starting in 1984, Karl produced icewine from Vidal grapes only. He felt that the thick-skinned, aromatic Vidal was ideal for winter harvesting of icewine. For years Karl used only Vidal grapes while adapting his original

Welcome to Inniskillin Estates Vineyards and Winery

Inniskillin's Brae Burn barn makes an enchanting wine boutique

icewine into two other styles: Oak Aged and Sparkling. His icewine portfolio today includes Riesling, Cabernet Franc, and Chenin Blanc. The Riedel Vinum Extreme icewine glass was designed specifically for Inniskillin by tenth-generation Austrian glassmaker George Riedel, President of Riedel Glass.

Inniskillin's production capacity is 120,000 cases annually. For aging, tight grain French barrels and water bent American Oak barriques are used. Inniskillin also uses stainless steel tanks.

After two decades of rapid growth for Inniskillin, Philip Dowell joined the winery as general manager to play a critical role in continuing that growth. His international perspective and experience in viticulture, winemaking, and general management augmented the roles of Ziraldo and Kaiser in the overall winery strategy. He concentrates on the production of table wines while Karl continues to focus on his internationally recognized icewines.

Inniskillin again brought world attention to the quality of Canadian wines at the International Wine and Spirits Competition (IWSC) in London, England, in 2001. Inniskillin earned the Best Icewine trophy for their 1998 Vidal Icewine, VQA Niagara Peninsula; and the Best Canadian Winery award was based on the judges' tasting of the icewine, together with the winery's 1998 Montague Estate Pinot Noir and 1999 Montague Estate Chardonnay, again both VQA Niagara Peninsula.

BALSAMIC VINEGAR HERB MARINATED PORK TENDERLOIN
Served with Roasted Yukon Gold Potatoes and Zucchini Summer Squash Stir Fry

—

from Izabela Kalabis, Inniskillin Resident Chef

—

Serves 4

PORK AND MARINADE
1½ lb (725 g) pork tenderloin
¼ cup (60 ml) balsamic vinegar
1 tbsp (15 ml) shallots, chopped
½ cup (125 ml) fresh herbs, such as oregano, basil, thyme, sage, chervil, tarragon
½ tsp (2 ml) garlic, minced
¼ cup (60 ml) olive oil

POTATOES
1½ lb (725 g) small Yukon Gold potatoes, peeled and halved
2 tbsp (30 ml) olive oil
coarse sea salt
freshly ground pepper
1 tbsp (15 ml) fresh rosemary

ZUCCHINI STIR FRY
¾ lb (375 g) zucchini, cut into 2-in (5-cm) strips
¾ lb (375 g) yellow summer squash, cut into 2-in (5-cm) strips
1 red pepper, cut into 2-in (5-cm) strips
2 tbsp (30 ml) olive oil
1 garlic clove, minced
1 tsp (5 ml) fresh thyme, minced
salt
freshly ground pepper

In a food processor, combine balsamic vinegar, shallots, herbs, garlic, and olive oil. Cut little nicks in pork, spread marinade over the entire tenderloin, rubbing it in well. Marinate, covered and refrigerated, overnight or for at least 6 hours.

Preheat grill. Cook the pork on a grill over medium coals until pink has just disappeared, about 10 minutes per side. The juices should run clear, but be careful not to overcook. Meanwhile, prepare the potatoes and vegetables.

continued on page 16

continued from page 15
Preheat oven to 400°F (200°C). Place the potatoes on a baking sheet, sprinkle with oil, salt, pepper, and rosemary. Roast for 30 minutes or until tender.

To make the stir fry, heat the oil in a large skillet. Add the zucchini, squash, and pepper. Sauté over high heat for 2–3 minutes, add garlic, thyme, salt, and pepper. Continue cooking for another 2–3 minutes or until tender. Remove from heat and serve with pork and potatoes.

WINE MATCH
1998 and 1999 Founders' Pinot Noir
1998 and 1999 Montague Vineyard Chardonnay

VQA, the Vintner's Quality Alliance, is the Canadian wine industry's appellation control system. Only those wines bearing the VQA logo guarantee that the grapes for the wine were sourced from Canadian vineyards.

In response to the great interest in agri-tourism and Inniskillin's concentration on culinary arts, a major expansion and renovation in the near future will include an increase in vineyard acreage and barrel aging cellars and the construction of a wine education center that will focus on the culinary arts.

Inniskillin wines include the following varietals: (white wines) Chardonnay, Riesling, Pinot Grigio, Chenin Blanc, Pinot Blanc, Viognier; (red wines) Pinot Noir, Gamay, Cabernet Sauvignon, Cabernet Franc, Merlot; (icewines) Riesling, Vidal, Cabernet Franc.

Inniskillin wines are available across North America, Asia, and Europe. Within the province of Ontario, wines are available at LCBO (Liquor Control Board of Ontario) outlets, Wine Rack locations, and the Wine Boutique in Niagara-on-the-Lake. A complete list of worldwide distributors can be found on the Inniskillin website at www.inniskillin.com.

What's in a Name?

Ontario wine industry archives would certainly recognize Donald Ziraldo as one of the founding champions who worked diligently to establish the Niagara Peninsula as a serious quality wine producer despite being a relatively small region. To emphasize just how small Niagara is, Donald often remarks that "Bordeaux spills more wine than Ontario makes."

Co-founder of Inniskillin Estate Wines, along with highly regarded winemaker Karl Kaiser, Donald didn't set out by intention to produce excellent Ontario wine. His partnership with Karl came about simply through serendipity.

Donald's parents had immigrated to Canada from Friuli in northern Italy. Settling in St. Catharines, Ontario, they started farming and, like many new Canadians from Italy, they made their own wine. Raised in a horticultural family where wine was a common beverage on the dinner table, Donald pursued a degree in horticulture at Guelph University, with a bent towards vine research. During his studies he began dabbling in various grafting techniques.

On a summer trip to Friuli, Donald visited his friend Manlio Tunutti, whose father was a close friend of Donald's father in the small village of Fagagna. Manlio designed and manufactured high-end wine labels for major wine producers. A visit to nearby Rauchado was also on the itinerary, and here Donald was introduced to

From left to right, Donald Ziraldo, Philip Dowell, and Karl Kaiser of Inniskillin Estate Wines

a village where the entire population was employed in the development, grafting, and cloning of grapevines. Donald imported some of these ideas and began grafting vines at the family nursery in Niagara. Others, such as the large wine company Bright's, were also doing research in this area.

Austrian Karl Kaiser had met his future wife, Silvia, a Canadian, while she was visiting Vienna. Karl was a teacher by profession and had learned winemaking through his association with a local monastery. Karl showed up at the Ziraldo nursery in early 1972 and asked Donald for grapes that "didn't taste Canadian." Months later, Karl returned to the nursery with a bottle of wine he had made from the grapes he bought from a local farmer. Tasting the wine, Donald was amazed at the remarkable quality.

Developing their friendship over a mutual interest in wine, Donald and Karl went for dinner at a local Fonthill

Sauvignon Blanc (soh-vihn-yohn blahngk) is known as Blanc Fume in the Loire Valley of France. Fume Blanc—as it was renamed by Robert Mondavi—is a tremendously successful Sauvignon wine and is distinguished by the characteristics of gentle oak aging.

When selecting wines to pair with food, winemakers often match the body and strength of the wine with the weight and flavors of the meal and any stock or sauces used.

schnitzel house and ordered what was recommended as a very good Ontario wine. With their more demanding tastes, they found the wine absolutely unpalatable. They knew that better wines could be made in Niagara and decided then and there to form a winemaking partnership. Karl would make the wine, and Donald reluctantly agreed to take on the role of sales and marketing.

Of course, in Ontario nobody makes or sells wine without the approval of the provincial government–owned Liquor Control Board of Ontario (LCBO). When Donald first knocked on their door seeking license approval, the LCBO hadn't issued a wine license in fifty years. Donald was laughed out of his first meeting with them.

A short while later, Donald received an invitation to meet with then chairman of the LCBO, General George Kitching. Donald had never attended a meeting in such a large, impressive, and somewhat intimidating office. Despite the opulence and prestige of the surroundings, General Kitching welcomed Donald with a warm handshake and came out from behind his mammoth desk to sit beside Donald. Years later, when asked why he eventually gave Donald the license, Kitching simply replied, "I liked him and didn't want to see him fail." Failure was never a consideration in Donald and Karl's endeavor.

They secured enough capital through private loans over the next year and a half to start the business, and the manufacturing permit enabled them to make the first lot of wine in the basement of the original Ziraldo family home on Ontario Street. Donald and Karl agonized over the naming of their new company. The two names in the running were Schloss Kaiser or Cantina Ziraldo. The co-owners were not enthusiastic about either of these options, and instead fate would play its unexpected hand.

In a meeting to finalize all LCBO requirements, with Donald and Karl still uncertain of the new wine company name, General Kitching asked if there were any historic names from Niagara they might use. Donald mentioned the name of his farm property, Enniskillin. Kitching recognized the name immediately, as it was a well-respected Irish military regiment. The name search ended and, with slight alteration, Inniskillin was born in 1975. It received the first Ontario wine license granted since prohibition.

Karl's first wines, released in 1974, were 500 bottles of De Chaunac, 500 bottles of Marechal Foch, along with several thousand bottles of a third blended wine called Vin Nouveau. At the time of Karl's first release, Chateau Gai (owned by the Labatt Brewing Company Ltd.) was

releasing its own Marechal Foch. Chateau Gai ran a substantial TV advertising campaign featuring its resident
winemaker, Paul Bosc, Sr. (who would later found
Chateau des Charmes estate wines in Niagara), a
renowned Burgundian French winemaker who informed
viewers of this higher-quality Ontario wine…and of "better things to come." Better things were very much on the
horizon.

With Inniskillin's Marechal Foch selling at $4.95 a bottle,
twice the price of any other Canadian wine at the time,
Donald and Karl thought it might be a difficult sell, but
the opposite proved true. In a wine-tasting review in the
Globe and Mail newspaper, wine writer Michael Vaughan
stated that Inniskillin Marechal Foch was better than
many imported French wines. With this positive press
and the benefit of the Chateau Gai Marechal Foch ads,
Inniskillin's first commercial supply of wines sold out in
only a few weeks.

By 1978 Inniskillin had produced its first vinifera
wines from 30,000 vine plantings of Riesling, Gamay, and
Chardonnay. In 1991 Inniskillin brought international
attention to the Niagara wine industry when it won the
distinguished Grand Prix d'Honneur trophy for its 1989
Icewine at Vinexpo, one of the world's most prestigious
and hotly contested wine competitions. For Donald and
Karl, there was no looking back.

*A wine is said to be "in
balance" if its alcoholic
strength, acidity, residual
sugar, and tannins complement each other in a way
that no single element
stands out or overwhelms
the other.*

Inniskillin Estate Winery is surrounded by vineyards

Icewine: Nectar of the Gods

Icewine's been called "Nectar of the Gods," and as Pierre Berton jested during one of our dinners, it's probably because "only the gods can afford it!"

Icewine, having originated in Germany, is one of those exotic beverages that spawn all sorts of stories, some more true than others. We've heard several different recollections of how icewine came to be. Our favorite recalls the monks who had passed out after imbibing in the vintages of the previous year and neglected to harvest the last of their grapes. A quick snap of extremely cold weather froze the grapes on the vine. They quickly harvested and crushed the frozen grapes so as not to suffer the scorn of their returning monsignor. (Stories like these add to the romance!)

The resulting fermentation revealed a remarkably luscious sweet wine that would become a highly prized and very rare sacramental beverage. Unfortunately, the weather in Germany rarely dropped to the subzero temperatures needed to freeze the grapes on the vine for making icewine. While Germany experiences the odd year that's cold enough, Canada is blessed with a constant and reliable subzero winter that enables the production of icewine. Ontario produces upwards of 350,000 liters of this celebrated wine, approximately 90% of Canada's total icewine production.

Many wine regions in the world produce sweet wines, usually as a result of picking select grapes weeks after the normal harvest, when they've sat on the vine and have developed highly concentrated sugar levels and enhanced flavors. Grapes used for these wines are more expensive to produce because they have to hang on the vines longer, under the threat of hungry birds, vineyard pests, and foul weather. Designated as late-harvest wines, they are very sweet, often preferred as dessert wines or apéritifs. As sweeter, more decadent wines with a full fruity richness, they are usually sold in 375 ml half bottles and are meant to be sipped slowly and in small portions. These late-harvest wines are made from various grapes in almost all wine regions. But then there's icewine!

Snow-covered vineyards, a prelude to glorious icewine harvesting

The odd vintage has suffered because of unusually warm winter weather patterns, but Ontario is usually cold enough to produce icewine every year. (The icewine crop in 1997 was all but decimated due to El Niño, and the extremely warm weather in the 2001/2002 season created great stress for winemakers.)

Opening a bottle of icewine can fill a room with an explosion of wonderful tropical aromas. A well-structured icewine, balanced with enough acidity to keep it from being overly sweet and heavy on the palate, is a dessert unto itself. The aroma and taste descriptors for icewine usually include apricot, peach, mango, grapefruit, and a host of exotic sensations for wine, such as honey, caramel, and butterscotch. For the sweet-toothed wine lover, icewine's got it all. (We've even heard of chocolate flavored icewine!)

The Vintners Quality Alliance (VQA) stipulates that to be authentic, grapes for icewine must freeze on the vine and be picked within a period of bitterly cold conditions ranging between –8 and –12 degrees Celsius. (Purists suggest that the grapes also be picked at night under a full moon!) The water remaining in the grapes crystallizes, and only the pure, sweet concentrated juice is pressed out for making icewine. (The second pressing of the same grapes would yield a secondary juice for what some would call a special or "select" late-harvest wine, not as concentrated as the first pressing for icewine but sweet just the same.) This legendary sweet wine has been compared to the ancient "mead," a honey-sweetened fermented wine-like beverage enjoyed by the gods and ancient Druids. It's valued for its rarity, and it's expensive to produce.

While most grapes for still or sparkling wines are harvested in September and October, grapes designated for icewine might have to hang on the vines through December, January, and sometimes into February if the weather isn't cooperating. This prolonged period of time

The determining factor in assessing the quality of icewine, as is true in assessing most sweet dessert wines, involves balancing the level of sweetness with a comparable level of acidity.

Jonathan is intent on guarding the icewine harvest—in uniform!

Try sipping icewine or a late harvest with some French or Danish blue cheese on bread or crackers. Let the wine and food melt in your mouth together. The experience is sensational and can convert those who dislike blue cheese on its own.

Celebrity icewine harvest at Inniskillin: (left to right) Donald Ziraldo, Jonathan, Jim Cuddy of Blue Rodeo, Executive Chef Christine Chamberlain, and CBC's Ron McLean

Icewine, from the German word **eiswein** *(ice-vyn), is made from grapes naturally frozen on the vine and pressed before they thaw. This resulting juice is highly concentrated with high sugar and acid content.*

Frozen grapes are netted for protection

reduces the amount of juice in the grape, and the longer it hangs the less juice there'll be when finally harvested. Then there are the pests!

Growers employ several tactics to prevent ravenous birds from devouring their vulnerable yields. One of the growers we filmed in early October was overseeing the installation of mesh netting to cover his vines. The cost of the netting, manpower, and equipment required was substantial. We had no idea that a roving flock of starlings could swarm into an unprotected vineyard and within minutes devour tens of thousands of dollars' worth of grapes. Mesh netting is the best method growers have found to protect the grapes. Icewine is also difficult to ferment because of the cold, and it requires special yeasts and a longer period for fermenting.

The exceptional icewine made in Ontario helped elevate international recognition of Canada as an up-and-coming wine-producing nation. Some might argue that icewine occupies too much attention and detracts from the many other great wines being produced in the province but few can disagree with icewine's sensual allure and worldwide sales success.

Icewine has become extremely popular in Asia, where rare delicacies command exorbitant prices on the open market. While filming on location it was not uncommon to see Japanese tourists taking a case or two of icewine with them to the airport. On one occasion we were filming inside a winery retail shop when a young Japanese travel guide started frantically banging on the door. It was 7 a.m. and the shop couldn't legally sell wine until 10 a.m. He was not happy and sat outside for three hours until he could run in and buy several cases of icewine for a departing tourist who was waiting at the airport. At an average $50+ a half bottle (375 ml), three cases can cost Can$1,800. He left with almost $6,000 worth of icewine in his car, but we have no idea if he made it to the airport in time for his client's flight. Why such a fuss?

Apparently, this is "chump" change because back in Tokyo that same 375 ml bottle of icewine has been known to cost as much as US$250. Talk about impressing your friends or family back home.

Jonathan's caught with his hand in the barrel!

Authentic icewine from Canada is also prestigious for Asian travelers because wine counterfeiters slip into the market with adulterated imitations. Throwing the grapes in a freezer and adding sugar to the process is not the same as tasting a real icewine. A forgotten bottle of Vidal left in the freezer pops its cork, and after thawing on the counter for a couple of hours the wine tastes much sweeter. By no stretch of the imagination does it compare to a real icewine or late harvest. The VQA enforces strict standards on icewine production in Canada, and its label is an assurance of authenticity.

If you want to try an icewine but are leery of the price tag, many wineries now release their icewines in small 50 ml bottles that are more than enough for a single serving test run. Where until recently Vidal and Riesling were the two common grapes used for icewine, today it's not unusual to find icewines made from a host of white grapes and even some red grape varietals. If you find icewine too sweet for your palate, the late-harvest wines offer a similar exotic fruit aroma and taste experience with much less concentration, and at 25% to 30% of the cost. It's quite an experience.

Laden with snow, frozen bunches await harvesting

The Underground Railroad

Let freedom's cry ring! "Following the North Star" to Canada was an arduous journey undertaken by nineteenth century fugitives escaping the tyranny and misery of slavery within the United States. They did this via the silent tracks of the Underground Railroad—neither underground nor a railroad but a symbolic term used by enslaved black Americans and firmly fixed in the mind's eye. Sanctuary! And, for many, that meant a dangerous trek north to the wilds of far-off Canada.

The "railroad" was a network linked by a passion to aid those thousands of African Americans seeking refuge from the miseries of slavery by escorting them to the free states of the North and to Canada in the years leading up to the American Civil War. The stories of hardship and abandonment are often hard to bear. Both the Niagara area and the Windsor area have a rich history in keeping the railroad open and moving. Many harrowing accounts of journeys "following the North Star" to sanctuary have been preserved in museums, and they are well worth the visit to observe the local activities of "conductors" on the railroad.

The St. Catharines Museum has a fabulous exhibit. The Niagara area was a terminal on the Underground Railroad for the simple reason that a strong black community was congregated around two churches in the town. The British Methodist Episcopal (BME) and the Zion Baptist became the focal points of

The congregation stands in front of the British Methodist Episcopal, c. 1920, Marjorie Dawson Collection, St.Catharines Museum, N8989

their social life. The Refugee Slaves' Friends Society (RSFS) was formed in 1852 to aid fugitives who arrived in need of immediate assistance after a treacherous journey.

Harriet Tubman, or "The Black Moses," was regarded as the greatest conductor to lead refugee slaves to freedom in Niagara. She escaped slavery herself in 1849 and went on to become a leading abolitionist prior to the American Civil War. She led hundreds of ex-slaves to freedom along the route of the Underground Railroad, and she ran a boarding house in St. Catharines. John Brown referred to her as "General" Tubman!

The Niagara area is rich in Black American history.

Harriet Tubman, reproduced from *Scenes from the Life of Harriet Tubman,* St. Catharines Museum, N8969

Marynissen Estates Winery

FAST FACTS

R.R. #6, Concession 1
Niagara-on-the-Lake, Ontario
L0S 1J0
Tel: 905-468-7270
Fax: 905-468-5784
E-mail: info@marynissen.com
Web: www.marynissen.com

One of the finest boutique wineries in Niagara, Marynissen produces wines only from its seventy-acre estate.

The winery also produces only VQA wines. Wines include (white wines) Chardonnay, Sauvignon Blanc, Riesling, Gewurztraminer, Vidal; (red wines) Gamay Noir, Cabernet-Merlot, Cabernet Franc, Merlot, Cabernet Sauvignon; (dessert wines) Vidal Icewine and Vidal Winter Wine.

The Winemaker's Daughter is a Winemaker

Winemaker Sandra Marynissen suspects that she may never be wealthy but she knows she'll never be thirsty. When she revisits the jobs she took on for the winery before her father retired, she remembers doing everything except actually making the wine. That was the domain of her father, John Marynissen.

John wasn't the offspring of a vintner or wine negotiant. He was the son of a Dutch dairy farmer who found a reasonable wage as a chauffeur. When he married Adriana Timmermans in 1951 they decided to save everything they earned to immigrate to Canada. The determined couple arrived in the middle of June in 1952 wearing overcoats and scarves. They had always heard that Canada was a cold place where everything froze! They arrived with $35 in their pockets.

John and Nanny found jobs as immigrant workers on the Schenk Farms in Niagara. The wages were low and the housing feeble but in their resolve to make the most of this new life, they began scrimping and saving their earnings. By 1953 they had saved enough money to jointly purchase a Niagara farm property with John's brother Adrian, who had moved to Canada that year. The property already had grapevines, tender fruit trees, and tomatoes, which they continued to farm. John even took a stab at raising pigs. Adrian eventually sold his share of the farm to John.

To support the farm activity John worked as a welder and

Marynissen Estates Winery and boutique

also blended feed for sale to local pig farmers. By about 1972 they had saved enough money to purchase a nearby property exclusively for growing grapes. As a grape grower, John had also begun dabbling in amateur wine-making. He had been selling his Marechal Foch grapes to winemaker Karl Kaiser at Inniskillin, and in their developing friendship, John learned a great deal about wine-making from Karl.

John's grapes included some of the earliest plantings of noble varietals such as Cabernet Sauvignon, Riesling, and Chardonnay. He came to also grow Merlot when the nursery mistakenly sent him Merlot plantings instead of the requested Gamay. (It's hard to distinguish one vine from another!) The noble varieties were doing extremely well, and John increased his vinifera plantings. His amateur wines were also starting to garner awards and praise from near and far, and his biggest fans were his daughters.

Sandra and Anne appreciated the quality wines their father was making—especially his reds—and constantly coaxed John to establish a commercial winery. The daughters' persuasive tactics finally worked, and in 1990 Marynissen Estate Wines released their first official commercial vintage. Sandra took on the task of sales and marketing but was always more enamored with the challenges of actually making the wine.

Marynissen has since established itself as a "cottage winery" and produces a limited selection of wines released each year. Like most smaller wineries, confining their annual production to around 10,000 cases means you won't usually find their labels in the large-volume wine shops, although some of their more select wines do end up on the limited-edition vintage shelves. Cottage wineries offer travelers an opportunity to taste wines that are not widely distributed.

Favorable reviews and positive word of mouth from consumers enable Marynissen to sell 80% of its wines through its winery retail shop, while the other 20% comprises direct sales to restaurants and hotels.

John Marynissen helped to establish Niagara's improvement in grape and wine quality standards, and received a Lifetime Achievement Award from the wine industry. Now that he has retired, he has watched his daughter take the reigns. When Sandra won her first award, John simply turned to her and said, "What do the judges know?"

Now that Sandra's the winemaker, she can say she's done it all.

GRILLED VENISON CHOP WITH A WILD BERRY DEMI

from Chef Tim Erskine,
The Kiely Inn and Restaurant,
Niagara-on-the-Lake

—

Serves 4

4, 10-oz (300-g) venison chops
  (red deer)
16 oz (500 ml) burgundy wine
6 tbsp (90 ml) white vinegar
6 tbsp (90 ml) sugar
juice from 1 lemon
1, 16-oz (500-g) jar of red currant
  jelly
blueberries and blackberries

In a sauce pot, add the wine, white vinegar, sugar, lemon juice, and red currant jelly and reduce to the desired consistency.

In a heavy pan, grill the venison chops to medium rare or about 4 minutes on each side. Turn only once.

Just before serving the sauce, add a mixture of fresh blueberries and blackberries. Serve with oven-roasted mini red potatoes, fresh asparagus, and baby carrots.

WINE MATCH
Marynissen Cabernet Sauvignon

While most labels on French wines profile the chateaux, North American and new-world wine labels tend to profile the specific grape varietal or varietal blends.

Sommelier. . . Hmmm

Main Entry: som·me·lier

Pronunciation: "s&-m&l-'yA

Function: noun

Inflected Form(s): plural sommeliers /-'yA(z)/

Etymology: French, from Middle
French, court official charged
with transportation of supplies,
pack animal driver, from Old
Provençal *saumalier* pack animal
driver, from *sauma* pack animal,
load of a pack animal, from
Late Latin *sagma* packsaddle—
more at SUMPTER

Date: 1829

: A waiter in a restaurant who
has charge of wines and their
service; a wine steward

—Merriam-Webster OnLine,
www.m-w.com

by Maria Moessner, Inniskillin Estate Sommelier

Perhaps dictionary definitions have confused you even more. What actually is the role of a sommelier? This question was asked on the television show "Who Wants to Be a Millionaire?" and fetched the sum of $125,000. So why is there such a mystery behind the name? Well, in France, this word is as common a term as "restaurant manager" is to North Americans. Simply put, a sommelier is a wine professional, an educator responsible for wine management, promotion, and sales. To be accredited as such, one dedicates years of study prior to attempting a grueling exam. One must maintain an average of 60% from each of three sections: written and essay, service, and a blind tasting.

Today in the new world, times are rapidly changing, bringing forth a new era of wine appreciation and fine dining *savoir faire*. Gone are the days of the condescending, pretentious, and somewhat stuffy male, sporting a black tuxedo with a silver chain around his neck with a cup (tastevin) attached. This individual made us feel rather ill at ease. Actually, most of us were terrified of selecting the wrong wine. It was almost as if he has waiting for those wrong words to be spoken, so he could take his silver cup and hit you over the head with it! Well, folks, you can breathe easier because times have changed. The door to a new century has opened to a new breed of fresh, innovative, creative, and extremely passionate sommeliers, there to guide you through your restaurant wine adventure. So, the next time you are the lucky candidate responsible for selecting the wine, don't be afraid to ask for assistance. Part of what you pay for in a restaurant is wine advice, and you should avail yourself of it.

You will likely, at one time or another, encounter the term "sommelier" or require the assistance of a sommelier—be it learning in a classroom, purchasing bottles at a winery or in a market, reading a newspaper wine column, or dining in a traditional restaurant atmosphere. Let's raise a glass and propose a toast to a new era of wine appreciation.

Restaurant Wine Tips

- Examine the wine list. Most restaurants briefly explain their selections, and they are organized in a logical manner.
- Wine lists may be categorized by country and region, or by grape varieties, but the most consumer-friendly menus usually present their wines by style and weight, lightest to heaviest.
- The wine cork rarely indicates quality or possible fault.
- Your best analysis is certainly the wine in the glass. A quick glance to note the wine's color and clarity, then a swirl to release its aromas, and finally, a sniff to assure the wine is clean. Simply put, it should smell like "wine" with no reflection of such aromas as chemical, must, vinegar, or sherry.
- Ask for assistance, even if the restaurant is "sans sommelier." Most staff know their list and are trained to help the consumer.

The word "varietal" refers to the specific grape from which a wine is made, and "vintage" indicates the year in which the grapes for a particular wine were harvested.

The term "hybrid" refers to a vine or grape created by breeding two varieties from different species, or the cross of two varieties from the same species. This produces a plant with the best traits of both parents.

Wine and Food Pairing Tips

- First and foremost, choose what you like!
- Balance the texture of the dish with the wine.
- Keep in mind the flavors of both food and wine and how they can react together.
- Pairing the weight of the dish or wine simply refers to the substance or heaviness found in both.
- Pair a wine to the most predominant taste on the plate.
- Match the wine with the occasion.
- Some food and wine opposites will attract.
- Strive for balance and regard between the two.

Cellaring Tips

- Ensure your wine is resting on its side in a cool, calm, dark environment, with a degree of humidity.
- Follow vintage charts for recommended aging.
- Research the wines you purchase.
- Most white, light reds, and rosé wines are not suited for the "rest" and usually drink best from one to four years from their noted vintage.
- Mainly full-bodied reds—maintaining high levels of tannins and alcohol—and some finer Rieslings are suited cellar styles.

The proper cellaring of wine requires careful attention

The Welland Canal

Visitors view a ship's passage as it "climbs the mountain"

The St. Catharines Museum is located at Lock 3 in St. Catharines, just beyond the Skyway Bridge. The Museum provides a bird's-eye view of the slow, majestic passage through the canal system at the foot of the Niagara Escarpment. The museum houses an extensive collection of nautical pieces related specifically to the rich history of the Welland Canal from its inception and construction from 1824 to 1828 through to the present day. Hailed as an engineering marvel, it still thrills viewers as they see the ocean-going vessels slowly "climb the mountain."

Take it from me, a visit to the Welland Canal is well worth it when traveling wine country. I grew up within sight of Lock 2 and never failed as a young boy to thrill to the mighty hoots of the giant boats as they announced their arrival. I've watched ships climb the mountain, and I have even perched on the forward deck of a freighter during its ascent, having hitchhiked a ride through the system from Lock 2 to Lock 8. I amassed an enviable collection of foreign coins tossed by sailors as they slowly rose in the locks. Ships from over forty nations regularly passed within arm's length, and the thrill has never left me. Just step outside the museum at Lock 3 to view this marvel of an engineering feat.

Inside the museum, trace the history of the many canals. Visionary William Hamilton Merritt was keen enough to capitalize on the canal-building

Jonathan points out the Niagara wine region

mania of the era. Improved transportation would open
up commerce to the American heartland, and so the idea
of joining lakes Erie and Ontario was floated! Merritt saw
it not only as a local channel but also as part of a Great
Lakes waterway—eventually to become part of the St.
Lawrence Seaway system.

In 1829 the first canal, with hand-worked timber along
with cleverly fashioned lift-locks, was opened. It contained thirty-nine locks with wooden gates. A ship was
dragged along by horses and pulled into the lock. The
second canal was opened in 1845 and the third in 1887.
The fourth and final canal was completed in 1932. The
complete system has a total of eight locks and is 27 miles
(43 kilometers) long. Portions of the old canals can still be
seen today in downtown St. Catharines and Port
Dalhousie, complete with lock tender shanties.

The shantytowns that grew up beside the canals were
home to the laborers—predominantly Irish immigrants
who rode the mania of canal building in the new world
(the Welland, Erie, and Rideau canals). These were generally poor, unskilled workers who toiled mercilessly for
upwards of fourteen hours a day for a pittance, if their
wages were even paid! (They were often owed wages for
months on end.) These intolerable conditions led to various troubles, among them the "Bread Riots" of 1844.

Most canal laborers and their families cobbled together
small shanties on public land as squatters. Constructed
from the detritus of local mills, discarded logs called
slabs, or outside pieces from milled logs, the clusters of
houses were known as "slabtowns." The accommoda-
tions were nothing better than hovels and lean-tos and
barely kept the elements at bay.

The "navvies" (Irish workers who dug the early chan-
nels) and the "tow boys" (who led the teams of horses
that pulled the sailing ships through the locks and along
the canal) had a rough life. The work itself was harrowing and hard, under appalling conditions. The museum
material notes that the workers "waded knee-deep in black
muck, wheeled, dug, hewed, and bore heavy burdens on
their shoulders, exposed at all times to every change of
temperature until stricken down with fever and then
taken to refuge in the shanties trembling with disease."

The St. Catharines Museum provides an in-depth
survey of those early years, so be sure to stop by. The
museum doesn't restrict itself to canal history but also
offers a wide range of memorabilia from various facets of
the area's rich history.

**The St. Catharines Museum
at the Welland Canals Centre at Lock 3**
SPEND SOME TIME

A special stop on the wine route.
Don't miss it.

Reif Estate Winery

FAST FACTS

15606 Niagara Parkway
Niagara-on-the-Lake, Ontario
L0S 1J0
Tel: 905-468-7738
Fax: 905-468-5878
Web: www.reifwinery.com

Located on the beautiful Niagara River Parkway, Reif produces wines only from its own 135-acre estate. Vinifera and hybrid grape varieties include Chardonnay, Riesling, Gewurztraminer, Vidal, Seyval Blanc, Pinot Noir, Cabernet Sauvignon, and Merlot. Reif is also well known for its award-winning Vidal and Riesling icewines.

The winery has a large underground barrel-aging cellar, which allows Klaus Reif to create some outstanding limited-edition wines that include premium oak-aged Chardonnay Reserve, three different barrel-segregated, unfiltered Chardonnays, and a unique barrel-fermented Gewurztraminer.

Reif has won a large number of national and international awards including gold medals at such prestigious competitions as VinItaly, Vinexpo in Bordeaux, France, and Concours Mondial in Brussels, Belgium.

The winery retail outlet is open daily to visitors, and public tours are held each day during the summer. Private groups are also welcome by appointment.

Tourists leaving Reif Estate Winery on a winery cycling tour, a pastime that is becoming increasingly popular

All Reif Estate wines are featured at the retail store, and a limited selection is available at LCBO outlets throughout Ontario. Reif also has distributors in other Canadian provinces, the United States, Europe, and Asia.

Klaus Reif: Wisdom Beyond His Years

Klaus Reif's family winemaking history dates back to 1638—that's over 360 years! Born into the Reif wines family from Neustadt in Southern Germany, Klaus is now the thirteenth generation of Reif winemakers, and the second generation Reif to make wine in Niagara. With over 360 years of winemaking in his bloodline and having worked in vineyards and the winery since he was a child, it's little wonder he's continuing the family business.

Klaus started picking grapes when he was five, and by the time he was fourteen he was managing the winery production line. As well as this hands-on experience and learning the craft from his father, Guenter, a university education in viticulture and winemaking was an essential ingredient in his training. Using an analogy, a parent can teach you to drive but a driver's education course will expose you to a more diverse array of driving experiences. And diversity was a must for Klaus.

Klaus graduated from the internationally acclaimed Geisenheim Institute, where he majored in viticultural studies, winemaking, and wine marketing. This solid education exposed Klaus to a wider range of ideas, experiences, disciplines, and practices, including the wine developments of the new world.

Groomed within the rigid traditions of his winemaking culture and primed with youthful ideals, Klaus became increasingly infatuated with the unconventional winemakers of California, Canada, and Australia. Their unlimited ability to experiment with any grape varietal in any manner they wanted was an exciting prospect.

In Germany, like most old-world European wine regions, winemakers were restricted in what they could do. Klaus was limited to working with the conventional wine varieties of the region and locked in to the centuries-old model of how German wines are made for the regional palate and food. Klaus was eager for greater winemaking diversity, and opportunity was about to knock on his door, thanks to his Uncle Ewald.

Ewald Reif had visited Canada during the 1960s for a holiday and had always remarked on how beautiful the Niagara region was. By 1975 Ewald wanted to step back from winemaking but continue his work in agriculture.

PAN-ROASTED VEAL TENDERLOIN
with Creamed Wild Mushrooms, Asparagus, and Red Wine Jus

—

from Chef Patrick Lin, Hemispheres Restaurant & Bistro, Metropolitan Hotel, Toronto

—

Serves 4

4 pieces of 5-oz (150-g) veal tenderloin wrapped with bacon slices
16 green asparagus stalks, peeled and blanched
1 cup (250 ml) shiitake mushrooms, sliced
½ cup (125 ml) seasonal mushrooms, chopped
1 tbsp (15 ml) garlic, minced
2 tbsp (30 ml) extra virgin olive oil
½ cup (125 ml) 35% cream
1 cup (250 ml) button mushrooms, sliced
1 cup (250 ml) oyster mushrooms, sliced
1 tbsp (15 ml) shallots, minced
1 tbsp (15 ml) parsley, finely chopped
1 cup (250 ml) chicken stock

SAUCE
½ bottle (375 ml) Reif Estate Merlot or Reif Estate Baco Noir red wine
½ carrot, peeled and coarsely chopped
½ leek, cleaned and coarsely chopped
4 shallots, peeled and chopped
1 bay leaf
½ thyme sprig
1 tbsp (15 ml) oil
½ celery stick, cleaned and coarsely chopped
1 onion, peeled and coarsely chopped
1 garlic clove, peeled and chopped
½ rosemary sprig
1 cup (250 ml) natural veal jus
1 tbsp (15 ml) unsalted butter

Wrap the veal tenderloin with the sliced bacon and sear it in a moderately heated pan with seasoning. Set the oven at 375°F (190°C) and roast the veal for 10 to 12 minutes. Take the veal out of the oven and let stand for 15 minutes.

continued on page 34

continued from page 33

For the sauce, slightly sauté the coarsely chopped vegetables and herbs with oil and pour in the red wine. Reduce to half and add the veal stock or jus. Sieve the vegetables and pass through a fine strainer. Season to taste and gently whisk in the unsalted butter. Sauté the mushrooms with the olive oil in a very hot pan. Add the shallot and garlic, then pour in the chicken stock and cream. Reduce until the cream is thick. Season to taste.

Cook the peeled asparagus in boiling water and season.

Place the veal in the middle of the plate with the creamed mushroom on top. Place the asparagus across the veal and dress the sauce around the plate.

WINE MATCH
Reif Estate Merlot

He sold his 50% share of the Reif Winery to his brother Guenter and moved to the Niagara Peninsula, where he purchased farm property along the Niagara River.

Klaus and his father paid many visits to Niagara over the next few years, and they agreed that the grape-growing conditions in Niagara were exceptional. By 1982 the Reifs had established an estate winery, which Ewald ran until 1987 when he retired. This was the door that Klaus had dreamed of walking through. Excited by the opportunity and bolstered with the pride of twelve generations of winemaking history, Klaus and his wife, Sabina, took on the task of managing the first Reif new-world winery.

Klaus knows that fine wine production isn't guaranteed—even with a distinguished family winemaking legacy—nor is it a realization of exacting laboratory analysis. Very few of the winemaker's decisions are made in the laboratory. Good wine can only come from healthy vineyards and well-balanced grapes. Like other farmers, winemakers are at the mercy of Mother Nature. Klaus looks at his role as that of an agricultural custodian, respecting the fruit and nature's ways. Winemaking isn't a formulated recipe but rather an intuitive process that is built upon a philosophy of harmony, balance, and passion that often defies bottom-line business strategies.

Where everything old is new again, Klaus notes that European old-world winemakers are learning from new-world attitudes and are now changing some of their ways. The competition in winemaking revolves around improving quality and constantly raising the bar of excellence. Klaus recognizes that Niagara, like every wine region in the world, is developing its own distinct style of wines that are unique to the soils, climate, and seasons of the area.

Klaus is satisfied that he's on track because when Guenter visits and tastes the wines from Niagara, Klaus can see the sense of pride in his father's satisfied smile. Vive la difference!

Red Green demonstrates a flare for fine wine

Stop and Go with Red Green

For those of you who don't know, Red Green (alias Steve Smith) is the duct-tape-loving man's man of TV. Red's weekly comedy television series "The Red Green Show" spoofs some

of the well-intentioned mis-
deeds executed by a bunch of
guys at the lodge. Red's plaid
shirt with mismatched sus-
penders and fisherman's hat
are a dead giveaway to his
preoccupation with outdoor life
at the lodge.

A native son of Hamilton,
Ontario, Steve has had an illustrious career in entertaining
and is without doubt one of the
grand masters of witticism.
That's to say he's really funny.

Steve agreed to join us along
with winemaker Klaus Reif
(Reif Estate Winery) in an
elegant restaurant for the taping of one of our shows. Talk
about your fish out of water! We were surprised when
he arrived already dressed as Red Green. Apparently, so
were dozens of commuters on the Queen Elizabeth
Highway who noticed Red—in full costume—driving a
Mercedes Benz.

Red and his lodge buddies once attempted to make wine in a
snow tire!

On time and ready to go, we quickly outlined the
format of the show. The chef was preparing three courses
and Klaus had brought wines to match with each dish.
Each course was being treated like an act in a play: the
beginning, middle, and end. Jonathan would trigger the
conversation and help guide it along, but for the most
part it was a free-flow conversation. Red was encouraged
to join in and ask questions whenever he wanted.
Opening up the format and encouraging Red to jump in
whenever he wanted was like serving him dessert before
the camera started taping.

Klaus Reif is an accomplished thirteenth-generation
German winemaker with a well-respected winery in
Niagara-on-the-Lake. Despite English being his second
language, Klaus has a wonderful ability to explain things
in easy-to-understand terms. Which was most fitting for
Jonathan and Red. In contrast to Red and Jonathan in
their fishing shirts, Klaus was wearing a handsome
double-breasted suit complemented with a silk tie. We
had told Klaus that the show was dedicated to demysti-
fying wine for viewers and that we wanted to have a
few laughs while delivering important information.
He embraced the objective, and once the tape started
recording he assumed the role of "straight man" and
played it perfectly.

You can recognize a mis-
matched wine and food pair-
ing when the combination
creates an unwelcome third-
party flavor that wasn't
present in the individual
wine or accompanying food.

Sauvignon Blanc is regarded as a wine varietal with distinctive characteristics often rooted in its naturally higher acidity, and depending on the winemaker's style, it often has a delicate, crisp, and refreshing finish.

A consideration that winemakers employ when selecting wines to match their foods is the weight or body of the wine, regardless of its color, and they always keep in mind the power of stocks or sauces used.

Red eased into the conversation and within minutes had Jonathan almost on the floor in stitches. With Jonathan already "on the hook" Red began working his quips on an unyielding Klaus. Red would taste the wine Klaus had poured and suggest it was very special…because nothing was floating in the glass. When a remarkable shrimp appetizer arrived Red mistook it for bait and, because it was arranged in a circle, pondered how he might turn it into a clock. When Jonathan suggested they dig in, Red thought the guys at the lodge would be impressed because the table was graced with cutlery.

Throughout the entire three-act taping, Red had everyone—except Klaus—in tears with laughter. At one point we almost stopped taping because the cameraman was laughing so hard the camera was shaking.

While Jonathan and Red bantered, Klaus offered all kinds of information on the origins of the wines, the influences of different kinds of oak on the flavors of the wines, and insights into how the wines would work with the meal. In the second act, featuring the main course of lamb, Klaus opened a door that Red couldn't resist going through.

Jonathan had brought up the topic of fishing and wondered if either of the wines being served with the featured lamb would go with fish. Klaus offered some sound advice and turned to prompt Red with a question about fishing at the lodge.

> *Klaus: I understand you have a lodge up north somewhere. How far is it?*
>
> *Red: Well, the government went metric on me and all I know is it's 140 beer stores north of Toronto.*
>
> *Klaus: Do you eat the fish you catch there?*
>
> *Red: Well, ya, we do,… we fish in Mercury Creek just outside the paint factory, but normally most people want a fish with just one head on it…but the fish are really colorful on the plate…and they magnetize the cutlery.*

When the taping was finished Klaus stood up and started laughing out loud, patting Red and Jonathan on the back. "That was the funniest time I ever had in my whole life!"

After having played the perfect straight man to someone as quick and gifted as Red, Klaus might some day consider a more theatrical career. If you ever have Red over for dinner, it's probably wise not to serve fish!

Vintner Klaus Reif (left) and winemaker Roberto DiDomenico

Vineyard site selection is the single most important aspect of grape growing, and it will affect yield, quality of wine produced, wine styles employed, and long-term profitability.

Winemaker's Matches
Klaus Reif, Reif Estate Winery

White Wine:	Dry Riesling
Food:	Pacific salmon with pasta in a cream sauce
Comment:	Contrary to some opinions, Klaus enjoys the Riesling's refreshing acidity, which helps to break down the heaviness of the cream while it cleans his palate.

Oversized barrels imported from Germany

Red Wine:	Cabernet-Merlot blend
Food:	Charbroiled fillet mignon with portabello mushrooms
Comment:	The charred flavors and texture of the beef match with the pepperiness and weight found in the Cab-Merlot. Ideal with a reduction sauce made from the same Cab-Merlot.

Pinot signifies a family of grape varieties, the most celebrated being the Pinot Noir. It is the grape wholly responsible for red Burgundy which is considered to be the most difficult wine to perfect.

Peller Estates Winery

FAST FACTS

290 John Street East, R.R. #1
Niagara-on-the-Lake, Ontario
L0S 1J0
Tel: 905-468-4678; 888-673-5537
Fax: 905-468-1920
E-mail: info@peller.com
Web: www.peller.com

Situated on forty acres in the heart of Niagara's wine country, Peller Estates Winery was designed to be the home of Canada's finest red wines.

Officially opened in 2001, the twenty-five acres of vineyards surrounding the winery feature vitis vinifera varietals such as Cabernet Sauvignon, Cabernet Franc, and Merlot. The 5,000 square foot underground barrel aging cellar and the 5,000 square foot press house are home to 1,000 barrels of next-generation Peller wines. They have the capacity for 60,000 bottles of Peller's sparkling wine, a blend of Classical Methode sparkling wine and icewine.

Winemakers Rob Summers and Jamie Macfarlane adhere to a meticulous winemaking process that uses small batches, minimum handling, and extensive barrel aging.

Only a select number of labels are available at Peller Estates: Andrew Peller Signature Series, Private Reserve

The impressive Peller Estates Winery in Niagara-on-the-Lake

Series, and Vineyard Series. These predominantly single-varietal red wines are carefully crafted through both traditional and contemporary winemaking techniques. The wines are often unfiltered, aged sur lie, or given extensive barrel aging. The result is the Peller style: big, bold, new-world red wines.

Peller varietals include (Andrew Peller Signature Series) Cabernet Sauvignon, Cabernet Franc, Merlot, Chardonnay Sur Lie, Riesling Icewine; (Private Reserve Series) Cabernet Sauvignon, Cabernet Franc, Merlot, Chardonnay, Sauvignon Blanc Barrel Aged, Gamay Noir, Riesling, Cristalle; (Vineyard Series) Riesling Semi-Sweet, Muscat, Chardonnay Non-Oak, Gewurztraminer.

Peller Estates has won a large number of national and international awards for its wines in such prestigious competitions as Cellars of the World, All-Canadian Wine Championships, International Wine and Spirits Competition in England, and VinItaly.

The winery is within walking distance of the Old Town of Niagara-on-the-Lake and the scenic Niagara Parkway. Visitors can participate in winery tours where they can visit the impressive underground barrel aging cellar, sample premium VQA wines in the tasting rooms, and browse through the winery boutique featuring wines exclusive to the winery. Groups are also welcome. The underground barrel aging cellar is a unique location for a wine tasting and the grand room, Founder's Hall, seats up to 100 guests.

Visitors also have an opportunity to enjoy exceptional regional cuisine at Peller Estates' own winery restaurant presented by Jason Rosso, chef de cuisine. Diners can enjoy a spectacular view of the Niagara Escarpment and surrounding vineyards.

RED WINE AND CARDAMOM POACHED PEARS

from Chef Jason Rosso, Peller Estates Winery Restaurant

Serves 4

4 Bosc or Anjou pears
½ bottle (375 ml) of Cabernet Franc
2 tbsp (30 ml) ground cardamom
1 stick cinnamon
4 tbsp (60 ml) fine sugar

Put the wine, cardamom, cinnamon, and fine sugar in a pot. Place on stove and bring to a quick boil. Take off the heat and let it steep for 10 minutes. Peel the skin off the pears using a sharp knife—be sure to follow the contours of the pear to keep its shape. Be gentle. Cut the bottom of the pear off to let it sit flat. Place the pears into the wine. Place back on the stove and bring to a boil. Reduce heat so there is no movement in the liquid (this is poaching). Let pears poach for about half an hour or until a knife slips easily into the flesh. The pears should be very red in color. Remove from the liquid and let cool. Serve the pears with warm chocolate sauce. The poaching liquid can keep for quite a while in the fridge to poach again.

WINE MATCH
Peller Estates Andrew Peller Signature Series Cabernet Franc

John Peller: When Your Name's on the Label

John Peller has more than an affinity for the Niagara wine region. When he talks about the future and making some of the world's greatest red wines, he's not just talking the talk. There's a fire in his belly that emanates from a deeply rooted respect for his father, Joe, and his late Grandfather, Andras (Andrew) Peller, the man whose vision and drive spawned one of Canada's most noteworthy wineries and wine family names.

Andras Peller (Andy to his friends) was born not far from Budapest in Gara, a small Hungarian town on the

Gewurztraminer is a pink-skinned grape varietal that produces fuller-bodied white wines known for their distinct heady aroma and exotic flavors of lychees and scented roses. The wine is commonly called spicey.

Where the term "aroma" often refers to the smells associated with the fruit characteristics of wine, "bouquet" indicates other attributes and complexities achieved by the winemaker during vinification.

Usually designated by the winemaker, the term "reserve" implies a superior or special wine, while the addition of "proprietor," "estate," or "family" reserve implies a wine of exceptional quality.

banks of the Danube River. He was born to poverty and with the early death of his father and being the only son, he had to work to support his mother and sisters. His dreams of going to school and running a business were secondary to his family's fundamental need for food and shelter. His entrepreneurial aspirations would have to wait.

Andy worked at several different jobs during the days while apprenticing as a millwright in the evenings. By the time he was seventeen he met his soon-to-be wife, Lena, the fourteen-year-old daughter of the local baker, and within three years they had three sons. The times were very difficult, and serious illnesses claimed the lives of the first and last son at the tender ages of one and three, leaving the last surviving son, Joe (age two), as the only heir. Andy realized that to build any future for his family would require desperate measures.

He and his wife worked a number of jobs and saved enough money to emigrate to Canada in March 1927. Settling in Kitchener, Ontario, Andy took on various jobs until he started working at Cosgroves Brewery, where he began training as a brewer. He excelled at the crafting of beer, and it wasn't long before he earned his Brew Master Certificate in Chicago. Andy worked for several brewers over the years before finally pursuing his own entrepreneurial dreams.

Andy established Pellers Brewery in Hamilton, Ontario, in 1945, located on the site that later became Amstel Brewery and is now Lakeport Brewery. The brewing venture was highly successful and provided Andy with a business foundation from which to develop other ventures. His entrepreneurial spirit soared, and he started grocery stores, machine parts companies, and car dealerships, to name a few. A generous offer to buy his brewery brought him even greater financial reward. By 1954 Andy Peller had established himself and was about to make one of the biggest decisions in his life—a decision that would see the annihilation of his hard-earned fortune!

In May of 1954 Andy entered the newspaper industry with the launch of the *Hamilton News*. Being loved by his employees and applauded for entering such a demanding field were short-lived pleasures. The newspaper bombed and he lost everything. At fifty-eight years of age, and never one to back away from circumstances, Andy began a new career in the wine business.

During those days, Ontario had not granted a wine license since prohibition. The political climate in Ontario was not receptive to the aspirations of Andy Peller, but British Columbia, under Premier W.A.C. Bennett (affectionately known as "wacky Bennett"), was open for business.

In 1961 Andy settled in Port Moody, where Andrés Wines was founded. He secured the services of viticulturist Helmut Becker, from the famous Geisenheim University in Germany, to initiate the growing of vinifera vines in the Okanagan Valley. By 1968 the political climate in Ontario had changed. Ontario was producing a great deal of fortified wines that appealed to the sweeter palate. Andy had a taste for higher-quality dry wines and a belief that they could be produced in Niagara.

Getting on in years but still fired by his drive and determination, Andy recruited his son, Joe, to help build the business. Joe left his internal-medicine practice after twenty years as chief-of-staff with Hamilton Civic Hospitals and joined his father's ambitious undertaking. Andrés Wines was to become an influential force in the new wine movement.

Today, John Peller, grandson to Andy and son of Joseph, is carrying the family banner into another important era for Canadian wines. While his law career and corporate business background have proven excellent tools in helping to steer the Andrés ship into the future, John's enthusiasm for wine is outmatched by his deep and profound respect for the vision of his forefathers.

Firmly committed to producing world-class wines, with a fondness for reds, John's focus and determination are soundly grounded in his grandfather's ability to overcome adversity and to build a better life for his family and friends. Andy's ability to survive, inspire, and rise to the challenge has instilled a sense of pride and dedication that guides John Peller through every moment of every day.

In his office he cherishes a trophy once presented to his grandfather from the employees of his newspaper venture. A bronze casting of two boxers standing fist to fist is graced with a small engraved message on the pedestal that reads, "To battling Andy Peller."

Where the enjoyment and appreciation of wine is often used as a metaphor for the wonderful gifts that life has to offer, this treasured statue reminds John that setting higher goals and never quitting are the fabric his grandfather was woven from. With the name Peller on the label and an illustrious family history that evokes tremendous pride in John, it's easy to understand that the apple doesn't fall far from the tree.

Aging of wines for long periods in oak barrels adds oak flavor and other complexities, while aging wine in the bottle helps to develop a pleasing taste and odor commonly known as "bottle bouquet."

Niagara Parkway

The Horseshoe Falls illuminated at night

The aerocar over the whirlpool and
the gazebo in the Botanical Gardens

The Niagara Parkway is the best example of "getting there is half the fun!" It's a twisty, two-lane black-top that hugs the Niagara River for a 35-mile (56-kilometer) stretch from historic Fort Erie to the period charm of Niagara-on-the-Lake. It is beautifully maintained with remarkable foresight by the Niagara Parks Commission, and there is not even a hint of Disney anywhere, for which you will be thankful. The Parks Commission was established in 1885 "for the preservation of the natural scenery about Niagara Falls." I salute them because they've stuck with the premise. Its stewardship has seen the attractions and services grow to include— free of charge—parks and gardens, picnic areas, concerts for all ages, a nightly illumination of the Falls, fireworks over the Falls, nature trails, and a world-renowned Botanical Gardens with even a fragrance garden for the visually impaired plus a year-round greenhouse featuring floral displays, tropical plants, and free-flying birds.

The Parkway Trails are all worth exploring. The Adventure Trail features the Falls itself with its breathtaking roar and thundering cataract that has thrilled millions of travelers since the first tourist, Father Hennepin, gazed on it and inked the first postcard in 1678. If you take the journey behind the Falls, you'll feel the mist of the water. The *Maid of the Mist* tug makes its journey to within yards of the Falls and is worth the wait. Or how about taking the Spanish Aero Car over the whirlpool rapids? Walk right down to the whirlpool itself if you're truly adventurous. I love the descent to the whirlpool.

The Horticultural Trail takes you to the Botanical Gardens, around the floral clock into the fragrance garden where you can stick your nose anywhere you like. Included in this tour are the Niagara Parks Greenhouse and the School of Horticulture (where gardeners can study), and you don't want to miss Queenston Heights with its commanding view of the sweep down the Niagara River to its mouth at Lake Ontario.

The Heritage Trail is fascinating. From Old Fort Erie, through the Chippawa battlefield of the War of 1812, on to the Laura Secord homestead in Queenston—home also to the Mackenzie Heritage printery, Canada's largest operating printing museum—and finally to McFarland House, one of the few buildings that pre-date the War of 1812. And don't forget Fort George in Niagara-on-the-Lake for reenactments during summertime.

The Nature Trail is one of my favorites. It includes the whole 35 miles of the Niagara Parkway to be enjoyed a number of ways. The best is by bike or, if you're adventuresome, by rollerblade. You'll have to take off the blades to enjoy a breathtaking experience at the Butterfly Museum and Conservatory; that is not to be missed. Picnic along the Parkway or in one of the many byways.

Jonathan charms the butterflies at the Butterfly Museum

The Recreation Trail has some of the best golf courses in Canada. The Legends on the Niagara gold course facility is located just south of the village of Chippawa. The 700-acre site features two eighteen-hole championship courses, a complete gold teaching academy, a nine-hole executive course, a 360-degree practice facility, and an eighteen-hole putting course. A spectacular clubhouse sits on a nineteen-acre lake and captures the spirit of this historic War of 1812 setting.

There is something for everyone on the Niagara Parkway.

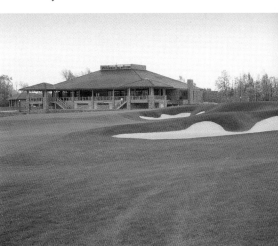

Clubhouse at the spectacular Legends on the Niagara

Kurtz Orchards

Any itinerary of wine country must include a picnic by the Niagara River, if time permits. The Niagara Parkway is a meandering roadway that is well worth a slow ramble along. You can walk it, you can bike it, you can rollerblade it, you can drive it. But do it.

To pick up supplies for a picnic, my favorite stop is just outside the Niagara-on-the-Lake town limits beyond Fort George at the corner of the East-West Line and the Niagara Parkway. It is the expanded fruit stand of Kurtz Orchards. You'll find all you require for a delightful picnic all in one place. This country market also has one-of-a-kind country crafts for those wanting to take home

Kurtz pond and picnic area

memories of Niagara. It's a lively spot with enough food to feed the busloads of tourists rolling along the Parkway. They serve lunches, soups, salads, fresh home-grown Niagara fruit, hot pastries, homemade ice cream, and travel snacks such as dried fruit and nuts. You can enjoy your lunch on the grounds within the orchards and gently cascading waterfalls or find a suitable spot along the Parkway overlooking the Niagara River.

Kurtz Orchards also offers a tractor-pulled tram ride through their orchards. It's an exciting break from wine touring, and you'll enjoy the spectacular colors of tender fruit trees in blossom come spring and at the other end the apple and cherry harvest. Peach and strawberry tours are also offered during the summer.

So if you want a picnic, a stop for lunch, or a tour of a fruit orchard, I recommend a stop here. Keep an eye out for the maple fudge!

Niagara-on-the-Lake History

The Niagara frontier is full of surprises for the curious traveler. Steeped in tradition, the sleepy little town of Niagara-on-the-Lake at the northern end of the Niagara Parkway is well worth a close inspection. Summertime

The stately Prince of Wales Hotel in Niagara-on-the-Lake

SINGING FOR MY SUPPER

During the filming of our series, I always looked forward to the dinners we filmed. I met a wide range of people and it was a real treat, as viewers continue to remind me. I enjoyed myself, sometimes a bit too much. "Yeah, sure, some job" is the response many people gave when I explained my job. But it was work. It appears relaxed and very upbeat, but eating and drinking can be hard work!

C.Y. Lai, the diminutive doyenne of a number of hotels in the quaint historic town of Niagara-on-the-Lake, was a delightful guest. She perched bird-like on the edge of her chair and was energetic and alert to every turn of the conversation. This was a dynamo who thrived on setting a breakneck pace and dared you to keep up. She was a whirlwind of industry and bursting with ideas and plans already far beyond the dream stage.

But beneath her steely gaze beat the heart of a romantic. I know because I coaxed a slow childlike smile of delight from her. How did I do it? I sang to her over dessert and she responded to the moment. The carefully hung veil parted to allow a glimpse of the shy girl within. Maybe she was startled by my mewling but, nonetheless, it was a magic moment. I saw the frightened refugee fleeing for her life, leaving behind the torments of a troubled China for the dream of freedom across the waters that divide the drab mainland from the glittering jewels of Hong Kong. She swam those treacherous waters to gain her freedom. And her determination to achieve all she could unfolds to this day.

The song I sang to her was Webber's "Love Changes Everything."

is always busy, as tourists come in droves. But don't let that deter you. A walking tour of the back streets is amply rewarded with peeks into a bygone era and a nod to the hardy settlers who carved this jewel from the harsh landscape. A slow ramble around the town will delight any jaded eye. A visit to Fort George will take you back to colonial times, and if you're lucky you'll catch a reenactment of one of the battles that this frontier outpost saw.

Between 1775 and 1783, the first loyalist settlers planted firm roots, and their handiwork can be gleaned from the town's Georgian design. The waterways were the highways of the era, and Niagara grew as a commercial hub for goods transported inland. The wars in Europe hastened an explosion of industry, and tourism was very much a part of the restlessness of the New Age. The world beckoned, and the best address in the world was "Niagara Falls"—a true wonder of the modern world. Niagara was a launching point for the avid and keen sightseer. Itinerant soldiers shipping from post to colonial post in the ever-expanding empire carried tales of the charms of this new world. The Industrial Revolution quickened society's pulse, and borders disappeared.

With commerce and travelers, the Niagara area grew rich and genteel but the construction of the Welland Canal in the early 1800s hastened the demise of this once-bustling outpost. The capital had shifted to York (Toronto) and the waterways were forgotten when the stitching of railroads across the land opened the interior. Towns became backwaters overnight.

The War of 1812 spawned many stories of heroism. But there were also some humorous stories for good measure. My favorite is about a Canadian cow that was sold by a farmer in Queenston to a farmer in Lewiston, New York, just across the Niagara River. It seems the cow was munching her cud staring off across the river when homesickness overtook her and she plunged in and swam back home to Canada. They called her a loyalist cow, at least in Queenston. It's not recorded what they called her in Lewiston.

The fertile soil saw its share of bloodshed as war took its toll on the area. The French-Indian wars, the American Revolution, and the War of 1812 have all left their mark.

The American Civil War (1861 to 1865) brought about an upsurge of commercial activity in the area. The American giant was hungry for agricultural and manufactured goods. And with its handy proximity to the border, Niagara became home to spies and scoundrels from Confederate and Union camps alike. Many plots were hatched along the Niagara frontier as Confederate saboteurs tried to storm the shipping lanes of Lake Erie, seeking to free prisoners of war or just to stir up trouble in enemy lines of defense. These daring escapades found a sympathetic public here, and some spies were lauded as heroes for their exploits. This created much tension along the border and almost plunged the colony into a war with the Union forces. It is said that these tensions were instrumental in hastening the birth of the Canadian nation. It was an invasion of sorts that finally tipped the balance and forged the disparate groups into a single nation.

It was a tense time along the borders of British Canada and its restless and hungry neighbor. With the end of hostilities in the States, thousands of veterans were discharged and entered the work force, but few jobs were available. Among these veterans was a large group of anti-British Irish-Americans who saw a golden opportunity to right smoldering grievances. They formed the Fenian Brotherhood in 1858 to fight for Irish independence. The Fenians planned an invasion of Canada, hoping to hold Canada for ransom for Ireland's freedom! This bold scheme had unfortunate results for all. A pitched and heated battle at Ridgeway in 1866 near Fort Erie ended any threat of harm to the infant nation of Canada.

Jonathan leaves the icewine harvest to the regulars after being shown the door!

It has been said that the American Revolutionary War spawned two countries—the United States and Canada—but Canada was truly born of those events of 1866! The 35-mile stretch that borders the Niagara River was long occupied and can lay claim to being the very heart of the country. Meander along and see for yourself.

The romantic side of Niagara Falls

An abundance of goodness!

Lailey Vineyard Winery

FAST FACTS

15940 Niagara Parkway
Niagara-on-the-Lake, Ontario
L0S 1J0
Tel: 905-468-0503
Fax: 905-468-8012
E-mail: tonya@laileyvineyard.com
Web: www.laileyvineyard.com

William Lailey was a pioneer of Canadian viticulture. In the early 1950s he planted some of Niagara's first French hybrid varieties on his farm, which also included peaches, pears, apples, and cherries. In 1970 Donna and David Lailey purchased the land from David's parents and began a steady transformation of the twenty-acre farm into a vineyard planting vitis vinifera and French hybrids and producing quality grapes for local wineries.

In 1985 David and Donna expanded their business to include the pressing of grapes for home winemakers and local wineries. Lailey Vineyard continues to supply amateur winemakers with premium juice and maintains a relationship with wineries such as Southbrook. Southbrook has established award-winning varietal wines from Lailey Vineyard grapes and credits Lailey on their labels.

Hand-picked grapes are ready for processing in the winery

In 2001 Donna and David, along with daughter Tonya and winemaker Derek Barnett and their spouses, opened the new Lailey Vineyard Winery. Derek was born in England and studied agriculture there. He was the winemaker at Southbrook Winery for ten years and was awarded the Air Ontario Winemaker of the Year Award in 2000.

The soil of Lailey Vineyard comprises a maximum of two feet of sandy loam covering ten feet (three meters) of clay. Below the clay is shale. The soil is a result of deposits from an ancient lake and the alluvium of a retreating river. Vitis vinifera varieties under cultivation include (red wines) Cabernet Franc, Cabernet Sauvignon, Merlot, Muscat Otto, Pinot Noir, Zweigelt; (white wines) Chardonnay, Riesling, Sauvignon Blanc, Gewurztraminer, Seyval Blanc, Vidal Icewine, and Riesling Icewine. Lailey Vineyard wines are 100% Vintner's Quality Alliance and are produced totally from grapes grown in their own vineyard.

Lailey's has already won numerous awards for its wines at competitions, including the All-Canada Wine Championships for its Merlot, Cabernet Sauvignon, and Cabernet Franc.

The retail store is open from 11:00 a.m. to 5:00 p.m. and educational wine and food events are held monthly at the winery. Wines can be purchased at the local winery or ordered for delivery by calling or faxing the winery.

Chardonnay is a green-skinned European grape variety used in making the great French white Burgundies, and while it is almost always a dry wine, it can finish in a variety of body weights.

Konzelmann Estate Winery

FAST FACTS

1096 Lakeshore Road, R.R. #3
Niagara-on-the-Lake, Ontario
L0S 1J0
Tel: 905-935-2866
Fax: 905-935-2864
E-mail:
wine@konzelmannwines.com
Web: www.konzelmannwines.com

A proud family name greets visitors to Konzelmann Estate Winery

Chardonnay vines were historically responsible for the great white Burgundian wines released under respected French chateau labels. They didn't gain notoriety until the late twentieth century, when they were transplanted around the world and released simply as Chardonnay.

One hundred years ago, Friedrich Konzelmann of Uhlbach, near Stuttgart in Wuerttemberg, Germany, was well known for his humor and foresight—and for his expertise in food and wine. A restaurant owner, Friedrich made and served his own wine. The demand for his excellent wines led him to expand, first using the cellars of the local minister and the city hall in Uhlbach to store wines and then, in 1893, to establish a full-scale winery.

Friedrich was soon producing 200,000 liters of quality wine, and the Konzelmann tradition was launched. Today, Herbert Konzelmann, Friedrich's great-grandson, continues the family tradition in Niagara-on-the-Lake.

In 1984, Herbert chose the site for Konzelmann Winery on the shores of Lake Ontario because the microclimate and soil conditions of the region are ideal for premium quality wines. According to Herbert, the morning dew that settles on the grapes in the Konzelmann lakeshore vineyards gives his wines a uniquely delicate and fruity character, comparable to those of the Alsace region of Europe. The Konzelmanns introduced vertical vine training to Niagara, a method that better allows the wind and sun to draw moisture from the fruit, thereby increasing sugar content and intensity of flavor while

maintaining the balance of acid that gives wine its freshness and spirit.

Konzelmann produces approximately 40,000 cases of
twenty-nine different wines and has a storage capacity of
500,000 liters. The white wines include Riesling, Vidal,
Seyval Blanc, Chardonnay, Pinot Blanc, Gewurztraminer,
Pinot Noir Rose, Riesling Icewine, Vidal Icewine, Riesling
Traminer Icewine, Peachwine, and Champagne. Red
wines include Pinot Noir, Merlot, Gamay Noir, Baco Noir,
Zweigelt Late Harvest, and Cabernet Sauvignon/Merlot.

Herb Konzelmann has won a large number of national
and international awards for his wines including a Gold
Medal at Concours Mondial de Bruxelles Brussels in
Belgium for his Vidal Icewine and the Trophée Civart at
Vinexpo in Bordeaux for his Riesling Traminer Icewine.

Konzelmann provides informative daily public tours
from May to September and a number of special events
year round. The tasting bar offers a wide selection of
thirty different varieties of VQA wines for tasting and
purchase.

Pristine Konzelmann vineyards point towards Lake Ontario

BAKED SALMON IN SAFFRON CAPER CREAM SAUCE

from George Campbell

Serves 4

4, 5–6 oz (150–175 g) Atlantic
  salmon fillets
½ Spanish onion, peeled and sliced
½ small package of saffron
2 tbsp (30 ml) vegetable oil
2 cups (500 ml) whipping cream
small jar of capers
½ bunch fresh dill
1 sliced lemon

Lay the salmon fillets on an oiled
baking sheet and place into a preheated oven at 450°F (230°C).
Cook for 20 minutes.

Pour the oil into a large
saucepan and add the onions. Stir
and add saffron to the mixture.
Continue to stir on high heat until
the onions are wilted but not
brown.

Reduce the heat and add the
whipping cream. Stir and watch
the mixture until it boils (be careful or it will overflow). Reduce the
heat to low and let simmer, stirring
until it thickens (coats the back of
a spoon). Remove the sauce from
heat and add the capers. Cover the
salmon with sauce, garnish with
dill and a lemon slice.

Serve with basmati rice and
seasonal vegetables.

WINE MATCH
Konzelmann Chardonnay Grand
Reserve

Old Fort Erie

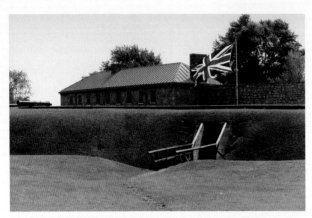

The redoubt at Old Fort Erie proudly flying the British Ensign

The shoreline of the Niagara River has been inhabited for thousands of years. In fact, recent excavations have led conservation authorities to suggest that Fort Erie was a major industrial center as long ago as 1300 to 1500. These excavations point to a thriving industry centered around the massive deposits of shale that Native tribes fashioned for arrowheads and spearheads. The shale of the Niagara area has surfaced throughout North America, and authorities surmise that it was shipped in bulk to be fashioned by other tribes, which suggests a massive export trade. Imagine an export industry in flint heads!

However, as the French explorers moved inland during their treks in the late eighteenth century, Native territories shrank and were ultimately displaced by settlers who introduced old world culture and methods.

A system of forts was built by the French for the fur trade. After the British displaced the French, the British took over the existing forts and planned new ones to assure their lines of communication remained open. Fort Erie was the first of these forts to be built, in 1764. It was located at the river's edge and served as a supply depot and shipping facility for the Great Lakes traffic. During the American Revolutionary War the fort was an important supply base for the British troops, loyalist rangers, and Iroquois warriors.

Storms wreaked havoc on the tiny fort and, in 1803, the British started building a new fort further back from the water and higher up the hill behind the original post. The supply of Onondaga flintstone available nearby made the new structure a formidable site but it was still unfinished when the War of 1812 broke out. The garrison distinguished itself at the Battle of Frenchman's Creek in

November of 1812, but the small contingent had to with-draw against a larger force in May 1813. Before they withdrew, however, they dismantled the old fort. The ruins were used by American forces until December when they were forced back across the Niagara River. Building was renewed by the returning British militia.

In the summer of 1814, a see-saw battle was waged along the Niagara frontier. The larger American forces were defeated by a smaller but veteran British army at the battles of Lundy's Lane and Chippewa, but Americans at Old Fort Erie remained defiant. The British forces attacked but were repelled with a huge loss of life, over 1,000 soldiers. Not deterred, the British laid siege but the Americans drove the British back to Chippewa by the end of September. Upon hearing of a full eastern seaboard attack on the United States and with winter approaching, the Americans destroyed the fort and with-drew to Buffalo for the last time. The Treaty of Ghent was signed in December, ending the War of 1812–14. Fort Erie remains the bloodiest battlefield in the history of Canada.

Reenactments of the War of 1812 are a feature of each summer's exciting events celebrated at Old Fort Erie, and I recommend a visit during any wine country tour.

Reenactments are a feature of each summer's exciting events

Jonathan on guard duty

Stonechurch Vineyards

FAST FACTS

1242 Irvine Road
Niagara-on-the-Lake, Ontario
L0S 1J0
Tel: 905-935-3535
Fax: 905-646-8892
E-mail: wine@stonechurch.com
Web: www.stonechurch.com

The Hunse family has been planting and developing vineyards since 1972 in one of the best wine-growing areas in Niagara close to Lake Ontario. In 1990 Rick and Fran opened Stonechurch and now have one of the largest estate wineries in Niagara. Winemaker Jens Gemmrich joined Stonechurch after years of experience in Germany.

On their 200-acre farm they have planted exclusively vitis vinifera and hybrid grape varieties. Eighty-five percent of Stonechurch wines are VQA. VQA wines include (white wines) Chardonnay, Vidal, Morio Muscat, Riesling, Gewurztraminer; (red wines) Cabernet Sauvignon, Cabernet Franc, Baco Noir, Pinot Noir, Merlot; (dessert wines) Vidal Icewine, Late Harvest Vidal.

Facilities at Stonechurch include a large retail store, a hospitality room that can accommodate up to 100, and an adjacent patio with weekend barbecues during the summer. A self-guided tour takes visitors on a pleasant

Stonechurch Vineyards in Niagara-on-the-Lake

ten-minute walk through the five-acre Chardonnay vineyard next to the winery. The winery also has a large number of special events during the year.

Stonechurch has won many awards for their wines at both national and international competitions including VinItaly and the All-Canadian Wine Championships. Wines are available at the winery store and some are also available through LCBO stores and in other Canadian provinces.

In Memory of Barry Morse

The late Barry Morse is remembered with much affection

During the taping of one of our episodes, we had the great opportunity to break bread with the late Barry Morse as one of our table guests. Most remembered for his continuing role on "The Fugitive" television series and having performed in many films and television programs, he also had a long distinguished career as a stage actor. The Shaw Theatre in Niagara-on-the-Lake was always a fond memory for Barry Morse, and his picture graced the walls of the Oban Inn dining room just down the street from the theater.

When he arrived on the set at the restaurant, his wonderful charm and sense of comradery were immediate. Within minutes his humor had unraveled the crew. Despite having worked in the industry for decades and knowing the rigors of production, Barry approached our shoot with the inquisitiveness of a young eager journalist. He wanted to know everyone by name, shake their hand, and learn about their jobs, family, kids, and pets. His

---

VIDAL ICEWINE SEMIFREDDO MAPLE TUILE BASKET WITH VINELAND BLACKBERRY COULIS

from Chef Barry Burton, Legends on the Niagara

Serves 4

SEMIFREDDO
5 eggs, separated
2 tbsp (30 ml) honey
2 cups (500 ml) 35% cream, whipped to a soft peak
⅔ cups (150 ml) sugar
1 cup (250 ml) Reif Estate Vidal Icewine

MAPLE TUILE
½ cup (125 ml) maple sugar
2 egg whites
½ cup (125 ml) pastry flour
½ cup (125 ml) butter, melted

BLACKBERRY COULIS
1 pint (½ L) fresh blackberries
1 oz (30 g) lemon juice
½ cup (125 ml) sugar
cornstarch

For the semifreddo, whip egg yolks with ⅓ cup (75 ml) of sugar until pale and fluffy.

Set aside. In a clean bowl, whip egg whites together with the other ⅓ cup (75 ml) of sugar until mixture forms a soft peak. Blend yolk mixture with the honey and Reif Estate Vidal Icewine. Fold in the whipped cream, then fold in the whites mixture. Spoon mixture into a muffin tin and freeze until needed.

To make the maple tuile, combine maple sugar and flour together. Stir in egg whites and melted butter. Chill batter for 30 minutes. Spread batter out in the desired shapes on a greased sheet pan. Bake at 350°F (175°C) for 8 to 10 minutes until they just turn golden. Quickly remove tuiles and mold them into a muffin tin making a cookie basket. Allow them to cool and harden, then set aside until needed.

continued on page 56

continued from page 55
To make the blackberry coulis, stew the berries and sugar together over medium heat. Add the lemon juice and thicken with cornstarch and water to the desired consistency (coats the back of a spoon lightly). Strain the sauce through a fine strainer to remove the seeds. Cool and reserve until needed.

To assemble, remove the semi-freddo from the muffin tin and place inside the tuile basket. Dust it with icing sugar. Pour blackberry coulis in the center of a dessert plate and place the semifreddo tuile basket on top of the coulis. Garnish with fresh whipped cream, blackberries, and a sprig of mint.

WINE MATCH
Stonechurch Vidal Icewine

Harvesting icewine is always done by hand

energy and enthusiasm were contagious, and he added an instant sparkle to the set.

His natural wit and charm were enriched by wonderful anecdotes from his thespian background. It was easy to see that he had a great joy for life and unconditional respect for everyone he met. When the makeup artist wanted to prep him with some powder, he took her hand and with a delicious twinkle in his eye suggested that the only thing mother ever allowed on his face was cereal.

While somewhat of a wine enthusiast himself, Barry wasn't in the least pretentious about wine appreciation. He was open to learning something and helped move the conversation along with some wonderful tales from his past.

Our featured winemaker was Sandrine Epp, a French winemaker with Stonechurch Winery in Niagara at the time. Once the table was set and the tape was rolling, Barry began to ask Sandrine all sorts of questions about her enological career. The only problem was that he called her "Francine." The chat was fun and light, and rather than interrupt the flow we let it pass and kept the tape rolling through the first fifteen-minute segment. Once the segment concluded, we reminded Barry that her name was actually Sandrine, not Francine. He apologized profusely and looked at Sandrine repeating her name out loud several times, "Sandrine, Sandrine, Sandrine...." He even complimented her on such a fascinating name and asked about its origins.

On set, from left to right, winemaker Sandrine Epp, producer Alan Aylward, guest Barry Morse, and host Jonathan Welsh

There were two more fifteen- to twenty-minute segments to be taped. We took the opportunity between segments to go over her name. "Sandrine, Sandrine, Sandrine…." Barry was curiously annoyed with himself, being a stage actor and having remembered countless lines and the most complicated of names. He found it odd that he couldn't retain her name despite repeating it and having written it down several times. Despite his best efforts, Barry called her Francine through each segment. Fortunately, it was not difficult to cut around this but it still puzzled Barry.

Finally, as the shoot ended Barry turned to Sandrine and apologized for the name mixup while on-camera. As he buttoned his coat and approached the door he turned to everyone for a final goodbye, and in his precise and clear English asked that, "if anyone discovered who 'Francine' was, could they please go to the trouble of letting him know."

Thank you for a wonderful time, Barry Morse. We remember you with great affection.

The use of the term "reserve" on the label suggests that the wine is made from a superior batch of grapes or select vineyards known for their high quality yields and determined to be superior to other wines made by the winemaker.

NOTES FROM THE CELLAR

BREATHE DEEPLY

What is decanting?
Decanting is the last step in the wine process, between the bottle and the glass. This procedure was originally used by the British to remove sediment from the bottom of the bottle. They consumed large quantities of Claret—wine from Bordeaux—and wanted to remove some solids that had developed during the maturation process. Since most wines today pass through a clarification process, decanting is generally only used when opening older bottles that have been cellared for a long period. However, it is still useful to expose a full bottle to

gentle oxidation all at once to allow the wine to breathe and fully develop.

Is there a special way to decant a bottle?
For old wines, pour the wine onto the inside walls of the decanter. This allows the wine to slide down the walls and maximizes the use of the surface area allowing for gentle oxidation, thus opening up the wine. If the wine is relatively young, splash the wine down the neck of the decanter. Young wines can improve with more rigorous oxidation. In the past, a candle was held under the neck of the bottle to see the sediment as it moved towards the mouth. Most

table wines today pass through a filtration process, which makes deposits unlikely, but some aged wines will still throw a sediment. This is a natural result of properly aging wines.

Decanters come in a wide variety of shapes: left, duck decanter; right, captain's decanter

Queenston

Mackenzie Heritage Printery Museum

Nestled at the bottom of Queenston Heights, underneath the watchful eye of General Sir Isaac Brock, is the Mackenzie Heritage Printery Museum. Located in the village of Queenston, the printery is devoted to displaying historic presses covering more than 500 years of the letterpress printing era.

The beautiful limestone building was the home of William Lyon Mackenzie, and from here he began his career as a publisher and agitator for political reform. He moved his family from York (Toronto) to Dundas and then to Queenstown (Queenston) in 1823. Disenchanted by the ruling clique, referred to as "the Family Compact," he soon gave up his lucrative mercantile career and took up printing broadsheets. His first newspaper, the *Colonial Advocate*, carried agricultural advice, poems, anecdotes, classified advertising, current events and, most importantly, Mackenzie's own political commentary. He rubbed the wrong people the wrong way. It was during these first issues that work had begun on a monument to Isaac Brock, commander of the British forces during the War of 1812, who was killed on the Heights above Queenstown. During the cornerstone-laying ceremony a bottle containing a copy of the *Colonial Advocate* was placed in the foundation stone. When Sir Peregrine Maitland, Lieutenant Governor of Upper Canada (and head of the Family Compact) heard this, he ordered construction on the monument stopped and a large quantity of the newly erected masonry pulled down in order to remove what he called a "colonial rag."

Mackenzie moved his family and press to York in 1824. He continued his agitation against the Family Compact and led the ill-fated rebellion of 1837. The desire for political change fomented during this rebellion finally was addressed by peaceful means, and responsible government was achieved in 1849.

His home in Queenston was neglected and deteriorated until all that was left were the skeletal remains of the

The whole family enjoys the interpreter's hands-on activity on a working hand press

walls and a single stone marker erected in 1935 by the Niagara Historical Society proclaiming the "Home of William Lyon Mackenzie. The Birthplace of Responsible Government, 1823–1824." In 1935 the Niagara Parks Commission undertook the restoration of the Mackenzie House. The beautifully restored home was officially opened in 1936 by William Lyon Mackenzie King, prime minister of Canada and namesake of his grandfather. Romantics will smile at the significance for the prime minister as it was here that his father proposed to his mother, William Lyon Mackenzie's daughter.

The original plans for the restoration called for a printing museum, and Mackenzie's original press was purchased. After a long journey the press was finally installed along with a collection of working heritage hand presses and an interpretive display on the history of printing. The museum features a hands-on environment with a working linotype, eight operating heritage presses, and the restored lithography studio of Canadian artist Frederick Hagan.

When you visit, take note of the two large locust trees growing at the entranceway, as they played a special part in our history. Mackenzie wrote in 1854, "Thirty years ago, I published at Queenstown, on the 18th of May, 1824, the first number of a public newspaper, voluntarily established to promote justice and equity in a sparsely populated, badly governed colony. To commemorate the day that had transformed a quiet, peaceful obscure trader into an ardent colonial politician and public censor, I then planted in front of my dwelling a row of acacia or locust trees, and a grape vine and had the pleasure last week of seeing them growing luxuriously." Two of his original five locust trees remain as living memorial to an early Canadian publisher and political activist, and while the grapevine is long gone I like to think his spirit had something to do with the success of the wine industry in some small way.

Laura Secord Homestead

When you travel by the town of Queenston in the Niagara area, consider stopping at the Laura Secord Homestead to explore the home of the famed heroine of the War of 1812. Costumed interpreters recount her adventures in the restored building.

Costumed interpreters greet visitors to the Secord Homestead

During the War of 1812, the hardest fighting was in Upper Canada. The American
forces struck at York (now Toronto), the
capital of Upper Canada. Wreaking havoc,
they stormed the Assembly building and
finding a scalp on display, seized it and sent
it on to Washington as proof of British bar-
barity. They then put the building to the
torch and withdrew. The British tried to
explain that the scalp was the ceremonial
wig of the magistrate or speaker of the
Assembly. In retaliation, the British attacked
Washington, burning down the Capitol.

Laura Ingersoll Secord came to Upper
Canada with her father and siblings in
1795. Her father was not a loyalist but had
hopes of regaining his family fortunes in
this new frontier to the north. The

Afternoon tea on the Parkway

Ingersolls settled in the Niagara Peninsula and opened a
tavern. Here Laura met her future husband, James
Secord, a loyalist settler. In the early 1800s Laura and
James moved to Queenston, and it was from this homestead that Laura set off on her journey to warn the British
troops of an impending attack by the Americans assembling a force in Queenston.

The Secords had been ordered to billet soldiers in their
home. They overheard an American plot to surprise the
British forces at their Beaverdams encampment. If the
attack succeeded, the Secords realized, the American
forces would control the entire peninsula. James Secord
had been wounded at the Battle of Queenston Heights
and could not attempt the journey. So it fell to Laura to
brave certain danger and unknown hardship to warn the
British troops. Her journey of roughly 20 miles (32 kilometers) over treacherous ground took her more than
eighteen hours. Her destination was DeCew House near
present Thorold. Through the smoldering night she
walked, risking death if discovered, but finally stumbling
into the encampment with torn clothing and bleeding
and blistered feet, able to deliver her vital message. The
British forces, with a strong Native contingent, turned
the tables and ambushed the advancing Americans at
Beaverdams, defeating them on June 24, 1813.

Laura Secord's heroism was soon forgotten, however,
and it wasn't until 1860—almost fifty years later—that she
was accorded recognition of her bold act by the Prince of
Wales. She died in 1868 at the ripe old age of ninety-three.
Maybe there is something to be said for long walks!

Jackson-Triggs Winery

FAST FACTS

2145 Regional Road 55
Niagara-on-the-Lake, Ontario
L0S 1J0
Tel: 905-468-4637
Fax: 905-468-4673
E-mail: info@
jacksontriggswinery.com
Web: www.jacksontriggswinery.com

JACKSON-TRIGGS
— NIAGARA ESTATE —

The state-of-the-art Jackson-Triggs Niagara winery set within a picturesque twenty-six-acre vineyard is dedicated to producing premium, super, and ultra premium VQA wines from the Niagara Peninsula.

Opened in the summer of 2001 and designed by the internationally acclaimed firm Kuwabara Payne McKenna Blumberg Architects, the 47,000 square foot winery is inspired by traditional farm buildings with their "post and beam" frames and wide barn doors. Its materials are a combination of natural stone at its base, native fir roof trusses, high-tech aluminum framing, and vast windows that showcase the vineyard.

The vineyard was planted in the spring of 2000 with individually selected vinifera clones and rootstocks custom grafted in France and features three varietals: Chardonnay, Pinot Noir, and Riesling. Jackson-Triggs winemakers— chief winemaker Rob Scapin and winemaker Thomas Seaver—work hand in hand with a number of independent grape growers in the Niagara Region to augment the supply of other vitis vinifera varieties such as Merlot, Cabernet Franc, Cabernet Sauvignon, and Sauvignon Blanc. All seven of the major varietals are showcased at

The impressive Jackson-Triggs Winery in Niagara-on-the-Lake

the front of the winery in a "demonstration vineyard," which forms part of the visitor education program.

The winemaking process utilizes a three-tiered gravity flow assisted system to maximize quality. Some of the most advanced equipment from France, South Africa, New Zealand, U.S., Germany, and Canada has been selected to provide flexibility and control in the wine-making process. All of the equipment is temperature con-trolled by a computer system that can be accessed by the winemaker both on- and off-site. Two large barrel cellars are located below ground for the aging of red and selected white wines.

The new winery is expected to support the growth of the winery's VQA wines to more than 100,000 cases by 2005. The product portfolio consists of VQA table wines, sparkling wines, and icewines carrying either the black Proprietors' Reserve label or the rarer gold Grand Reserve label available exclusively at the winery.

The winery offers a comprehensive wine education experience, with private guided tours in an intimate set-ting where visitors in small groups learn how premium wines are made. Tours begin in the impressive two-storey Great Hall, which separates the wine production area from the front-of-house hospitality and retail sections. On the tour, every aspect of winemaking is explored, from the pressing of grapes to barrel aging in the cellars. Guests then have the opportunity to enjoy a food and wine experience in the Tasting Gallery and visit the gift boutique where they can purchase Jackson-Triggs award-winning limited Grand Reserve wines.

Founded by Don Triggs and Allan Jackson less than a decade ago, Jackson-Triggs vintners produces wines in both the Niagara Peninsula and in the Okanagan Valley in British Columbia. Jackson-Triggs' Proprietors' Reserve and Grand Reserve wines have won numerous domestic and international awards including Best Canadian Producer and Best Icewine in 1999 and again in 2000 by the International Wine and Spirit Competition in England. In 2001 Jackson-Triggs won the Best Red Wine Trophy at the All-Canadian Wine Championships for its 1998 Grand Reserve Meritage made by chief winemaker Rob Scapin.

Jackson-Triggs varietals include Chardonnay, Riesling, Gewurztraminer, Sauvignon Blanc, Vidal, Merlot, Cabernet Franc, Cabernet Sauvignon, and Pinot Noir.

Jackson-Triggs wines are widely available across Canada. They can be purchased in LCBO stores, in private wine boutiques, and at leading restaurants and hotels.

ALASKAN KING CRAB LEG WITH PARSLEY SALAD, AVOCADO, VANILLA, AND GRAPEFRUIT MONTE

—

from Stephen Treadwell,
Executive Chef,
Queen's Landing Inn,
Niagara-on-the-Lake

—

Serves 4

salt
freshly ground white pepper
8 oz (250 g) king crab leg meat
1 ripe avocado
pinch of hot serrano pepper,
   finely chopped
juice of 1 lime
grapeseed oil
juice of 2 red river grapefruits
4 oz (125 g) unsalted butter
1 tsp (5 ml) fresh vanilla bean seed
small servings of baby greens with
   flat Italian parsley leaves and
   chives

Season crabmeat with salt, finely ground white pepper, and serrano. Refrigerate.
   Peel and roughly mash avocado. Add lime juice and season with salt.
   Whip butter, and add vanilla seed.
   Bring grapefruit juice to a boil. Cool. Using a hand blender, emulsify butter into juice.
   To serve, place avocado in middle of a plate—using 2½-inch (6.5-cm) ring or similar. Top with crabmeat.
   Season baby greens with grape-seed oil and salt, and place on crab. Remove ring.
   Spoon sauce around and garnish with sprigs of chervil.

WINE MATCH
Jackson-Triggs 1999 Proprietors Grand Reserve Chardonnay

Allan Jackson: One Step at a Time

Founders Don Triggs (left) and
Allan Jackson

*The French term depicting
the blending of different
wines is known as* **assemblage,** *and is most famous
in Bordeaux red wines.
North America often uses
the term "meritage" to indicate a blended red wine.*

*A wine is considered "in
balance" or "in harmony"
when each of its major
components—acid, sugar,
alcohol, and tannins—
complement each other so
that no single one is over-
powering.*

A native son of Hamilton, Ontario, Allan Jackson grew
up just around the corner from McMaster University,
where he hoped to one day pursue a degree in medicine.
The making of Dr. Allan Jackson, MD was not to be.
During his studies Allan found himself increasingly smit-
ten with the challenges of chemistry. Changing career
paths he pursued a PhD in this newly chosen field.

Allan's supervisor was a wine buff, and it didn't take
much to ignite Allan's interest in wine. During the mid-
1970s very little, if any, analysis was being conducted on
the flavor components of Canadian wines. Allan turned
this open opportunity into his thesis. With this unique
accomplishment and an enhanced interest in wine, Allan
secured a position with the Labatt-owned Chateau Gai
Wines, where he first met Don Triggs.

Don was the manager of the Canadian Wine Division
for Labatt and recognized the tremendous value of
Allan's work and the need to improve the quality of
Canadian wine. This was at a time when Canadian wines
were frequently the brunt of bad jokes in the press and
on comedy TV shows. Chateau Gai had instituted several
research programs to study all aspects of grape growing
and the many elements of the vinification process.

Their experimental vineyards in Winona were planted
with the noble European varieties like Merlot, Cabernet
Franc, Cabernet Sauvignon, Pinot Noir, Chardonnay, and
Riesling. To elevate the quality of Canadian wines, they
knew they'd have to use the better-quality grapes but there
were many skeptics who believed Niagara's cold winters
would thwart any such attempts. Despite the naysayers,
the research and development continued and yielded
promising results that excited the winemaking community.

When Labatt decided to return to its core business of
making beer, Allan and Don joined others to form a management acquisition of Chateau Gai Wines. From the very
beginning Allan and Don agreed that they would dedicate
their efforts to recognizing and appreciating the characteristics of each varietal. They were intent on making fruit-
forward wines that weren't dominated by oak—"woody"
flavored wines that Allan recalls as "lumberjack" wines.
They also recognized the shortcomings of old-world wines
saddled with a complex and confusing labeling system.
Such structures were dedicated to protecting and enhanc-
ing high-quality standards, but for the average consumer,
they were also intimidating. Bordeaux wines were certainly a standard to rise to, but for consumers faced with

hundreds of hard-to-remember Chateau names and a complex appellation structure, there was a need for greater simplicity. True to the new-world wine order, Jackson-Triggs concentrated on releasing wines by their varietal names, a development that consumers have responded to with great enthusiasm.

Don believed that in putting their personal names on the label, he and Allan would be highly motivated to produce the highest-quality wines possible. They focused on using the noble European vinifera grapes, which in turn would elevate the quality bar. Their dedication to these founding principles has been responsible for Jackson-Triggs establishing itself as one of Canada's most recognizable brands with an equally impressive array of international awards.

Allan appreciates the need to constantly strive for quality improvement. The old-world European wine industry became quite comfortable in dominating the wine shelves of the world. Jackson-Triggs and other new-world winemakers redefined the rules of an established industry and caught the Europeans napping.

Such an achievement wasn't easily come by. Allan can recall the lean years when it was all they could do to keep the company afloat. Today Jackson-Triggs is a state-of-the art winery in Niagara, blending old-world know-how with modern technology and a passion for winemaking that has never waned.

Favoring cooler climate wine regions, Gewurztraminer does well in the Alsace, Germany, Austria, Hungary, Rumania, Ukraine, Canada, and in the cooler sub-regions of California and New Zealand.

Winemaker's Matches: Allan Jackson, Jackson-Triggs

White Wine: Niagara Gewurztraminer
               Jackson-Triggs Proprietors' Reserve
Food: Chicken and vegetable stir-fry
Comment: The spicy nutmeg and sage notes in the Gewurztraminer complement the seasonings in the stir-fry, and it is easy to prepare.

Red Wine: Okanagan Meritage
               Jackson-Triggs Grand Reserve
Food: Pot roast with pan-roasted potatoes, carrots, and onions
Comment: The perfect winter "comfort food." The Meritage is a big, fruit-forward wine that stands up to the beef and onion without dominating.

Dessert Wine: Niagara Gewurztraminer Icewine
               Jackson-Triggs Grand Reserve
Food: Strawberry scone shortcakes
Comment: The intense fruit highlights of the icewine are beautifully offset by the strawberries and cream, and the textures of both wine and dessert meld extremely well.

Joseph's Estate Wines

FAST FACTS

1811 Niagara Stone Road
Niagara-on-the-Lake, Ontario
L0S 1J0
Tel: 905-468-1259
E-mail:
info@josephsestatewines.com
Web: www.josephsestatewines.com

Joseph's Estate Winery in Niagara-on-the-Lake

Appreciated for its low acidity, Pinot Gris—known as Pinot Grigio in Italy—often produces soft, dry, rich wines without overpowering aromas and has good food-pairing attributes.

Joseph's, founded by owner/winemaker Joseph Pohorly, opened its doors in 1996. But his dream of starting a winery began many years before.

In 1979 Joseph Pohorly founded Newark Winery in Niagara-on-the-Lake, one of only six original wineries at that time in the province of Ontario. Renamed Hillebrand Winery in 1983, and now one of the largest boutique wineries in Canada, Joseph sold his share to other investors in 1986.

But his love for the wine business brought him back again. In 1992 he purchased a twenty-acre peach farm. Today there are eighteen acres of grape vines and two acres of fruit trees surrounding the winery and boutique. Joseph harvests grapes from his own vineyards and from neighboring grape growers for a total of eighty acres. A 10,000 square foot building houses the winemaking operations. Production has increased to 30,000 cases per year.

Joseph's offers a wide range of wines, from the bold, rich classics to clean, crisp, fruity wines, and the elegant sweet nectar of award-winning dessert wines and icewines. Varieties include (white wines) Pinot Gris, Vidal, Chardonnay, Gewurztraminer, Riesling; (red wines) Pinot Noir, Cabernet Sauvignon, Cabernet Franc, Gamay, Merlot.

He also features two other red grapes, Petite Sirah and Chancellor, which are rare in Ontario. Two popular house wines include Festival Blanc and Festival Rouge.

The winery also offers a wide selection of fruit wines. These unique wines are produced from the freshest fruit grown in their own orchards and include peach, pear, apple, and apricot. Strawberry is a big favorite.

Customers can purchase wines at the local winery boutique, at restaurants, and through the LCBO.

The public tours at Joseph's are informative, entertaining, and fun, offering a look at the history and geography of Niagara viticulture, the science of grape growing, and the art of winemaking. A hospitality room can accommodate up to sixty-five people for bus tours and smaller groups.

Joseph Pohorly has received about 100 awards over the past few years at Canadian and international wine competitions. A man who in 1983 was the first winemaker in Canada to make Vidal Icewine has seen his dream of producing affordable, premium wines become a reality.

The Clock Tower in Niagara-on-the-Lake welcomes visitors to this quaint, historic town

GRILLED SPICE RUBBED CHICKEN IN OREGANO DIJON SAUCE

—

from George Campbell

—

Serves 4

The chicken can be cooked on the barbecue or baked in the oven.

4, 5–7 oz (150–210 g) boneless, skinless chicken breasts
½ tsp (2 ml) dried thyme
½ tsp (2 ml) chili powder
½ tsp (2 ml) garlic powder
½ tsp (2 ml) black pepper
1 tbsp (15 ml) sesame oil
2 tbsp (15 ml) vegetable oil
½ Vidalia onion, peeled and sliced
1 cup (250 ml) chicken stock
2 tbsp (30 ml) oregano
3 tbsp (45 ml) Dijon mustard

Combine and mix all the spices except the oregano.

Place the sesame oil, spices mixture, and chicken in a bowl and rub the spices on the chicken. Let stand for at least half an hour. Grill or bake the chicken until cooked.

Sauté the onions with vegetable oil in a large saucepan until tender.

Add the chicken stock and oregano and bring to a boil. Add the Dijon and stir, reduce heat to a simmer.

WINE MATCH
Joseph's Pinot Gris

Strewn Winery

FAST FACTS

1339 Lakeshore Road
Niagara-on-the-Lake, Ontario
L0S 1J0
Tel: 905-468-1229
E-mail: info@strewnwinery.com
Web: www.strewnwinery.com

Strewn Winery and the Wine Country Cooking School

Winemaker Joe Will and his wife,
Jane Langdon

In the three and a half years that Strewn has been open,
the winery has carved out a niche as a premium producer
of wines made exclusively from vinifera grapes in
Niagara.

Strewn's portfolio of more than twenty wines provides
a choice of wine ages and styles, from a mature barrel-
aged Chardonnay to a young, zesty Riesling.
Winemaker/president Joe Will produces wines from the
classic grapes of Chardonnay, Pinot Blanc, Sauvignon
Blanc, Gewurztraminer, Riesling, Merlot, Cabernet
Sauvignon, and Cabernet Franc. His flagship red wine is
Strewn Three, a classic blend of Merlot, Cabernet Franc,
and Cabernet Sauvignon. Icewine and Select Late
Harvest—barrel-fermented Riesling icewines—are made
from Vidal and Riesling in an original Strewn style.

The Strewn vineyards are located near the south shore
of Lake Ontario. More than half of the grapes used by
Strewn come from the winery's two vineyards and the
remainder are purchased from independent growers
located within six miles (ten kilometers) of the winery.

Strewn is a modern facility within a historic building.
It was originally home of the Niagara Canning Company,
a local enterprise that was started in the late 1930s to
process the area's abundant supply of tender fruits such

as peaches, cherries, and plums. In 1997 part of the original building was restored to serve as the winery cellar and another portion was rebuilt as the new visitor complex. Facilities include a spacious tasting room, wine store, Wine Country Cooking School—Canada's first cooking school at a winery, operated by Joe's wife, Jane Langdon—and a highly acclaimed Niagara Provençal restaurant called Terroir La Cachette.

Strewn has drawn accolades and won more than a dozen medals in major international competitions from Hong Kong to Verona.

Strewn offers visitors tours of the winery and wine tastings as well as an opportunity to savor regional cuisine and enjoy informative cooking school classes.

Strewn wines can be purchased at the winery retail store, LCBO stores, SAQ stores in the province of Quebec, and selected private stores in the province of Alberta.

Guided winery tours cover all aspects of winemaking, and no question is dumb!

CABERNET CHICKEN

from the Wine Country
Cooking School at Strewn

Serves 4

8 chicken thighs, bone-in or boneless
1 tbsp (15 ml) olive oil
1 clove garlic, finely chopped
1 tbsp (15 ml) fresh ginger, finely
    chopped
1 tbsp (15 ml) fresh chives, chopped
¼ cup (60 ml) blackberry jam
½ cup (125 ml) Strewn Cabernet
    Merlot
1 tsp (5 ml) grated lemon zest
juice from 1 large lemon
1 tsp (5 ml) Dijon mustard
fresh chives and blackberries for
    garnish (optional)

Remove skin from chicken thighs. Set skinless thighs aside. Heat olive oil in a large skillet over medium heat. Add the garlic, ginger, and chives. Sauté until soft, about three minutes.

Place chicken thighs in skillet and brown on both sides. In a small bowl, combine the jam, wine, lemon zest, lemon juice, and mustard. Stir to mix. Pour the mixture over the chicken in the skillet. Cover and cook over medium low heat 7 to 10 minutes (cook bone-in thighs the longer time).

Remove cover, turn chicken thighs over and cook 5 minutes longer.

To serve, place 2 thighs on each plate and spoon the blackberry Cabernet sauce on top. Garnish with fresh chives and blackberries if desired.

WINE MATCH
Strewn Cabernet Merlot

Wine and food attract summer tourists

The Shaw Festival

Jonathan with hair in an early promotional shot

Niagara-on-the-Lake holds special memories for me: Sunday drives, visits to many fruit stands with my parents, ice cream forays on Queen Street, the 1958 World Scouting Jamboree, a race along Lakeshore Road in a police car chasing robbers. And in 1967 I was hired as one of two apprentices for the Shaw Festival.

The Shaw Festival owes its beginnings to Brian Doherty, a successful lawyer who had moved to Niagara in 1955. He was in love with the theater and was determined to found a summer theater festival in the sleepy town with a blue-ribbon heritage. With the Davis family in Toronto and other intrepid souls, Brian sought to develop and nurture live home-grown stage productions in Canada. He enthusiastically supported the Straw Hat Players, the Red Barn Theatre, and the New World Theatre companies. His support and the production of *Father Malachy's Miracle* on Broadway in 1937–38 were strong credentials that opened many doors in his determined pursuit of a showcase summer theater in Niagara.

He and a small group of like-minded souls saw the theater as a way to help preserve the heritage of this unique town still mired in economic doldrums. The plan was hatched almost overnight, and the first Shaw Festival offering was presented in eight performances in 1962. It was a ramshackle affair but it launched the theater. The next four seasons saw a magical enterprise take shape, inspired by both the town and a hardy bunch of determined pioneers. These included Andrew Allan, of CBC fame, actor/director Sean Mulcahy, and a young Christopher Newton appearing on stage in 1964. And in 1966 internationally acclaimed actor Barry Morse assumed the artistic directorship for a year and set a standard that continues to thrill audiences from far and wide.

The phenomenal growth of the Shaw Festival couldn't have happened without the support and encouragement of the local community. The spirit of volunteerism was the hallmark of the early years, and without the open arms, wallets, and hearts of the townsfolk it simply wouldn't have happened.

As the productions grew so did the need for more staff in every conceivable area. During the summer of 1967 I was hired as an apprentice (stagehand) along with Pamela Brooke—who would subsequently become a noted actor and teacher—at the princely sum of $30 per week. During the daylight hours, we painted sets, made props, cleaned the playhouse, ran errands of every nature, located errant actors for rehearsals, and fetched clothes and prop donations. In the afternoons, we readied the Court House for the evening performance, took tickets, and ushered patrons to their seats before rushing backstage to change sets and create sound cues, among other things. We also fetched the actors for their entrance cues.

It was exhausting but exhilarating work. I was billeted in a room at the Prince of Wales Hotel for the summer, for which I paid $15 per week. The Prince of Wales Hotel is currently a deluxe five-star accommodation. But in 1967 it was very much in need of a face-lift. I had a large room on the second floor that was said to be haunted (a number of local residences are said to be haunted), but I heard and saw nothing unusual—except an ugly stain on the wall. The fact is, I wasn't in the room long enough to allow any haunting. My work was scheduled from morning till night!

The Shaw Festival Theatre as seen from above

From the beginning, a permanent building was sought for the Shaw Festival performances since the old Court House could only be a temporary location. With each success, the crowds continued to swell and the need to expand came quickly. Finally the site was chosen at its current site, and the new theater was opened to great "hurrahs" in 1973. The talented company continues to enchant and thrill audiences of all ages. Other theaters are also used: The Royal George on Queen Street was beautifully restored to all its Victorian elegance, as was the venerable Court House.

I was a part of it, and I heartily encourage all to pay a visit to both the town and the theater. That's what wine country is all about; opening your mind and sharing the adventure.

Contemplating Fort Niagara, New York, and Lake Ontario at the mouth of the Niagara River

Hillebrand Estates Winery

FAST FACTS

1249 Niagara Stone Road
Niagara-on-the-Lake, Ontario
L0S 1J0
Tel: 905-468-3201; 800-582-8412
Fax: 905-468-4789
Web: www.hillebrand.com

Founded in 1979, Hillebrand Estates Winery is Canada's leading producer of VQA wines. Based in the historic town of Niagara-on-the-Lake, Hillebrand produces a full range of world-class wines and provides a complete wine-country experience.

Nestled between the Niagara Escarpment and Lake Ontario, Hillebrand consistently combines the quality vinifera grapes from the growers of the Niagara region with the skill of winemaker J.L. Groux and the state-of-the-art winemaking equipment and extensive barrel

Hillebrand Estates Winery in Niagara-on-the-Lake boasts a great restaurant and several summer music concerts

Clusters of grapes ripening under the Niagara sun

aging facilities. Hillebrand produces award-winning varietals that include Chardonnay, Riesling, Cabernet, Gamay
Noir, and blends such as Trius Red.

Using the unique local microclimate, Hillebrand was
the pioneer in the Niagara production of icewine and has
produced this special wine every year since 1983.
Hillebrand uses only the Vidal grape to produce icewine
because of its thick skin and strong stem necessary to
mature and survive until harvest in late December
through January. The winery continues to experiment
with different aspects of the growing, harvesting, and
winemaking processes to improve its icewine.

The winery has won more than 300 medals at both
national and international wine competitions, including
the first gold medal for an Ontario table wine at the prestigious Intervin International Wine Competition; the distinguished Pichon Longueville Comtesse de Lalande
Trophy at the International Wine and Spirit Competition
in England; and a gold medal at VinItaly.

During the past few years Hillebrand has undergone
extensive upgrades and expansion of its wine production
facilities including equipment, barrel room, underground
cellars, press house, and the addition of a new welcome

"QUACKER BOX" DUCK

from Chef de Cuisine
Tony De Luca,
Hillebrand's Vineyard Cafe

—

Serves 4

DUCK
2 duck breasts
8 ½ cups (2 L) wine lees
2 tbsp (30 ml) olive oil
2 tbsp (30 ml) butter
salt and pepper to taste

SAUCE
1 tbsp (15 ml) butter
2 tbsp (30 ml) olive oil
2 shallots, peeled and finely diced
1 clove garlic, peeled and finely
*   minced*
1 cup (250 ml) red wine
1 cup (250 ml) red wine Ver Jus
1 cup (250 ml) veal stock (or
*   chicken stock, duck stock, etc.)*
3 tbsp (45 ml) cedar jelly
2 sprigs fresh thyme, picked and
*   finely chopped*

SPAETZLE
salt
1 cup (250 ml) olive oil
2 cups (500 ml) flour
1 cup (250 ml) milk
1 cup (250 ml) water
salt and pepper

SMOKED ONION SPAETZLE
2 tbsp (30 ml) butter
1 large onion, peeled, smoked, and
*   cut into julienne*
1 clove garlic, peeled and finely
*   minced*
3 cups (750 ml) spaetzle
salt and pepper

Submerge duck breasts in the lees
and refrigerate for 48 hours.

Preheat oven to 400°F (200°C).
Add the butter and the olive oil to
an oven-proof sauté pan. Remove
the duck breasts from the lees
and pat dry. Season with salt and
pepper. Place the sauté pan on
medium heat and, when the butter
is frothy, add the duck to the sauté
pan, skin side down.

continued on page 74

continued from page 73
Place the pan in the oven and roast for 15 minutes. Using a pair of kitchen tongs, turn the duck over and cook for another 5 minutes.

Remove the pan from the oven and remove the duck from the pan. Keep the duck warm until ready to slice.

For the sauce, in a small sauce pan heat the butter in the olive oil until frothy. Add the shallots and stir. Add the garlic and sweat for a few seconds, stirring frequently. Add the wine and reduce to 1 tbsp (15 ml). Add the veal stock and reduce until 3 tbsp (45 ml) of liquid remain. Add the Ver Jus and reduce until thick. Pass the sauce through a fine mesh sieve. Return the passed sauce to a small sauce pot and bring to a simmer. Add the chopped thyme and the cedar jelly and stir until dissolved. Keep the sauce warm until the duck is ready.

For the spaetzle, bring a large pot of water to a rapid boil. Add a pinch of salt and the olive oil. Combine the flour, milk, and water and stir to a paste. Place a large whole colander over the boiling water and pass the spaetzle batter
continued on page 75

center for visitors and the creation of its on-site gourmet restaurant, Hillebrand's Vineyard Cafe.

Diners at the cafe have a view of the barrel aging room, the picturesque Stone Road vineyard, and the impressive Niagara Escarpment. The restaurant features fine wines matched with locally grown food to create a regional cuisine that is unique to Niagara. Chef Tony De Luca has a full-time forager on the kitchen staff whose job is to find and procure the finest products of the region for the chef's exclusive creations.

Hillebrand offers many wine-related activities during the year. The annual Vineyard Jazz is held in the winery vineyards in the summer and features live music, fine wine, and great food. This is now part of a Vineyard Concert Series that includes Vineyard Blues. Each January Hillebrand hosts an Icewine Celebration at the winery.

Merlot—often noted as a grape for blending with Cabernet Sauvignon and Cabernet Franc in Bordeaux wines—is also vinified on its own, producing some of the most sought after, expensive red wines in the world such as Chateau Petrus and Pomerol.

Hillebrand's courtyard hosts thousands of visitors each year

Hillebrand Estates wines are available at the winery boutique, at Hillebrand's restaurant, through home delivery from WineCountry At Home, via the Internet at www. hillebrand.com, and through the LCBO as well as The Wine Shoppe locations throughout Ontario.

Hillebrand hosts a wide range of daily winery tours for visitors with tastings that cater to everyone from beginner to expert. In addition, the winery offers a series of more in-depth, specialized tours for parties of ten or more. With more than 200,000 visitors each year, Hillebrand has become one of the premier destinations for visitors to the Niagara Region.

NOTES FROM THE CELLAR

OPEN AND POUR

Should a special method be used to open a bottle of wine?
Most wine bottles today have corks, and since corks are usually a natural wood product, they can cause problems. Use a good corkscrew, much like a carpenter uses sharp tools. Choose one that has a good worm, or helix, so that it cuts into the cork properly. Also, the corkscrew should have a lever that allows the cork to ease straight out.

Is there a way to prevent yanking or bending a cork?
Today, a lot of high-profile winemakers are requesting longer corks to be certain of the seal. A longer straight pull is needed to ease the cork out of the neck. Many corkscrews, because of a short-lever action, twist the cork sideways and snap it halfway out. I always suggest a two-staged lever corkscrew that keeps the pulling action parallel to the bottle. The screwpull and rabbit use a rack-and-pinion lever to keep the cork coming straight out during the entire process. Little physical effort or experience is needed when using these types of corkscrews.

Remember to cut the foil, plastic, or wax away from the neck of the bottle before opening it. Cut the decorative seal so that the wine will not touch it when poured. And always be sure to wipe the exposed neck and cork with a clean cloth.

How should a wine be poured?
Although pouring wine appears simple, it is wise to follow a couple of rules to ensure success. The wine bottle should not touch the edge of the glass. It's partly a matter of simple etiquette, but also, touching the glass may cause it to chip. Pour slowly to make sure that there is no splash.

The golden rule is, never fill the glass more than a third or a quarter with wine. This allows room to swirl and to nose, or sniff, the wine without spilling any. A slow and pleasurable approach to drinking wine can awaken the senses. Allow the wine to speak first by observing its color and then by smelling the aroma or bouquet. Having a glass only partly full allows for this opening dialogue. Pretty simple stuff. Remember to relax and enjoy.

continued from page 74
through the colander into the boiling water. Cook for a few minutes, stirring frequently. When the spaetzle rise to the surface (float), remove them from the pot and plunge into ice water (use a slotted spoon). When the spaetzle have chilled thoroughly, remove them from the ice water and reserve.

For the smoked onion spaetzle, melt the butter in a large sauté pan and heat to medium high. Add the smoked onion julienne and the garlic. When the onions have become golden brown add the spaetzle and stir. Add salt and pepper to taste. Cook until the spaetzle have warmed through and serve.

TO ASSEMBLE
Place a few spoonfuls of spaetzle in the center of 4 large dinner plates. Slice the duck and arrange the slices overtop the spaetzle. Spoon the "Great Canadian Sweet-and-Sour Sauce" around the plate and garnish with garden thyme.

WINE MATCH
Hillebrand Estates Showcase Merlot "Glenlake Vineyard"

*Blending, or **assemblage** as it's called in France, means bringing together wines of different individually fermented varieties or mixing various barrels or lots of wine from the same grape variety.*

Pillitteri Estates Winery

FAST FACTS

1696 Niagara Stone Road
Niagara-on-the-Lake, Ontario
L0S 1J0
Tel: 905-468-3147
Fax: 905-468-0389
E-mail: winery@pillitteri.com
Web: www.pillitteri.com

Pillitteri Estates Winery offers local market fare and homemade goodies

Usually vinified as a wine to be consumed young, Sauvignon Blanc's most distinct characteristic is its almost instantly recognizable herbaceous aroma, often described as grassy or musky. It is grown worldwide.

For Gary Pillitteri the opening of Pillitteri Estates Winery in 1993 was the culmination of a lifetime dream. His goal since arriving in Canada from Sicily in 1948—through many years as a grape grower in Niagara and award-winning amateur winemaker—was to open his own winery.

The turning point had come five years before opening Pillitteri, when Gary won a gold medal for his icewine in Niagara's amateur wine competition. He knew then that his dream could come true. But he had been thinking about early retirement and could only build a professional and high-quality winery with the expertise and full commitment of his family. That commitment was provided by Gary's son Charles as vice-president of sales and marketing; daughter Connie as vice-president of operations; and son-in-law Jamie Slingerland as manager of the family vineyards.

Pillitteri wines are produced primarily from the family's fifty-three acres of vineyards planted with vitis vinifera and French hybrid grape varieties. Following the exacting standards of the VQA, production has steadily increased to approximately 250,000 liters annually with additional production capacity available. Pillitteri produces more than twenty VQA wines.

PILLITTERI ESTATES WINERY

The Pillitteri logo contains a Sicilian cart, called a *carretto*, which is intricately painted with scenes of Pillitteri ancestors. The original antique, a cherished family heirloom, is displayed in the winery's reception area. During spring and summer, visitors can take a trolley ride through the vineyards and orchards, receive a guided tour of the winery, and participate in formal tasting lessons.

The Pillitteri family is proud of their heritage and their accomplishments. In the past eight years the winery has won more than 220 medals in both domestic and international competitions. These include the coveted Civart Trophy from the Challenge International du Vin in Bordeaux, France, and a rare Double Gold Medal from the American Wine Society.

Pillitteri wines are available in their Niagara-on-the-Lake winery store. Certain listings are available at LCBO stores or LCBO Vintages. Their wine list includes (sparkling wines) Duemila, Spumante; (dry white wines) Pinot Grigio, Chardonnay Unoaked, Chardonnay Barrel Fermented, Chardonnay Barrel Aged, Chardonnay Family Reserve, Sauvignon Blanc Family Reserve; (semi-dry white wines) Vidal, Gewurztraminer, Riesling; (sweet white wines) Riesling Sweet Reserve, Vidal Sussreserve, Riesling Dolce; (rosé wine) Rose; (red wines) Chariot Dolce, Cabernet, Carretto Rosso Secco, Cabernet Merlot, Merlot, Cabernet Sauvignon, Merlot Reserve, Merlot Family Reserve, Cabernet Franc, Cabernet Franc Family Reserve, Cabernet Sauvignon Family, Trivalente; (dessert wines) Riesling Late Harvest, Vidal Late Harvest, Vidal Select Late Harvest, Gewurztraminer-Riesling Select, Riesling Icewine, Vidal Icewine, Gewurztraminer Icewine.

Sue Ann Staff: Watch Out for the Rookie!

Sue Ann Staff, winemaker at Pillitteri Estates Winery, doesn't consider any gender delineation in the ability to make wine. The fact that women winemakers are uncommon may have something to do with the European traditions, where winemaking was a male domain. Sue Ann, however, does have a lineage with the grapevine that goes back almost 200 years and several generations. That's a long time in a Canadian historical context.

Almost 200 years ago Canadian General Brock and his loyalist troops marched past Sue Ann's ancestral farm while on their way to Queenston to fight back invading

MUSSELS AND SOUP À LA PILLITTERI
—
from Pillitteri Estates
—
Serves 4

5–8 lb (2.5–4 kg) mussels, well rinsed
1 anise bulb (fennel), diced, including the tops
1 Spanish onion, diced
2 cloves of garlic, minced
¼ lb (125 g) butter
1 cup (250 ml) whipping cream or milk
1 bottle (750 ml) Pillitteri Estates Pinot Grigio

In a large stockpot over medium low heat, melt the butter. Combine the melted butter with diced anise bulb, diced Spanish onion, minced garlic, whipping cream or milk, and a ½ bottle (375 ml) of Pillitteri Estates Pinot Grigio. Bring to a boil, then simmer at medium low until slightly al dente (25 to 30 minutes).

Add the mussels and the rest of the bottle of Pinot Grigio. Stir every 2 minutes to completely cover the mussels in the base. As the mussels open, keep stirring and simmering for a few more minutes so that some of the mussels fall out of the shells.

Serve the mussels in a large soup bowl, and ladle the soup over the mussels. Serve with crusty bread.

WINE MATCH
Pillitteri Estates Pinot Grigio

From left to right: Sue Ann Staff, Charlie Pillitteri, and Connie Pillitteri

*The French name "Pinot"
(pee-noh) is the first word
of dozens of varieties
worldwide, but the only
real family members are
Pinot Blanc, Pinot Gris,
Pinot Noir, Auxerrois,
and Meunier.*

Americans in the War of 1812. Today, the Staff family vineyards have vines that are over 100 years old. Prior to the free trade agreement with the U.S., Sue Ann's family owned one of the largest privately held vineyard properties in Canada with 800 acres. Today the Staff vineyards of 250 acres continue to grow Concord grapes for jams, jellies, and juices.

Growing up in a grape-growing family seemed a natural footing from which to enter the wine business. At sixteen years of age—before she could legally drink wine—Sue Ann knew she wanted to be a winemaker. The University of Guelph gave her the horticultural and biotechnology foundation she wanted. Upon graduation she journeyed to the University of Adelaide in Australia, where she received her graduate diploma in enology, followed by a practical hands-on crash course in the realities of winemaking.

Having graduated during the Australian harvest, and rather than return to the cold Niagara winter, Sue Ann worked for Simon Gilbert's Wine Services. It was a privately owned cooperative winemaking facility that serviced dozens of grape growers who wanted to make wine for their own enjoyment and commercial labels. The facilities offered growers all the tools and space they required without having to endure the heavy capital costs of buying their own equipment. With grapes arriving from all over Australia and the company employing only a handful of employees, Sue Ann had the chance to work at just about every aspect of the vinification process. She took up the position of trainee winemaker under winemaker and proprietor Simon Gilbert for six months. She jumped from the pan into the fire; or is it, in this case, from the vineyard into the vat?

Upon returning to Niagara Sue Ann worked under short-term contracts for various wineries until she was offered the winemaker position at Pillitteri Estates Winery in the spring of 1997. She was quite astonished that this established family wine business would take a risk on a twenty-six-year-old greenhorn, but neither has regretted the decision. Sue Ann notes that one of the ties that bind the winemaker with the owner is a shared philosophy about the style of wines they wanted to produce. With highest possible quality as the starting point, they were in sync.

The always important barrel cellar

Sue Ann has always appreciated the true character of the varietal whites, and works to preserve their unique fruit characteristics, but her burning passion lies in the vinification of red wines. The complexities of red wine throw down a gauntlet of critical decisions and risky challenges that she relishes.

Her mark on Pillitteri was quickly celebrated when her 1998 Cabernet Franc Family Reserve took the gold medal in the New World category at the Challenge International du Vin in Bordeaux. It was a triumph for several reasons. Sue Ann had no idea how difficult a category this actually was. With five judges on the international panel, each with a different palate, from a different country, and with their own cultural and historical references on how wine should taste, the variations in the scores can be dramatic. When averaged out, the highest ranking of Gold is actually the wine that best pleases a truly international palate.

Brock's Monument

Still a relatively young winemaker, Sue Ann didn't fully appreciate the impact that a distinguished award or critical acclaim could have on a wine until an issue of *Wine Access Magazine* published Canada's list of top 100 wines. Pillitteri tied for first, second, and third highest ranking out of 100 points in the red wine categories. The 1998 Cabernet Franc Family Reserve scored ninety-one for a third position; the 1998 Family Reserve Merlot took a second position with a score of ninety-two; and a first place position with a score of ninety-three was awarded for her 1998 Trivalente (Italian for the "blending of three"), a Meritage- or Bordeaux-style blended wine. While all wines sold extremely well after the publication, the 130 cases of Trivalente (selling at $12.95 a bottle!) sold out in only two months.

Not bad for a rookie, eh!

Winemaker's Matches: Sue Ann Staff, Pillitteri Estates

White Wine: Sauvignon Blanc (not Fume style)
Food: Goat cheese salad with citrus-based dressing
Comment: Mixed greens (no tomatoes) with toasted almonds and creamy goat cheese offer both a complement and a contrast in one dish. The wine offsets the creamy rich cheese and cleanses the palate while the salad greens pair with the wine's herbaceous flavors. (The Sauvignon Blanc could be used as an alternative to vinegar in the dressing.)

Red Wine: Cabernet Franc
Food Oven-braised rack of Ontario lamb with rosemary and thyme, salt and pepper
Comment: A medium-bodied Cabernet Franc with some elegance and herbal qualities matches the weight and flavors of the lamb, and the wine has enough tannins to smooth out any oiliness in the lamb while refreshing the palate.

Chateau des Charmes

FAST FACTS

1025 York Road
Niagara-on-the-Lake, Ontario
L0S 1J0
Tel: 905-262-4219
Fax: 905-262-5548
E-mail:
info@chateaudescharmes.com
Web: www.chateaudescharmes.com

"Toasting," or charring the inside of a barrel according to the winemaker's specifications, provides a buffer between the alcohol in the wine and the tannins in the wood.

Niagara's first French-style chateau, Chateau des Charmes, on the St. David's Bench in Niagara

Chateau des Charmes traces its roots back over five generations to the Alsace region of France and the vineyards of French Algeria. It was there that the ancestors of Paul Bosc began a heritage of fine winemaking that would serve the Bosc family for generations. The tradition of excellence continues today in the vineyards of Niagara-on-the-Lake, where Paul and his family carry on this rich heritage of meticulous vinification by harmonizing science and art.

A graduate of one of Europe's finest winemaking schools, the University of Burgundy at Dijon, Paul came to Canada from France in the 1960s. He brought the old-world tradition of winemaking to Canada and grafted that knowledge and tradition onto the soils of Niagara.

After studying the Niagara Peninsula for fifteen years, Paul concluded that the soil and climate of the area were ideal for fine wine production. Chateau des Charmes' vineyards are ideally positioned south of Lake Ontario and north of the Niagara Escarpment at 44 degrees latitude, providing superb growing conditions. In fact, the Niagara Peninsula is further south than France's famous Burgundy region where Paul was educated and trained. He is joined by his wife, Andrée, and his sons, Pierre-Jean and Paul-André, who represent the sixth generation of winegrowing expertise.

The Chateau was opened in 1994. Besides housing state-of-the-art wine production facilities, the winery is home to three hospitality rooms, an outdoor vineyard courtyard surrounded by rose gardens, a wine boutique, a tasting bar, and a theater.

Chateau des Charmes produces a range of outstanding wines. Varietals from the St. David's Bench Vineyard include Chardonnay, Sauvignon Blanc, Gewurztraminer, Viognier, Merlot, Cabernet Sauvignon, and Cabernet Franc. From the Paul Bosc Estate Vineyard varietals consist of Chardonnay, Cabernet, and Riesling for icewine. Estate bottled varietals comprise Chardonnay, Aligote, Auxerrois, Late Harvest Riesling, and Pinot Noir.

The winery has won numerous national and international awards at competitions including the International

Wine and Spirit Competition in England, All-Canadian Wine Championships, and Vinexpo in France.

Overlooking the eighty-five-acre St. David's Bench Vineyard, visitors can join daily public tours. The chateau also hosts a series of wine and food seminars, special events, and private functions throughout the year.

Chateau des Charmes wines are available at most LCBO stores, the winery boutique and Chateau des Charmes boutiques in Ontario; through sales agents in Eastern Canada, Quebec, Alberta, Manitoba, and British Columbia; and in the United States, United Kingdom, Germany, France, Japan, and Taiwan.

The Unique Bosc Family

The Bosc family is unique in the Canadian wine industry. Paul Bosc, Sr. is fixated on producing world-class wines from the relatively young soils of the Niagara region. He set himself goals he continues to eclipse beyond his fragile dreams. He has had many hardships, obstacles, and uneven roads to travel, but he succeeds because he is surrounded by a loving family who share his impossible dream. This family has carved out a niche for themselves in the face of much opposition and has managed to put the lie to all the naysayers who doubted the rich farmland of Niagara could produce world-class wines.

Andrée, Paul, and their two sons are intent on coaxing magic from their soil. The glue that holds this family together is an exuberant joie de vivre that engages all. They are proud owners of an imposing chateau near historic Queenston on the St. David's Bench.

Paul took me aside one time and confided in me at his sweeping grand entrance. "Look!" he pointed. "At what?" I thought. "Look," he said again, forcefully, pointing across the front roadway. "Very nice," I offered, not sure what I was supposed to be looking at. He proudly told me that the house across the street was his. Then he boldly bellowed, "My front door is exactly on line with this front door, perfectly aligned." I nodded. He continued to explain: "When I first arrived here I looked around and wondered, couldn't anybody draw a straight line? Everywhere I looked it was crooked. Zig-zags everywhere. Nobody could plant straight! Ridiculous!"

He saw not neat vineyards but sloppy design, and it offended him in no small way. Within this environment he was determined to make his statement. So whenever you visit the Chateau des Charmes, see this for yourself. Be sure to stand at the doorway and notice the straight line.

SAUMON À LA BOSC

by Madame Bosc

Serves 4

4 salmon steaks
1 large tomato, sliced
1 lemon, sliced
1 clove of garlic, diced
½ cup (125 ml) fresh mushrooms
½ cup (125 ml) fresh parsley
½ cup (125 ml) bread crumbs
½ cup (125 ml) butter
1 bottle (750 ml) Chateau des Charmes Sauvignon Blanc, St. David's Bench Vineyard
salt and pepper to taste

Cover the inside of a baking dish with aluminum foil and baste with butter. Place salmon steaks evenly in the dish. Place tomato and lemon slices on steaks. Arrange the mushrooms, garlic, and parsley around the steaks, sprinkle them with bread crumbs, and season to taste.

Add one glass of Sauvignon Blanc. Bake in 350°F (175°C) for 30 minutes or until tenderness is achieved. This dish is best served with wild rice and a tossed salad.

WINE MATCH
Chateau des Charmes Sauvignon Blanc, St. David's Bench Vineyard

---

Although oak is primarily used with red wines, Sauvignon Blanc and Chardonnay are the rare white grape varietals that can be enhanced with oak treatment during fermentation and vinification.

Henry of Pelham Family Estate Winery

With 150 acres of vineyards, Henry of Pelham Family Estates is a small premium winery on the Niagara Bench.

The winery was a founding member of the VQA, and with its first vintage in 1988 was one of a very few estate wineries dedicated to producing premium quality wines made from 100% Ontario-grown grapes. The focus continues to be on vinifera grape varieties including Chardonnay, Riesling, Cabernet Sauvignon, Baco Noir, and Riesling Icewine.

The Henry of Pelham philosophy is "to do as little as possible in the production of our wines." Paul Speck, president, says that from the vineyards through the bottling "we are naturalists allowing nature to take its course." For example, Henry of Pelham grape-hoes in the vineyards as much as possible instead of spraying for weeds to maintain a high grape quality. The production

Henry of Pelham Estate Winery resides in this historic inn on the Niagara Bench near St. Catharines

area of the winery, including the crusher, press, tanks, and bottling line, is a state-of-the-art facility to meet the high standard of quality set by the Speck family.

Old-world winemaking is matched with new-world technology. Typical of bench wineries, Henry of Pelham wines display the distinctive character produced from the clay, climate, and growing season along the ridge of the Niagara Escarpment.

The persistence for high quality has been rewarded with more than fifty international awards for outstanding wines, including awards at prestigious wine competitions such as VinItaly and the London Wine Trade Fair. Henry of Pelham winemaker Ron Giesbrecht has also been recognized for his achievements, including Ontario Wine Society Winemaker of the Year Award at the Air Ontario Wine Awards in 2001.

Henry of Pelham products are available at their local winery store, at LCBO stores, and through distributors in the rest of Canada, the U.S., and the rest of the world. The winery website at www.henryofpelham.com has a distributors' listing.

Their VQA products include (white wines), Riesling, Vidal, Sauvignon Blanc, Chardonnay, Gewurztraminer; (red wines) Cabernet Merlot, Cabernet Foch, Gamay, Merlot, Pinot Noir, Baco Noir, Rose; (sweet wines) Botrytis Affected Riesling, Late Harvest Vidal, Late Harvest Riesling, Riesling Icewine, Vidal Icewine.

ROASTED FILLET OF HALIBUT ON GOLDEN BEET MASHED POTATO

with an Asparagus Cream and Truffle Oil Drizzle

———

from Chef Eric Peacock, Wellington Court

———

Serves 4

4, 6-oz (175-g) fillets of halibut
6 medium golden beets
1 lb (500 g) Yukon Gold potatoes, peeled, quartered
10 stalks of asparagus, bottoms snapped, roughly chopped
1 small onion, finely diced
1 cup (250 ml) chicken or vegetable stock
1 cup (250 ml) heavy cream
2 tbsp (30 ml) butter
2 tbsp (30 ml) olive oil
white truffle oil
salt
pepper

Preheat oven to 300°F (150°C).
Place the golden beets in salted, boiling water with skins on for approximately 30 to 40 minutes. Beets should be fork tender when cooked. Drain and place in an ice water bath to cool completely. Once cooled, peel beets, roughly chop, and set aside.
In a saucepan over medium heat, melt the butter. Add the diced onion. Allow the onion to sweat for 3 to 4 minutes until softened. Add the asparagus and stock. Bring to a boil. Reduce heat and allow to simmer for 20 minutes. Blend the contents with a hand-held emersion blender. (You may need to move the contents from the saucepan to a bowl to avoid spraying the liquid.) Add ½ cup (125 ml) of heavy cream and blend again. Pass liquid through a sieve to remove any asparagus or other bits not blended.
Place the potatoes in a pot. Cover with salted water. Bring to a boil and cook until fork tender, approximately 20 minutes. Strain the potatoes and allow to thoroughly dry in a strainer. Place the potatoes, beets, and remaining
continued on page 84

continued from page 83
cream in a bowl and mash with a potato masher or fork. Do not over-mash the mixture. Season to taste with salt and pepper. Keep the potatoes hot until ready to serve.

Moisten the top of the halibut with olive oil, spreading it evenly. Sprinkle with salt and pepper. Place on a parchment-lined baking sheet in the oven. Bake the fish for 12 minutes.

While the fish is cooking, reheat the asparagus cream in a saucepan and keep it hot until ready to plate. Once the fish is cooked, remove it from the oven along with the potatoes. Place a 4–5 oz (125–150 g) scoop of potatoes in the center of a plate. Center a piece of fish on top of the potato. Surround the plate with asparagus cream and drizzle with white truffle oil. Serve with vegetables of choice.

Serving suggestion: This dish is perfect with cooked baby carrots and steamed green beans.

WINE MATCH
Speck Family Reserve Chardonnay

The Specks: Three Sons and a Winemaker

The Speck brothers—Paul, Matthew, and Daniel—were growing up in Toronto during the early 1980s when their father decided to purchase a piece of retirement property in Niagara. The fifty-five-acre parcel of land would enable their father to become a "gentleman farmer" with a nice home in the quiet countryside where he could relax, tend his garden, and enjoy life away from the hectic business world he had always known in Toronto. It didn't take the Speck family long to find out that the land was prized Niagara grape-growing "bench" property. Their wine journey was about to begin.

In 1984 Paul and Matthew were drafted by their father to begin planting Baco Noir, Chardonnay, Riesling, and Gamay vines. Both sons were at university pursuing studies in philosophy and would spend much of their spare time in the vineyards. By 1988 the family had produced its first vintage with 2,400 cases of wine, but it was obvious their father couldn't manage the winery and vineyards by himself.

After graduating, Paul thought he'd take a year off—before pursuing studies and a career in law—to help his father with the winery. Needless to say, he never returned to his studies. Another native Niagara son was bitten by the wine passion bug. In 1984 they purchased a building that their great-great-grandfather Henry Smith (of Pelham) built in 1842 and ran as a carriage house for over seventy-five years. By 1987 they had established the Henry of Pelham winery, with the former inn serving as offices and a retail shop.

Two different winemakers helped Henry of Pelham for the first two vintages, but it wasn't until the Speck brothers hired local winemaker Ron Giesbrecht in 1990 that the winery started to draw serious critical acclaim. Ron had worked for a much larger commercial wine company and saw Henry of Pelham as an opportunity to have greater hands-on influence with a smaller volume of wines. It was a relationship founded on a focus for quality, craft, and mutual respect.

Their 1991 vintage of Baco Noir was released in 1993 and met with critical acclaim. Sales took off, and the Henry of Pelham Baco Noir established an almost cult-like status and consumer following. In the shadow of the noble vinifera, the hybrid Baco Noir surprised almost everyone and Henry of Pelham garnered substantial notoriety.

From left to right: Paul, Daniel, and Matthew Speck with winemaker Ron Giesbrecht

Following their newly earned accolades, Paul initiated a distinct new label design to reflect the winery's growth and coming of age. During a wine tasting in London, England, Paul had an opportunity to pour the Henry of Pelham 1995 Cabernet Merlot for Hugh Johnson (internationally acclaimed wine critic and writer). Delighted by what he was tasting but thinking that it couldn't possibly be a Niagara wine, and suspicious that someone was trying to dupe him, Johnson demanded to verify the label.

With their substantial growth happening over a relatively short period of time and a firm appreciation for the risks of running an agricultural business in a highly competitive, oversupplied market, the team at Henry of Pelham won't be found napping. With Paul as the business manager, Matthew overseeing the vineyards, Daniel at the sales helm, and Ron Giesbrecht guiding the wines, they are determined to help raise the bar of wine excellence.

Running a business in a low-margin industry means that Paul's earlier dreams of owning a high-performance racecar have been supplanted by dreams of producing the highest-quality wines that each vintage will allow. For now, he can take some solace in knowing that their Baco Noir is Canada's number one selling VQA red wine. Zoom, zoom!

Baco Noir (bah-koh nwahr), created by Maurice Baco, is a hybrid made by crossing a French Folle Blanche with an American vine. He also developed Baco Blanc, which is used in producing the brandies of Armagnac.

Hernder Estate Wines

FAST FACTS

1607 8th Avenue
St. Catharines, Ontario
L2R 6P7
Tel: 905-684-3300
E-mail: wine@vaxxine.com
Web: www.hernder.com

Well into their third generation of grape growing, the Hernder family has transformed a love of viticulture into one of the largest family estate wineries in Canada.

Growing up on the family farm, Fred Hernder's success began early when he was crowned as the youngest "Grape King" in 1977. Over the years he began selling grapes, juice, and winemaking supplies to the home market as well as wineries.

After the first vintage of 7,000 bottles of Vidal produced in 1991, Hernder Estate Wines was officially opened in 1993. The entrance to the winery is across Niagara's only covered bridge to reach stone wall patios

The picturesque Hernder Estate Winery hosts weddings and special occasion celebrations

surrounding a charming 1867 Victorian barn. Hernder has become known as Ontario's "wedding winery" with reception rooms that can accommodate 500 people and outdoor patios for another 150.

The winery has expanded over the years and now produces more than twenty-five varieties of VQA wines. Plantings on Hernder's 500 acres of land in Niagara focus on vitis vinifera varieties including Chardonnay, Riesling, Gewurztraminer, Cabernet Sauvignon, Merlot, Cabernet Franc, and Pinot Gris. Other popular varieties include sturdy French hybrids such as Vidal, Baco Noir, and Marechal Foch.

Hernder has won numerous awards for its wines at national and international competitions including the All-Canadian Wine Championships and the International Wine and Spirits Competition in England.

Many of Hernder's wines are available at the winery and through LCBO outlets throughout Ontario. They can also be ordered for delivery within the province by calling the winery.

Hernder offers public tours and wine tastings daily. They also have full banquet and conference facilities.

HERNDER'S CRANBERRY GLAZED HAM STEAKS

Hernder Estates

—

Serves 4

4 small ham steaks
1 cup (250 ml) Hernder's Cranberry Wine
1 small can of pineapple tidbits
½ cup (125 ml) dried cranberries
½–¾ cup (125–180 ml) light brown sugar

Combine the drained pineapple, cranberries, and wine. Set aside for at least 1 hour.

Place the ham steaks in a shallow baking dish sprayed with non-stick spray. Sprinkle the ham with the brown sugar then pour the fruit and wine combination over top.

Bake at 350°F (175°C) for 50 to 60 minutes, basting several times.

WINE MATCH
Hernder Cranberry Wine

NOTES FROM THE CELLAR

WINE CELLAR HINTS

When is a wine cellar considered useful and economical?
I think the largest wine cabinet will hold about 500 to 600 bottles. It becomes economically viable to move on to the next stage when approaching or exceeding those numbers and especially when getting close to keeping 1,000 bottles.

Is it wise to keep an inventory of bottles in a cellar?
It's amazing how many bottles of wine can be ruined without a proper inventory system. As an example, years ago, clients discovered that the 1982 Bordeaux vintages were promising to become the finest ever. Conditions, climate, yield, everything was perfect. It was the first Parker-rated vintage that attracted new collectors to leap onto the bandwagon and buy in bulk. People also added many bottles of the '83 vintage when they heard it was "drinking well," then more bottles of '85 and '88 vintages, which were all great. But as people were purchasing and storing all of this wine, they lost touch of a simple principle: Wine matures and is a perishable commodity. They didn't label and track their inventories so they lost many bottles of wine that became "over the hill." Wastage won't happen if a record is kept even of those two bottles stuffed away in the back of the closet or under the holiday wrappings.

What's the best way to track the inventory in a cellar?
It's simple, really. Get a piece of paper and make a grid, then plot where the wine bottles reside in the cellar or rack. For the next step, take the grid and create a spreadsheet. Perhaps write the year on wine tags placed on the necks so that the bottles are not disturbed. Computer programs can graph and plot the wine by region or even by varietal. Don't forget to include a "no-problem rack," a list of bottles that can be pulled without incurring the wrath of the collector. It all makes sense!

St. Catharines

Spa Central

The lonely years after Abraham Lincoln's assassination were very difficult for his wife, Mary Todd Lincoln. She found much-needed comfort in the rejuvenating waters of the salt mineral springs of St. Catharines!

Between 1850 and 1900, the tiny town of St. Catharines was celebrated far and wide as "the Carlsbad of America." North Americans flocked to experience the relaxing balm of the salt springs by "taking the waters" at one of the imposing hotels that catered to the needy travelers. The world-famous spas—such as Stephenson House, the Welland House, and the Springbank Hotel—did a brisk business providing saline baths, massage, and a pleasant sojourn. The ad said it all: "The celebrated waters of St. Catharines will cure all the ills of life but poverty. Rules for taking: If one bath does not cure, try ten." Known popularly as "the Saratoga of Canada," the town itself was very much a part of the general attraction. It was said that the town was "the most American town in the Dominion"! The major attraction was always the mighty Falls but word had spread about the delights to be found not ten miles (15 kilometers) away. The water was the actual draw that brought visitors back again and again.

Visitors were a who's who of America as well as Canada with a special interest exhibited by southern U.S. citizens. During the American Civil War, the whole Niagara area was a hotbed of intrigue that catered to a host of mysterious characters in various guises of both Union and Confederate combatants. It became common knowledge that the large hotels were listening-posts alert to the activities of both sides. It was a well-known fact that sympathy for the southern cause was strong, and plots and criminal activity filled the mineral-laced air. The local papers even reported the comings and goings of notorious agents in a sympathetic tone. The president of the short-lived Confederacy, Jefferson Davis, worshipped at St. George's Anglican Church and later held court at

"Indian at Spring," Stanley Raptis Collection, St. Catharines Museum, N4167

St. Catharines c. 1875, St. Catharines Museum, N4170

Welland House
Hotel c. 1895,
St. Catharines
Museum, N1037

the nearby Welland House Spa. We've been able to glean
information about daily life during a spa visit from letters
written by Mrs. Robert E. Lee visiting in 1860. She com-
mented on the high cost of a visit and was against the
very thought of rising prices as its fame spread!

Spas waned in the years after the Civil War as the restless young nation sought relief in other pursuits such as
visiting seaside resorts that were springing up along the
Atlantic coastline. While the comforting restorative pow-
ers of mineral waters continued to draw many, closer
attention was being paid to the health benefits of outdoor
activity and healthy exercise.

Only the Welland House remains as mute testimony to
the forgotten charms of taking the waters. I'll bet some
enterprising spirit will some day stumble over a rock and
release the elixir of the St. Catharine Well, and maybe
we'll see a resurgence of weary travelers coming for
relief. The bubbling waters still churn beneath the well-
worn byways of the Garden City of Canada.

Entrance to the Welland House
Hotel, The Valentine & Sons
Publishing Co. Collection,
St Catharines Museum, N1093

Lacrosse

Lacrosse is often referred to as the game older than sport!
Let me tell you a bit about the ancient game, and then
you can visit the St. Catharines Museum for its superb
lacrosse collection.

St. Catharines
MUSEUM

Viewers enjoy displays at the Ontario Lacrosse Museum, in the St. Catharines Museum

Lacrosse was a popular "Indian summer" game throughout what is now southern Canada and most regions of the United States. It certainly qualifies as the oldest team sport in North America. It was invented by First Nations people and played for many reasons: to settle disputes among Native communities; to pay homage to the Almighty Creator; to promote the healing of individuals and communities; or for the welfare of the entire community. At first, the game was steeped with religious meaning but by 1790 it developed into a more recreational sport.

The game appeared simple. Any number of people could play as long as both sides were relatively equal. The playing field had no boundaries. The number of goals needed for victory was determined beforehand and the game itself could go on for days at a time. One rule has remained dominant down through to the present time: No player may touch the ball with his or her hand.

After "game day" was designated, much preparation was undertaken with religious zeal. Provisions had to be set aside for the journey to the game site and to last for the duration of the game. Articles for wagering would be made or gathered together by the whole community, which was very much a part of the ritual. Also part of the ritual, players had to fast and avoid contact with women!

The ball was made from animal hairs wound tightly together and wrapped in deer hide. This ball of fur sometimes included a sacred object sewn inside the center. The healers of each community would prepare special potions or cleansing tonics for players to drink or use as salves to anoint their bodies for the coming spectacle. Players approached the playing field with the utmost reverence, for it was taken to heart that to play the game well was a gift unto itself, and enjoyment flowed from exerting a superior effort.

A Mohawk faith keeper explains that "We called the game 'Tewaarathon.' It was a gift from the Creator. We played it to strengthen our medicine when someone fell sick. Then we played it with all our life force. We ran from field and village, through streams and woods. There were few rules and no boundaries. Our bodies were strong and unprotected, and we invoked the spirits of the swift and powerful animals to guide us."

Of course, the Native people played among themselves when their communities were threatened and especially when British interlopers made their presence known. Fort Michilimackinac (in present-day Michigan) was a British outpost in 1763. In June of that year the Native people played lacrosse on the acreage a distance away from the fort. It was a hot day. The game was played in the morning, under the noonday sun, and late into the afternoon, without stopping. Slowly the garrison emptied as the British troopers went to watch the game. The ball was arched over the walls of the fort and the players shucked aside their sticks, took up weapons, and fell upon the stockade, killing thirty-five soldiers and capturing the fort!

Grape and Wine Festival

Everyone along the many byways of Ontario's wine routes looks forward to celebrating the end of another vintage by joining in the much ballyhooed Grape and Wine Festival in St. Catharines. It remains the annual focus of celebration within the wine community. It is harvest time and time to raise a glass. The festivities stretch over two weeks.

The REO

This is St. Catharines' very own contribution to the horseless carriage era! The REO, named for Ransom E. Olds (also the inventor of the Oldsmobile), was manufactured in St. Catharines around the turn of the century. Just one of the many firsts for the city!

The St. Catharines Museum at Lock 3 on the Welland Canal boasts the only known 1912 REO Roadster still in existence. The car has been lovingly restored over a period of forty years by Mike Guzei at a cost of over $30,000. The REO Roadster was renowned for having been driven all the way across Canada in 1912, a feat deemed impossible by many. I'd love to take it for a spin, wouldn't you?

Jonathan with the REO

Creekside Estate Winery

FAST FACTS

2170 Fourth Avenue
Jordan Station, Ontario
L0R 1S0
Tel: 905-562-0035; 877-262-9463
Fax: 905-562-5493
Web:
www.creeksideestatewinery.com

Creekside Estate Winery in Jordan Station, Niagara Peninsula

Sauvignon Blanc wines are light to medium bodied and usually dry. Descriptors often used to describe their aromas and flavors include grassy, herbaceous, crisp, and even fruity.

Founded in 1988 by Peter and Laura Jensen, Creekside Estate Winery has quickly become a Niagara leader for premium VQA wines.

Situated along the Beamsville Bench, the winery boasts a state-of-the-art production facility and underground barrel cellar, where Australian winemaker Marcus Ansems vinifies a wide variety of wine styles, from well-structured, aromatic Sauvignon Blancs to long-lived Bordeaux blends.

Along with the thirteen-acre Creekside vineyard with Sauvignon Blanc, Shiraz, and Cabernet Sauvignon varieties, the winery has also developed a strong network of vineyard partners who share Marcus' vision of low yields and rigorous bunch selection to achieve wines of distinction.

Production levels have risen dramatically from 5,000 cases annually in 1998 to approximately 25,000 today. Grapes are sourced from both Niagara-on-the-Lake and the Bench area and are most often blended together to provide greater complexity. The winery is particularly known for its Sauvignon Blanc, Pinot Noir, and Laura's

Blend, a combination of Cabernet Sauvignon, Merlot, and Cabernet Franc.

One of the region's first underground barrel cellars has the capacity to store 600 barrels and hold special events such as winemakers' dinners and specialized tastings. The winery has approximately 350 barrels, half obtained from France and the other half from the United States.

Creekside has captured a number of domestic and international awards at wine competitions such as the Concours Mondial Bruxelles, the International Wine Challenge, the All-Canadian Wine Championships and the International Eastern Wine Competition.

During the summer, visitors can relax on the outdoor patio and enjoy the ambience of wine country while sampling Creekside vintages. On weekends a small selection of gourmet lunches is available.

A complimentary tour of the winery is available at 2:00 p.m. each day during the summer and fall seasons. For larger groups, Creekside offers various educational tours designed to highlight the multifaceted world of wine.

Creekside wines are available through Vintages (special LCBO outlets), the winery boutique, and at fine restaurants.

Wineries often host vineyard picnics and luncheons for special events

GRILLED SCALLOP SALAD WITH ASIAN NOODLES

from The Grill at
the Epicurean,
Niagara-on-the-Lake

—

Serves 4

SALAD
1½ cups (375 ml) somen noodles
½ cup (125 ml) carrot julienne
½ cup (125 ml) cucumber julienne
½ cup (125 ml) sweet red pepper julienne
2 tbsp (30 ml) coriander, chopped
salt
freshly ground pepper
8 large sea scallops, fresh

DRESSING
2 tbsp (30 ml) soy sauce
1 tbsp (15 ml) mirin
1 tbsp (15 ml) rice wine vinegar
½ tsp (2 ml) dark sesame oil
½ tsp (2 ml) sambal
½ tsp (2 ml) ginger, peeled and finely diced
½ tsp (2 ml) garlic, peeled and finely diced

Combine all ingredients for the dressing, whisk, and set aside. (It is important that the dressing stand so that it can absorb the ginger and garlic flavors.)

Combine the noodles, carrot, cucumber, and red pepper in a large bowl.

Season the scallops with salt and ground pepper then coat lightly with oil. Grill the scallops over a high flame until they are cooked but still soft.

While the scallops are grilling, dress the noodles with coriander and most of the dressing.

Put a small pile of the noodles in the middle of a plate. When the scallops are done, slice them in half with a sharp knife so there are 2 thin disks. Arrange the scallops, 3 pieces around the salad and 1 on top, and drizzle with the remaining dressing.

WINE MATCH
Creekside Sauvignon Blanc

Riesling: All Hail the Queen!

"Putting Riesling in oak barrels would be grounds for divorce!"
—A. Schmidt, winemaker

The Riesling grape is a varietal that came out of Germany. In wine circles, Riesling is considered the queen where Chardonnay is the king. It was probably the first white that gained serious international recognition for Ontario white wines and local recognition as a serious premium variety. It's a classic grape that's native to cool climate regions, and Ontario is well suited to nurturing wonderful Rieslings. Virtually all of its characteristics are really coming from how Mother Nature treats the vineyard.

In a good vintage you will get very good, tasty fruit acids and very flowery aromas rather than bouquet—Riesling has a very definitive smell. It's like smelling a single rose, which is an aroma, whereas in a bouquet of flowers you're getting several different scents coming from the different types of flowers. The term "bouquet" would be much more appropriate in describing a Chardonnay, where several smells come about from the influence of oak and a host of other procedures.

The aroma of Riesling is very distinctive and can be produced in many styles, from very sweet as an icewine or late harvest dessert wine, to off-dry with a slight residual sweetness, to very dry with no residual sugar at all. Angelo Pavan at Cave Spring Cellars makes as many as six different styles of Riesling. This is a wine that is appreciated for its good acid backbone and fresh fruit flavors. Even in a fully dry

Riesling and roses

The famous German Riesling grape does exceptionally well in Ontario

Riesling, people often mistake the forward fruit for residual sugar levels.

The Riesling grape has been greatly underrated. In the late 1800s and early 1900s Rieslings from Germany were some of the most expensive, highly coveted wines on the market. Today they're experiencing resurgence due to higher-quality practices and a newfound respect for the unadulterated flavor components of the grape itself.

You'll find it has a pleasant crisp, fruity flavor that goes well with light meats and is an excellent wine to drink as an apéritif before dinner.

Riesling likes to be stressed. When you stress Riesling in a vineyard it creates character and backbone that is reflected in the quality of the wine. Rieslings grown on the clay soils of the Niagara Bench tend to get some apricot character, some citrus tones, and a bit of grapefruit on the nose and especially on the mouth and on the finish. In good years there can even be hints of lime, and depending on the age of the wine, it can also develop a kind of a mineral earthiness character and a petrol or gasoline aroma as it ages. This petrol essence is highly prized by wine aficionados. (Don't ask us why!)

Riesling is one of the rare white wines that can age very well. Hot dry summers and cool evenings help build the acid backbone and ageability in Rieslings, and for Niagara the 1991 and 1993 vintages enjoyed these ideal conditions. Most are made to drink young while they are

CAVE SPRING

Reserve 2000 *Réserve*

RIESLING

VQA NIAGARA PENINSULA VQA
ESTATE BOTTLED

CAVE SPRING CELLARS, JORDAN, ONTARIO, CANADA
WHITE WINE/PRODUCT OF CANADA • VIN BLANC/PRODUIT DU CANADA

12.5% alc./vol. 750 mL

One wine may taste sweet in comparison to another because it contains less acidity, while the alcohol in a totally dry wine can create a sweet taste, as though sugar had been added.

Trellising and leaf trimming help grape clusters ripen fully on the vine

Well-balanced white wines with a good measure of acidity taste crisp and refreshing, while those without enough acidity can taste fat, flabby, and cloying in the mouth.

still refreshing and fruity. If you're interested in ageability and want to experience that petrol characteristic, it's often best to ask the wine shop purveyor or the winery if that particular vintage would improve in the cellar.

Even though Riesling is a thin-skinned grape, it's a cold, hardy variety, which makes it the quintessential cool-climate white-wine grape. When the fruit starts to ripen you get extremely tight bunches where the skins are quite thin, and as the fruit gets closer to harvest, the clusters tighten up. The berries start to push against each other and eventually they can start breaking or popping out of the bunch. The berry itself can be finicky and deli-cate, and sometimes the Riesling will develop what's called noble rot, or botrytis.

As those berries open up and rot, a mildew will start to grow, a green type of rot that basically punctures the skin of the remaining berries and gives them a raisin-like appearance. Generally, Ontario has enough humidity during harvest to promote the growth of noble rot. It's not pretty to look at, but when it evolves under the right circumstances in the right amount, it enhances the won-derful concentration of fruit flavors, which will be detected in the finished wine. It adds another taste dimension and interesting complexity to the fruit, and you get nutty and caramel-type characters in the finished wine. Many winemakers promote this event by putting the term "botrytis effected" right on the label.

However, with every blessing comes a curse. If the rot develops too early it will diminish the crop yield. It's one of those things growers need to control and want to have developed slowly and no more than a few weeks before harvest so that they can benefit from the great taste attributes it imparts. Botrytis also reduces the volume of juice in the grape and subsequently the volume of wine that can be produced.

Unfortunately, if it rots too early, it reduces yield and (here's the kicker) could possibly turn into what is known as brown rot. This produces an acidic vinegar-like odor that wafts across an entire vineyard. Needless to say, growers and winemakers have an aversion to anything that smacks of vinegar.

Riesling is sometimes considered the honest grape variety because it is a wine that is definitively made in the vineyards. Winemakers have very little ability to change the style of the Riesling and are best off when they respect the fruit they harvest.

Where a wine like Chardonnay is malleable and invites the winemaker to put it in oak or to do whatever they think might work best, the Riesling is a hands-off proposition. Riesling has been described as an adventurist and one of the most versatile grape varieties to work with. Most winemakers insist it is a wine to be made in inert stainless steel tanks where nothing can affect the lovely flavor profile of the grape.

The French term **terroir** *is universally used by wine-makers to distinguish one grape-growing location from another, and includes natural elements such as climate, soil type, drainage, winds, and humidity.*

Riesling icewine grapes

NOTES FROM THE CELLAR

LEARNING ABOUT WINE

What's the best way to gain information about wine?
All that's needed is some basic knowledge before attacking the critical heavyweights. Novices should learn the terminology and fundamentals, and start off by keeping a journal. Get to know your own taste buds by simple experimentation. It all boils down to personal preference. By all means, read the critics and discover whose taste buds you agree with the most. If you generally feel the same way as some "expert" does about certain wines, follow their recommendations. But always use your own judgment. You are the expert at what you enjoy. Use atlases and maps to provide a base from which you can explore on your own. Use your journal and explore on paper. When you feel comfortable with your idea of the basics, pick up a wine buyer's guide and become familiar with how the various wine-producing regions market their product. We've come a long way from Italian wicker baskets and easy brand names such as Blue Nun and Black Tower. But at least these bulk offerings introduced us to Riesling and Gewurztraminer, in however raw a form.

Cave Spring Cellars

FAST FACTS

3836 Main Street
Jordan, Ontario
LOR 1S0
Tel: 905-562-3581
Fax: 905-562-3232
E-mail:
tpenna@cavespringcellars.com
Web: www.cavespringcellars.com

Located in a historic winery dating back to 1871, Cave Spring Cellars boasts the oldest functioning wine cellars in Ontario. Cave Spring Cellars was founded in 1986 but the winery's history goes back many years earlier.

As a youngster growing up in the area, Leonard Pennachetti had a keen interest in grapes. His grandfather Giuseppe, an immigrant from the Marche region of Italy, regularly took Leonard with him to care for the family vineyard near St. Catharines, Ontario. In 1978 Leonard and his father, John T. Pennachetti, planted some of Ontario's first vitis vinifera grape vines at the Cave Spring vineyard.

Located along a gently sloping terrace of the Niagara Escarpment around the town of Beamsville—known as the Beamsville "Bench"—this vineyard quickly became renowned as one of the region's best. The Bench is ideal for growing grapes because of the well-drained,

Niagara escarpment "bench" vineyards along the Peninsula are considered prime grape-growing properties

mineral-rich soil, its close proximity to Lake Ontario—which helps to moderate winter temperatures—summer temperatures, and optimal air flow patterns. Leonard Pennachetti believes Cave Spring wines are unique because they capture the *goût de terroir* or taste of the land from which they come.

The focus of Cave Spring Cellars is to produce wines from the classic European vinifera grape varieties grown at the 130-acre Cave Spring vineyard and other selected Escarpment vineyards. Varietals include (white wines) Gewurztraminer, Sauvignon Blanc, Chenin Blanc, Semillon, Riesling, Chardonnay; (red wines) Gamay, Pinot Noir, Cabernet Sauvignon, Cabernet Franc, Merlot.

In 1986 the winery produced only 500 cases, enough to acquire a winery permit. In 1987 the winery was moved to the historic Jordan Winery building in the village of Jordan and produced 6,000 cases of wine. Today Cave Spring Cellars produces approximately 60,000 cases annually.

Cave Spring has earned an excellent reputation as one of Ontario's leading producers of premium wine, with all of its wines bearing the VQA prestigious mark. Winery president Leonard Pennachetti was a founding board member of the VQA at its inception in 1988.

Cave Spring has also forged new ground in Niagara's agri-tourism industry. In 1993 the winery opened Ontario's first winery restaurant—On the Twenty—rated one of the finest anywhere. With an elegant ambience and beautiful views, On the Twenty features regional foods, which include local tree fruits and berries, quail, trout, and organically grown vegetables, herbs, and greens matched with Cave Spring wines. In 1996 Cave Spring expanded its hospitality venture by opening Inn On the Twenty, with luxurious rooms, suites, and a winemaker's cottage.

Over the years the wines of Cave Spring have garnered awards at top European competitions including Vinexpo in Bordeaux, France, VinItaly in Verona, Italy, and the International Wine and Spirits Competition in London, England. Cave Spring wines also consistently rank among Canada's best in national wine competitions.

Visitors can tour the winery's expansive underground cellars and enjoy a tasting of fine wines. Afterward, they can stroll along the charming village of Jordan's tree-lined main street, which features antique, craft, and gift shops, Jordan Historical Museum's authentically restored pioneer settlement, and an impressive array of nineteenth century period homes.

Wines are available at LCBO stores, at the local winery boutique, through distributors in all Canadian provinces,

SEARED SCALLOPS ON YUKON GOLD CELERY ROOT ROSTI
with 12-Year-Old Balsamic and Whitefish Caviar

———

from On the Twenty Restaurant, Cave Spring Cellars

———

Serves 4

SCALLOPS
16 scallops
2 tbsp (30 ml) vegetable oil
4 oz (125 ml) white wine
3 tbsp (45 ml) butter

ROSTI
2 large Yukon Gold potatoes
½ celery root
salt
pepper
grapeseed oil

VEGETABLE SOFFRITO
1 carrot
2 celery stalks
1 onion
1 red pepper
1 leek
2 tbsp (30 ml) olive oil
1 tbsp (15 ml) butter
2 thyme leaves, picked and chopped
1 yellow pepper

Place a heavy bottom fry pan on high heat. When the pan begins to smoke, add the oil and carefully add the scallops. After 1 minute loosen scallops from the bottom of the pan. Continue to cook for another minute.

Flip scallops over and cook for another 2 minutes. Remove from pan and keep in warm oven.

Pour off the oil from the pan and add wine. Scrape the bottom of the pan while the wine is bubbling, loosening all the bits of cooked scallops. Once the wine has reduced by half, add the butter off the heat and whisk it in.

To make the rosti, peel the potatoes and the celery root. Cut into julienne-size strips (using a mandolin is easiest), and sprinkle with salt to prevent from turning brown.

continued on page 100

continued from page 99
Heat pan over medium high heat and add about a quarter inch of oil in the bottom of the pan. Place the shredded potatoes in the oil and cook, pressing regularly to pack potato and celery root together. Once browned, carefully flip the potato cake over and cook it until brown on the other side. Remove and place on paper towels to drain off the excess oil.

For the vegetable soffrito, finely dice all vegetables. Sauté very quickly in olive oil and butter, season with salt, pepper and thyme.

TO ASSEMBLE
Place the sofritto in the center of a plate. Warm the rosti in the oven and then place on top of the vegetables. Place the scallops on top of the rosti, and pour pan butter sauce on top. Place half a teaspoon of caviar on top of each scallop and drizzle the plate with balsamic vinegar.

WINE MATCH
Cave Spring Riesling Reserve

and in the states of New York, Massachusetts, D.C., Virginia, and Washington. Cave Spring wines are also available in Denmark and Holland.

Angelo Pavan: Elementary and Unassuming

Angelo Pavan was too small to play professional football, his schoolboy passion. And without a musical note in his body, he could never be the rock star he dreamed of. Winemaking wasn't even on his radar when he graduated from high school in his native St. Catharines, Ontario.

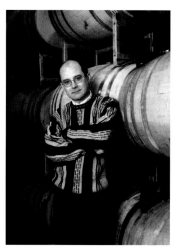

Winemaker Angelo Pavan

Angelo's strength was always in the intellectual arena (as he tells the story), and if he couldn't sing or pass the ball for a living he would use his academic gifts to select a career. One that wouldn't see him tied to a corporate chair.

Cited as one of Niagara's most talented winemakers, Angelo once scorned the very thought of "wine appreciation." While undertaking his doctorate in philosophy and preparing his dissertation, he noticed a promotion for an evening course in wine appreciation. Having grown up with an Italian heritage, where wine was a common beverage at every meal, Angelo scoffed at such a course as something akin to navel gazing. What could there possibly be to appreciate?

It was his skepticism combined with his natural curiosity that prompted him to take the evening course, just so he could find out what it could possibly offer anyone, let alone him. Angelo had opened Pandora's box. He became a wine appreciation junkie!

The introductory course led to a mid-level program and an advanced course. Angelo credits the course teacher, Peter Gamble, with inspiring him to see the magic that wine holds. He was amazed at the taste nuances between various wines. They would line up four different Burgundian reds and taste them blindfolded, their instructor guiding them through aromas, textures, mouth feels, taste sensations. It was like a giant jigsaw puzzle that wanted solving. It was like art history and fine literature. He was learning about the world by looking through a wineglass. It was a fascinating book of life he couldn't put down.

This was the perfect challenge. Angelo began honing his taste buds. Over and over, again and again, he would take different wines home to explore. He'd mask the bottles and have others pour the wines into different glasses so he could try to identify the variety, the origin, and the age, from behind his blindfold. With so many wines from so many places and different vintages it was like preparing for an exam that could never be completed—the ultimate challenge. His studies in wine appreciation were about to take him on a more serious journey.

Fascinated by the complexities and variations that wine offered, Angelo started to make wines with his life-long friend Len Pennachetti, who supplied the grapes from his own vineyard. The results impressed both Angelo and Len. Their musings about starting a wine company became reality in 1986 when Len managed to pool enough resources to start Cave Spring Cellars.

Cave Spring Cellars derives its name from the bench property that the Pennachetti grapes are grown on. The area where the vineyards are situated is called Cave Spring because of the ice caves in the escarpment adjoining the property. The Neutral Indians who had inhabited the region for centuries had used these natural refrigeration ice caves as storage units.

A wine referred to as "woody," or "wood juice," is one that has been kept in oak too long, taking on an exaggerated oaky flavor and bouquet that overwhelms the fruitier components.

The current Cave Spring Cellars Winery was originally home to the now defunct Jordan Wines Limited in the village of Jordan. It was being used as a warehouse when

The village of Jordan offers tourists first class wines, foods, accommodation, and a host of unique shops

Angelo, Len, and their colleagues moved into a small section in the south end of the building in 1987. Already established as a wine production facility, the building had a below-ground European-like cellar that was ideal for winemaking. The success of their wines lead to rapid expansion, and by 1990 Cave Spring Cellars owned the entire Jordan complex where they joined forces with Chef

Michael Olson to establish the acclaimed restaurant On the Twenty, which helped to pioneer indigenous Niagara cuisine married with Niagara wines.

Angelo finds Riesling to be his favorite white grape, from which he makes six different wines. With Chardonnay having occupied the number one spot in the wine world for so long, he's quick to point out that Rieslings were the most sought after, expensive wines in the late nineteenth and early twentieth centuries. Riesling is making a dramatic comeback as consumers discover its diversity.

Riesling's earlier fall from grace had much to do with the clever marketing of wines such as Black Tower, Blue Nun, and Leibfraumilch, which left a limited impression on consumers and cast Riesling into an undeserved light. Angelo believes Riesling has much more dimension than Chardonnay, which he finds more neutral on the flavor front and bulky or stocky by comparison to Riesling.

"Yeasty" is the winetasting term used to describe the fresh-bread bouquet found in wines that have been aged "on the lees." Wines not aged sur lie but having yeasty aromas are considered flawed.

Jonathan with the Pennachetti family: from left, Thomas, Leonard, and matriarch Dorothy

Tending to side with the underdog, Angelo prefers the unheralded Gamay as his favorite red grape for Niagara. Another under-appreciated wine, Gamay has the ability to step outside its traditional light, fruity nouveau style. In cutting back on his crop yields and introducing barrel aging, Angelo produces Gamay wines that are fuller in body with forward fruit character and greater ageability. He loves the concentration of cherries and the spiciness of black pepper that shows up, and Angelo sees tremendous depth and diversity in Gamay.

Angelo's winemaking style is qualitatively rooted in the European old-world model. Where others might strive to be big, bold, and opulent, Angelo prefers to strive for a taste profile that is less assuming, almost humble in its respect for the character of the fruit. He appreciates making wines that are known for their natural subtleties and elegance rather than fashioning wines that might be considered rich or pushy. Angelo makes wines to be appreciated with food, family, and friends as part of a healthy lifestyle.

We'll toast to that.

The wide selection of growing soils and climates for Chardonnay throughout the world produce a vast array of Chardonnay styles ranging from the tastes of apple, lemon, melon, and pineapple to flavors that seem buttery, creamy, smoky, and nutty.

The Farmer/Chef Connection
by Michael Olson

Michael Olson is regarded as one of Niagara's founding chefs, helping to establish a distinct level of cuisine excellence in the region. In establishing Cave Spring Cellars' renowned On the Twenty restaurant, Michael continued to help define the movement to create regional dishes that reflect Niagara's bounty.

When I first arrived on the scene in Niagara in the early 1990s, I was immediately overwhelmed by the connection between the chef and the farmer. To cook in an area that excels in growing wine grapes and wonderful produce is truly a great opportunity to not only source the best, freshest product, but also to get to know the characters who toil behind the scenes in quiet dedication to their craft.

You can really identify with the flavor of peaches after standing in a room with sixty tonnes of the garnet beauties, sucking in gasps of cold air, thick with their aroma. When a bushel of tomatoes arrives at the back door, vine ripened and still warm from the afternoon sun, you tend to take a little extra pride in the soup that is coaxed out of their fragile architecture. And when the herb man gives

Chardonnay's remarkable versatility means it can grow in climates as dissimilar as those found in the cooler northern districts including Switzerland and England on one hand, and in warmer southern locations such as Chile and Spain on the other.

While today's delectable food sauces are highly prized, early sauces—in the days before refrigeration—were actually used to smother the taste of foods that had begun to go bad.

you total grief for allowing his marjoram to wilt and die instead of ushering that bowl of tomato soup from good to great, the chef sees food production a little differently.

I feel strongly about choosing fresh produce that is grown in your own neighborhood. If you can find fruits or vegetables that are grown with respect and integrity, then prepare them as simply as you dare to show off the true natural taste. When the tomatoes are peaking in August, they need very little to make them stars—a pinch of salt and a basil leaf is all you need to make that slice of goodness sing! We often reach for one or two ingredients more than is necessary, and this tends to clutter and confuse the palate. Do not play with your food.

To really get a sense of what Niagara is all about, simply drive down the back roads and stop at any of the wonderful fruit stands at the farm gate. You're likely to find homegrown produce at its peak and some solid advice—by a member of the family who grew it—on when and how to eat it. On the other hand, many of the stands work on the honor system, where you leave the cash in a metal box and take your fruit or vegetables. Do not even consider being a

Jonathan shares a pear with Michael Olson of the Niagara College Culinary Institute

"bad guy"! Niagara farmers take their business seriously, and the penalties are steep for farm-gate robbery. After all, who would want to steal from such an honorable pillar of society as the farmer?

The winery restaurant community is growing in Niagara, and the food culture has seen a steady rise as a result of wine fans who visit the area to get a glimpse of the production of their favorite nectar. Something I really enjoyed about working with a winery was the constant banter between chef and winemaker—winemaker Angelo Pavan became my favorite guinea pig for new dishes. We would talk and taste and compare sweetness, tannins, oak aging, and acidity to the characteristics of the food and look for the balance achieved between contrasting and complementary tastes.

A good food and wine match is one where each helps the other but leaves a clean, pleasant finish on the palate. In some instances, you desire a contrast to "lift" something such as foie gras; the rich, fatty character is balanced by a sweet, acidic late harvest or icewine made from Riesling.

Chardonnay that is barrel fermented has a buttery, almost sour cream scent that complements a nice tangy cheese like Balderson's vintage cheddar. Light reds usually have a decent acid component that can stand up to zesty tomato sauces or spicy foods, so when we have pasta or peppery grilled foods at home we pop some corks on Gamay or Pinot Noir.

Speaking of popping corks, I'm always guilty of cellaring wine for only a week so we often end up opening young tannic reds that would have otherwise mellowed into smooth, complex wines. However, a young Cabernet is a perfect accompaniment to rare beef, as the rich-mouth feel and proteins temper the wine's tannin. In the end, though, you like what you do, and if you really want your favorite wine with a particular dish, then by all means, have it your way! It's your palate!

Note: In January 2001 Michael Olson left On the Twenty to join the chef professors at Niagara College, where he trains the next generation of chefs for the Niagara region and beyond. A special thanks to Michael for this contribution and for his untiring dedication.

"Confit" (kohn-fee) is an ancient method of preserving meat whereby it's salted, cooked, and preserved in its own fat in a crock or pot, and can then be refrigerated for up to six months.

The Hamlet of Jordan

A favorite spot of mine in wine country is the beautiful hamlet of Jordan. It is located about 5 miles (8 kilometers) up the Twenty Mile Creek, nestled on a high bank overlooking the running waters. It is a gem recently enjoying a renewal that promises to delight travelers. Jordan lies at the center of a rejuvenation project that will focus on the burgeoning travel and tourism industry. The dynamic Len Pennachetti and his wife, Helen Young, are spearheading an effort to reveal the many charms of this unique area. Wine is only a passport to discovery as the many attractions unfold for visitors within walking distance of the rushing waters of the Twenty Mile Creek. It is the jumping off point for many excursions by foot, bike, or car. Yet Jordan retains a sleepy quality, almost as if time has sidestepped it.

Its rich and fertile soil, along with its enviable situation on water, attracted the early settlers. The earliest European settlers were ex-Butler's Rangers who fought on the British side during the American War of Independence and were granted land on retiring from service. United Empire Loyalist Jacob Beam settled in what is now Beamsville in 1788. Mennonites (Pennsylvania Dutch) walked north from the United States in 1799 to found the villages of Jordan and Vineland. Ancient trails were clearly marked.

Jonathan with Helen Young and Len Pennachetti on the steps of the newly-renovated Vintage House

The Jordan Harbour was a crowded and bustling metropolis during these heady days of shipping farm produce to a hungry continent. Industry grew quickly as agriculture flourished. Tanneries, grist mills, saw mills, and woolen mills sprang up in the surrounding countryside. The natural harbor at the mouth of the Twenty Mile Creek saw Jordan and Jordan Station bustle as thriving shipping centers for the export of logs for masts, tan bark, hides, ashes used for the manufacture of soap, as well as grain, flour, fruit, and fruit products. A small ship-building industry existed for a time on the banks of the Twenty during the early nineteenth century.

A strong sense of community was ingrained in the small populace and no matter how far they ranged native sons and daughters carried a little piece of home with them. At age eighteen, Moses Rittenhouse, who was born in Vineland Station in 1846, went to Chicago and founded a lumber business. He distinguished himself in his industry and extended a ready hand when he received calls for financial assistance for various projects "back home." For example, he purchased 500 books, two sets of encyclopedias, twenty bound periodicals, and subscriptions to twelve magazines to endow a library in a school he had built in Vineland Station. The endowment of $20,000 from his estate in 1915, a heady sum at that time, was an enviable legacy for a native son.

Many pioneer descendants still farm the original plots of land. Their legacy extends beyond the soil as they have continued to nurture the community down the years. As more and more wineries spring up to urge nature's bounty, a sense of tradition plays out in the many celebrations that thrive today. You'll pass many roadside fruit stands dotting the byways. It's a treat that is a mainstay of any journey through wine country. The baskets and bushels brimming with produce are a welcome salve to city eyes and an invitation to stay and explore. Many farms allow picking.

The area is linked as only rural communities can be. Antiquing for collectibles, nature trail rambling, birding, roaming the nearby conservation area, Ball's Falls, and exploring our Mennonite heritage at the Jordan Museum are only a few suggested delights for the wine country traveler during a stopover. Jordan presents a starting point for this portion of wine country. Make sure you taste all the flavors! And be sure to visit the museum for a current schedule of events and exhibitions of note.

Jordan Museum Fry House

The fertile soil around the Twenty Mile Creek Valley attracted many settlers from the recently formed United States around 1790. Have a look at the Fry House on the Jordan Historical Museum grounds to get a sense of the time.

Jacob Fry and his family left Pennsylvania in 1800 along with thirty other families seeking religious freedom and the good farmland said to be had in Upper Canada, as the region was known in those days. Of German Mennonite background, the immigrants were hard-working, faithful, and very community oriented. The Connestoga wagon on the grounds of Fry House allows viewers to picture the hardships of long journeys on foot and in wagons. Imagine having to take off the wheels to ford streams and rivers when on the move.

Samuel Fry (seated) and family

The house Jacob built, with its central chimney plan and double attic, was based on medieval German architecture, and was a statement of the strong traditions of his community. The Fry family lived there until 1895 when it was replaced by a brick home less than 200 yards (180 meters) away. The little log house was left as a playhouse for the children and even served for a time as a chicken coop! In the late 1950s, volunteers rescued the house and moved it to its current site on the museum grounds.

The charming house was restored and turned into a showcase for the artifacts and lifestyle of the Fry family, including the well-known weaver Samuel Fry, one of Jacob's sons. Samuel produced beautiful coverlets and other items. He also has the distinction of being the best-documented weaver, with his original pattern and account books, even his wedding suit, still in existence. The house achieved celebrity status for having the most complete set of original furnishings in a pioneer craftsman's home. Of particular interest are the beautiful "schranks" (clothes presses or wardrobes) made by Jacob Fry. Helen Booth, the director of the museum, tells me that pieces produced by Jacob Fry, along with those of other local cabinet makers of Pennsylvania German Mennonite origin, launched the rage for antiques collecting in Niagara.

The house is continually being restored and added to. Visitors can tour with costumed interpreters and have a peek at the original beds used by the Fry family. I enjoyed the craft activities displayed during the summer months. Visitors can try food baked on an open hearth, see spinning and weaving in the weaving room, or pick up scissors or a brush for "scherenschnitte" (paper cutting) or "fraktur" (painted folk art). Workshops featuring activities such as hearth cooking and candle making for adults and tin punching and fraktur painting for children are offered on a regular basis. Something for all to enjoy.

Pioneer Day

Jordan's meek and humble setting is deceiving. To the discerning eye, a closer look will reveal an unusual and unique heritage that has been lovingly restored as a living piece of pioneer history. Canadians have a very strong attachment to the land. To the dedicated pioneers it appeared a mass of unforgiving brambles that resisted taming but, once harnessed, yielded a bounty that continues to be harvested to this day. The Niagara Peninsula has earned its name as the Garden of Canada.

Jordan proudly displays its strong community roots. Cave Spring Winery continues to draw visitors from far and wide to sample their award-winning wines, but it is the unpolished heritage treasure that provides the startling reminder of the hardy band of souls who put down roots and cultivated the soil. Grapes are only the latest bounty yielded by the rich soil.

The Jordan Historical Museum provides a peek into yesteryear with its many exhibits and hands-on activities that bring the pioneer lifestyle alive. Steps from the Cave Spring Winery, a majestic maple tree stands sentinel and anchors the grounds of the museum. It appears to be a special tree, both for its incredibly rich coloring and also for its uncanny ability to blossom and burst into its fall colors just in time for Pioneer Day.

The first Pioneer Day was held as a Centennial Year (1967)

Jonathan in costume during Pioneer Day

Folk crafts come alive...

...during hands-on activities...

...and feet too

event. It was designed as a festival, showcasing the rich folk traditions of the area's past through demonstrations of its crafts, skills, and activities as handed down through the close-knit community. The Pioneer Festival has been proudly celebrated every year since.

The Pioneer Festival is held at the beginning of each October, either the Saturday before or after Canadian Thanksgiving. The event runs from 10:00 a.m. through 4:00 p.m., and a nominal admission fee is charged at the gate. The entire community is involved, and parking and shuttle buses are available for the short trip into the village of Jordan from the parking site at the local arena. It's an enjoyable romp into the past, and you're guaranteed to catch the spirit of the festival if you give yourself over to exploring how the pioneers existed!

The day is brimful of activities for all. The village is usually closed to traffic so you can saunter along and savor the sights, sounds, and tastes of yesteryear. You'll see antique steam engines, corn shellers in action, wood branding exhibitions, booths of all sorts, as well as various community groups in period dress to entertain and inform in an old-fashioned frolic.

Throughout the museum grounds you'll encounter craftspeople explaining needlecrafts, blacksmithing, and children's games of the time, and you'll see Victorian dancing demonstrations to the lively accompaniment of the early sounds of the original settlers. There are plenty of hands-on activities to keep the children occupied. And everyone can enjoy a pleasant stroll through the museum grounds and to the embankment overlooking the Twenty Valley itself with its brilliant display of fall plumage.

To stir up your taste buds, Pioneer Day is renowned for its delicious food offerings. Apple fritters are a true standout and sure crowd pleaser! Some say the apple fritters are the best reason to attend Pioneer Day. Another mouthwatering delight to sample is hot soup cooked in a cauldron over an open fire. Or how about roast pig-on-a-spit, a Pennsylvania German sausage on a hot bun, fresh roasted peanuts, or freshly popped cauldron popcorn? It promises wholesome fun for all; a treat not to be missed.

The Museum Schoolhouse

In an old-time schoolhouse, come relive a childhood of yesteryear. The original brick structure, situated steps west of the current building, was burned to the ground in 1858. The following year, the school trustees built this new schoolhouse, utilizing local limestone. It was a model of its time: large, roomy, and bright. Huge windows were designed and the color scheme was carefully chosen to encourage attention and obedience. It also featured a sloped floor, angled up and away from the teacher's raised platform allowing students at the back to see clearly over the children down front.

Interior of schoolhouse

As with most schools of the time, it became the center of the community, used for various purposes including the Ladies' Intellectual Club meetings, adult German classes and, of course, the much anticipated annual Christmas pageant.

The school developed a reputation for having "difficult" students. Education at that time was a patchy effort at best. Most of the children came from farms, and often more pressing duties at home called out. Many children would appear exhausted from having risen early to attend to chores. The spring plantings and fall harvest were especially difficult times. Some children were hard on young teachers fresh to the vocation from teacher's college. It was common for a teacher to stay no longer than one term!

Exterior of schoolhouse

The school was in continual use for eighty-nine years, until a larger, more modern school was completed nearby. The stone structure was abandoned, denuded of its interior. In 1953, a local winery, Jordan Wines, purchased it and restored it to the community. It became a museum, stored with agricultural tools and artisan equipment, and it opened to the public in 1959.

The restoration to its 1908 setting was painstaking. Desks were found; the ceiling was replaced, as was the dividing wall and the girls' and boys' separate entrances. All the details of a one-room schoolhouse of that period carefully emerged. A school field trip program has been set up whereby children can role play students of 1908.

Lessons on blackboard

During the summer months the schoolhouse is open to the public. It will appeal to the forgotten child in all of us. Step back in time and imagine what it would have been like to attend as a child writing on slates, undergoing a hygiene inspection, and participating in a spelling bee! It's worth the stop.

Chardonnay: All Hail the King!

"Complexity" is a complimentary term, most often used when describing red wines with multiple layers and nuances of bouquet and flavors, many elements in balance, and a harmonious, interesting taste experience.

In most wine circles, Chardonnay is considered the king of the white grape varieties and Riesling is considered the queen. Chardonnay tends to be a little more robust and has a more boisterous character to it. As a wine it can have a very big ego, as can the people who endlessly drool over its complexities.

The world is Chardonnay crazy, and some people have long predicted a Chardonnay burnout. When offered their choice of a glass of white wine, some wine enthusiasts will respond, "ABC"—anything but Chardonnay! Well, the burnout hasn't happened yet and for good reasons.

Chardonnay offers a diverse taste adventure. The styles, flavors, and characteristics can range dramatically within any wine region and within a single winery. Chardonnay's very popular with consumers because it is usually dry and can work well with a wide range of foods. Winemakers love it because it's like putty or clay. They can influence the outcome, and Chardonnay will let them have their way with the greatest latitude of any white grape.

The influence of Oak barrels adds to the complexity of wines

Some winemakers have referred to Chardonnay as the Gucci grape. As much as 50% of the attributes of a Chardonnay can come from a winemaker's hand. The influences of barrel fermentation, barrel aging, leaving the wine on the yeast and secondary malolactic fermentation, bottle aging—these are all components that drastically change the character of Chardonnay and are not a result of the viticultural practices in the vineyard. These winemaker influences can also affect the price, especially if the wine is kept in barrels over a long period of time before being bottled.

The Burgundian Chardonnay grapes are now grown around the world and offer a wide variety of taste profiles

When it comes out of the vineyard and into the winery, it's up to the winemaker to decide what kind of Chardonnay to make. At its most basic, Chardonnay is essentially one of two different styles: oaked or unoaked. It can be an apply-crisp, possibly grapefruit-like Chardonnay that reflects the fruit from the vintage and is treated only in stainless steel tanks. At the other end of the spectrum—where the wine has been vinified and aged in oak, possibly on the dead yeast cells (the lees)— it produces a full, round, very buttery, soft, and mellow oaky Chardonnay. These heavily oak-influenced Chardonnays also beget descriptors that include toasty, caramel, vanilla, toffee, nutty, and butterscotch. These are the most complex Chardonnays, and invite the connoisseur to conjure up all kinds of descriptors.

Sur lie (soor lee) is a French expression meaning "on the lees," where the wine is left to age in a container with the dead yeast cells and grape particles accumulated in the bottom.

Of all the white wines, most young winemakers are usually most enthusiastic about making their first Chardonnay. It is this malleable grape that will let winemakers play with all sorts of techniques to declare a signature style. This is where oak plays an important role.

Where toasted oak barrels would ruin the more delicate, aromatic Riesling or other more fruit-defined white wine grapes, Chardonnay can be modified with the lightest or heaviest of oak treatments. How the winemaker handles it usually depends on the attributes of the grapes

An escarpment view overlooking Niagara's rich farmland

at harvest. Chardonnay grows everywhere in the world but does especially well in cool-climate regions such as Ontario. Burgundy, the historic home of the great Burgundian Chardonnays released under chateau labels is also a cool-climate region. The average growing season in Ontario is blessed with enough sun days and heat units to ripen most wine grapes. Chardonnay does well in Ontario, and the sugar levels are often up around twenty-three brix (sugar units), which is quite high on the world standard scale.

"Vintage" is the term describing the year in which the grapes were harvested and vinified. The term "vintage wine" is used to indicate a year of superior quality.

When you smell a Chardonnay that's been treated without oak, you'll note the aroma that reflects the attributes of the Chardonnay's fruit characteristics. When you smell an oak-influenced Chardonnay you'll note more of a bouquet of several scents that reflect the complexities added by the winemaker's hand. Wines that have too much oak presence can be tannic and described in unflattering terms such as "woody" or "wood juice." Recent trends have seen winemakers moving away from the heavy oak influence towards unoaked, more fruit-driven Chardonnays.

A winemaker working with a Chardonnay is akin to a chef cooking in the kitchen. A winemaker uses oak to flavor wine the way a chef uses spices and herbs to flavor different foods. Foods are cooked to rare, medium, or well done, depending on how the chef thinks they're best served. This is how the winemaker uses oak. You don't want to smell one predominant spice in your food, and the winemaker uses that same philosophy with oak-aged Chardonnay. Winemakers have to keep tasting the wine during its contact with oak to decide when enough is enough.

It's important to remember that of all the white wines, Chardonnay will offer the most diverse range of taste profiles and the greatest latitude when matching with different foods.

NOTES FROM THE CELLAR

GLASSES AND STEMS

Does the type of glass make a difference to the enjoyment of wine?
In the past, stemware was frequently used for decorative purposes, designed to showcase the wealth of the family. Today we focus on stemware that enhances the experience and enjoyment of wine. Glass manufacturing houses such as Riedel and Spiegelau have shown that the shape of the glass does affect the wine and the experience of its taste.

Select a glass that fits the wine. Both houses make stemware designed for individual varietals such as Chardonnay or Merlot. Generally speaking, lighter-style red wines taste better in a larger, rounder glass. As the wine is poured into the front of the mouth, the lighter red is allowed to open as it rolls across the different taste zones of the tongue. However, a lighter white wine will lose its intensity in a big glass.

What's the difference between glass and crystal?
The difference between crystal and glass is that crystal contains lead. Lead adds a brilliance and clarity. It also adds flexibility to the glass

and the ability to make the walls of the bowl thinner.

It was only recently—at the end of the eighteenth century—that a standard glass service came into play. Wine can be imbibed from any vessel but a glass is the pedestal on which the "art" is viewed. Stemware should be inert and clear, allowing the wine—its color, depth, and clarity—to engage the eye. Simplified, to get started, use a small glass for white wines and a larger glass for reds. From there, varietal-specific stems are available, such as Champagne flutes or Port, Brandy, or Madeira snifters.

Is there a proper way to care for stemware?
Generally, any stemware made these days can be put through the dishwasher with no ill effects.

Hold glasses carefully, and avoid rough handling when hand drying. Also avoid twisting the stem while drying; instead, cup the bowl of the glass in one hand (covered by a drying linen, of course) while drying the inside of the glass with the other. Holding the bowl with both hands will avoid twisting and snapping the delicate stem. Stemware often breaks when it's overhandled. Make sure to wipe the edges to get the fingerprints off. Lightly wipe the glass, and don't worry about cleansing agents attaching to it. The stems should be well rinsed before drying and lightly polishing. The trick is to never wash the stemware on the night of consumption! Pour a little water in the bottom of the bowl so the wine doesn't cake, and leave it until morning.

Riedel stemware: (left to right) Chardonnay, Spirits, Viognier/ Chardonnay, and Shiraz

Willow Heights Estate Winery

FAST FACTS

3751 King Street
Vineland, Ontario
L0R 2C0
Tel: 905-562-4945
Fax: 905-562-5761
E-mail:
willowheights@sympatico.ca
Web: www.willowheights.on.ca

Located on more than twelve acres on the Niagara Bench and leasing another forty acres, Willow Heights produces wines only from 100% Ontario grapes.

Willow Heights began producing VQA wines in 1995. The winery focuses on varietal VQA wines that are characteristic of the Niagara terroir including Chardonnay, Riesling, Cabernet Franc, and Merlot. Producing approximately 18,000 cases of wine annually, Willow Heights uses both American and French oak barrels, depending upon the varietal.

Three years ago, the winery moved to its current location with its appealing Mediterranean décor, where visitors can enjoy fresh, authentic antipasto while sipping matching wines on its patio overlooking the vineyard. The mouth-watering menu includes such dishes as Marinated Vegetable Mista of Artichokes, Eggplant, and

Willow Heights Estate Winery in Vineland, Niagara

Roasted Peppers Topped with Sweet Basil; or a Meat Trio of Authentic Cured Sausage and Hot Capicollo Circled with Fresh Prosciutto and Melon.

The adherence of Ron Speranzini, president and vintner, to old-world, time-honored, and visionary wine-making has resulted in significant recognition of the winery with a large number of awards over the past few years. In 2001 Willow Heights won a gold medal at the Air Ontario Awards for its 1999 Chardonnay Reserve. In 2000, the winery won an honourable mention at VinItaly, one of the world's most prestigious competitions, for the same wine.

Willow Heights wines are available at the local winery boutique, at LCB0 stores, through distributors in Alberta and British Columbia, and through licensees including hotels and fine restaurants in Canada.

Willow Heights' VQA varietals include (white wines) Seyval Blanc, Chardonnay, Riesling, Gewurztraminer, Auxerrois; (red wines) Cabernet Franc, Gamay Noir, Merlot; (dessert wine) Vidal Icewine.

Ron Speranzini: From Steel to Vine

Graced by his Italian ancestry, Ron Speranzini grew up with wine at the dinner table. A native of Hamilton, Ontario, Ron worked for the steel industry as a quality assurance manager. Steel was his product, but winemaking was his preoccupation.

Ron continued as an amateur winemaker for twenty-five years before venturing into the field as a professional. Frequent trips to Niagara for wine grapes enabled Ron to meet the movers and shakers of the wine industry. Having won several awards for his amateur wines, he drew the praise of noted vintners such as Donald Ziraldo of Inniskillin and Len Pennachetti of Cave Spring Cellars. Both had suggested that Ron consider getting into the wine business and possibly start his own winery.

Finally garnering enough nerve and capital backing, Ron applied to the LCBO for a winery license in 1992, but policy reorganization delayed the granting of his license by two years. Down but not out, Ron leased a portion of the winemaking cellars and facilities at Cave Spring Cellars in Jordan for the next two years. He had a used French oak barrel and a small steel tank in which to vinify his wines. Ironically, the licensing delay kept his wines in a holding pattern, which—as time would tell—served to improve the quality of his Chardonnay. More than he could have hoped for.

SHELLFISH RISOTTO

from Ron Speranzini,
Willow Heights

A gentle risotto—the cooked seafood is folded in at the end of the cooking time.

Serves 4

½ cup (125 ml) white wine
1 dozen littleneck clams
1 dozen mussels
2 tbsp (30 ml) olive oil
4 large scallops
8 large shrimps

RISOTTO
5 cups (1.25 L) chicken stock, approximately
2 tbsp (30 ml) olive oil
2 tbsp (30 ml) butter
½ cup (125 ml) onion, finely chopped
1½ cups (375 ml) Vialone Nano rice
½ cup (125 ml) white wine
2 tbsp (30 ml) chives, chopped
salt and freshly ground pepper

To cook the seafood, add wine to a heavy pot. Bring to boil on high heat. Add clams, cover and steam until clams open, or about 5 to 7 minutes. Remove clams with tongs. Separate meat from shells and discard shells. Add mussels, cover and steam until open, or about 3 minutes. Toss out any that do not open.

Remove with tongs. Remove meat from shells and discard shells. Reserve cooking liquid and cool. Add clams and mussels to cooking liquid.

Heat oil in skillet on medium high heat. Add scallops and shrimps and sauté for 2 minutes. Add to clam and mussel mixture in bowl. Reserve.

For the risotto, bring the stock to a simmer on the stove. Heat the oil and butter in a heavy pot on medium heat. Add the onions and sauté for 3 minutes or until softened. Add the rice and sauté until the rice is coated with oil.

Pour in the wine and cook until the wine is absorbed. Add 1 cup (250 ml) of chicken stock, stirring until most of stock is absorbed.

continued on page 118

continued from page 117
Continue to add stock in 1-cup (250-ml) quantities, stirring.

After 15 minutes, when the rice grains are still a bit firm in the middle, add the seafood fixture and broth. Stir until the rice is creamy with a slight bite in the center, about another 3 to 5 minutes. If the rice seems too dry, add more stock or water for a creamy consistency. Stir in the chives.

Remove from heat. Taste before seasoning well with salt and pepper. Serve immediately.

WINE MATCH
Willow Heights 2000 Chardonnay Sur Lie

His first release under the Willow Heights label in 1995 was a 1992 Reserve Chardonnay, which won the Best White Wine of Show at the coveted Cuvee Awards in Niagara. The subsequent notoriety fast-tracked Willow Heights' credibility in the wine industry and before consumers seemingly overnight.

Ron continued to balance his full-time work in the steel industry with his desire to make premium wines from Niagara grapes. His weekly workload of forty hours in steel and forty hours in the wine cellar eventually became too much to handle. The success of Willow Heights and increasing consumer demand by 1998 had already consumed the efforts of Ron's wife, Avis, who manages the retail shop and his daughter, Nicole, who heads up marketing and sales. Ron finally bowed out of the steel business and stepped into the role of full-time winemaker.

Escalating production from 200 liters of wine a year as an amateur to over 15,000 cases a year was a substantial leap. The days of scouring vineyards and paying premium prices for lower quantities were now supplanted by more formal and affordable grape-purchase agreements with growers. Turning a hobby into a full-time career also brought the harsh realities of inventory, sales, and cash flow—a delicate balance and tremendous challenge for any industry that relies on Mother Nature and a highly competitive market.

With Chardonnay as his flagship wine and Pinot Noir his revered soul mate, Ron remembers being warned by several people about how expensive and time consuming establishing a winery can be, but he also recalls that he didn't really listen. Passion won out over economic uncertainties, and Ron and his family have few regrets.

Sur lie *aging is thought to impart desirable complexities to certain wines, such as Chardonnay and Sauvignon Blanc, and is also used in the production of sparkling wines made in the* **methode champenoise.**

Willow Heights Winery retail shop and boutique

Winemaker's Matches
Ron Speranzini, Willow Heights

White Wine: Chardonnay Reserve
Food: Lobster bisque
Comment: Both are rich and creamy and complement
              each other in balance and flavor.

Red Wine: Pinot Noir Reserve
Food: Ontario rack of lamb
Comment: Weight, flavor, and elegance of both match
              extremely well.

Attributed to two businessmen talking over lunch: "If you want to make a small fortune in the wine business, you have to start with a large fortune."

NOTES FROM THE CELLAR

STAGES OF STORAGE

How should wine be stored?
Wine is very sensitive to storage conditions. It can be stored professionally or in a simple wine cellar. Most wine drinkers go through three stages with storage.

STAGE 1: Putting wine on a counter or in a closet is the first stage. But when there are a few more bottles, they are usually organized in a rack. Wood is the best product for a rack because wood does not conduct heat. Racks generally hold twelve, twenty-four, or thirty-six bottles. The rack's position is all important: It should be placed in an area away from vibrations, odors, heating units, and harsh, direct (natural) light. It's better to keep wine at a constant temperature (even if it's warmer than it should be) than at a fluctuating temperature.

Try to maintain the integrity of the wine by providing suitable conditions for aging. Wine is a natural "living" entity and therefore is drawn to the conditions of the "womb" of the earth. Ideally, wine should be placed in a dark basement corner, preferably where there is relative humidity of 70% to 80%, and where the wine is free from vibration and odors and can be kept at around 56°F/13°C (which is the constant temperature of the earth below the frost line regardless of season). In a pinch, a dark corner of a closet will do, but avoid a wooden closet because of odors. Choose the most inert space in the home.

STAGE 2: The goal at this stage is to emulate conditions similar to a Mediterranean cellar. But not everybody has the space or the budget to install a custom wine cellar in their home. However, free-standing temperature-controlled wine cabinets come in all shapes and sizes. They artificially create an ideal environment for the long-term storage of wine. When considering buying this product, shop around and compare units. (And beware of those products that are passed off as temperature-controlled units but are just colored fridges.)

It is important to keep wine at the right temperature. Wine that is kept cold for too long will end up being cold-stabilized; crystals will form and the wine will not age properly. In some restaurants, white wine is stored in refrigerators and when served it may show tartaric crystals. This is an indication that the wine's maturation process has been arrested. If this happens, the wine won't necessarily taste bad, but it certainly won't get any better.

At the opposite end of the scale, wine can become "cooked" if the temperature is too high, thereby artificially increasing and randomizing the maturation process. Also, when a bottle is opened too soon, its decline is accelerated and its best qualities are sacrificed.

STAGE 3: Stage 3 is, of course, a proper wine cellar. There are two ways to go: a passive wine cellar or an environmentally controlled cellar. A passive wine cellar uses the natural subterranean soil temperature conditions. Below the frost line, the earth maintains a constant temperature and humidity level, and it is dark and free from vibration—all of these conditions are ideal for aging wine. However, this type of wine cellar must be well insulated against the home's controlled climate and humidity levels. It is certainly risky in the Canadian climate and other cool climate viticultural regions. With an environmentally controlled room, an envelope is created surrounding the room that artificially creates the ideal humidity and temperature conditions.

Vineland Estates Winery

FAST FACTS

3620 Moyer Road
Vineland, Ontario
LOR 2C0
Tel: 905-562-7088
Fax: 905-562-3071
E-mail: wine@vineland.com
Web: www.vineland.com

Known as "Ontario's most picturesque winery," Vineland Estates Winery is located on the "bench" of the Niagara Escarpment overlooking rolling vineyards and Lake Ontario.

The seventy-five-acre estate was planted in 1979 by Herman Weis from the Mosel region in Germany with the first vintage in 1983. In 1992 John Howard purchased the winery and expanded its vineyard holdings. Today, with more than 350 acres of vineyards, 80% of the winery's grapes come from Vineland's own vineyards that are planted with vinifera varieties.

White vitis vinfera grapes include Riesling, Chardonnay, Gewurztraminer, Pinot Gris, and Sauvignon Blanc. Red vitis vinifera plantings include Pinot Noir, Merlot, Cabernet Sauvignon, and Cabernet Franc. White hybrids include Seyval and Vidal, with Vidal being one of the varieties used to make Vineland's award-winning icewine. Riesling is the hallmark of Vineland, with the growing area of the bench particularly suited to this grape.

Current winery production is approximately 30,000 cases annually with plans for significant production increases.

The historical location of Vineland Estates Winery dates back to 1845, when it was a Mennonite homestead. The original buildings have been transformed into the visitor and production facilities while retaining their original character. The original barn was converted into the winery boutique where guests can shop for award-winning wines and unique accessories and join a complimentary guided tour and wine tasting. The winery boutique is the exclusive outlet for the majority of Vineland premium and reserve wines.

The Carriage House, dating from 1857, and the 1877 Balcony in the winery boutique are available for group tours and private group functions. The winery also has a bed-and-breakfast cottage nestled on the edge of the vineyard.

The historic Carriage House at Vineland Estates is a popular setting for celebratory dinners and corporate functions

The view from Vineland's terrace offers diners an impressive view over their vineyards, Lake Ontario, and the skyline of Toronto in the distance

NORTHERN PECAN CRUSTED RACK OF FALLOW VENISON

—

from Chef Mark Picone,
Vineland Estates Restaurant

—

Serves 6

1 rack venison (have butcher clean and "French" the bones)
2 tbsp (30 ml) olive oil
½cup (125 ml) grain-style mustard
1 cup (250 ml) northern pecans, chopped
1 cup (250 ml) bread crumbs
2 tbsp (30 ml) mixed herbs (fresh thyme, rosemary)
salt and pepper to taste

In a hot frying pan, add the oil and sear the rack making sure all sides are browned. Dry the rack with a paper towel and brush on the mustard. Season with salt and pepper. In a bowl, mix together the nuts, bread crumbs, and herbs. A pinch of salt and pepper here is important.

Coat the exposed meat side of the rack with the crumb mixture.

Bake in a preheated oven of 450°F (230°C) and roast until the internal temperature is 130°F (55°C) for medium-rare doneness. Rest 10 minutes before serving.

Serving suggestion: Candied sweet potatoes, roasted root vegetables, red wine reduction as a sauce.

WINE MATCH
Vineland Estates Winery Cabernet

Chef Mark Picone

Guests can also enjoy fine dining, either indoors or outdoors, in Vineland Estates' restaurant. Under the direction of Mark Picone, a pioneer of gourmet regional cuisine, they can savor a superb meal with a stunning view of the surrounding vineyards.

The winery has won a large number of national and international awards at such prestigious wine competitions as VinItaly and Rieslings of the World Competition in Strasbourg, France.

Vineland wines are available through the LCBO and winery boutique, at fine restaurants, and through sales agents in the provinces of Alberta, Manitoba, and Quebec, and in the United States, Hong Kong, and Taiwan.

A Long Line of Schmidts

Brian Schmidt isn't just the winemaker at Vineland Estates. His older brother, Allan Schmidt, isn't just the general manager of and a partner in Vineland Estates. These two British Columbia native sons are the heirs to a family that's been involved with the Canadian wine industry for quite some time. You could say that wine's in their blood!

Their grandfather, Frank Schmidt (1913–1979) was born in Unity, Saskatchewan (a place better known for its wheat than its grapes). As a young man during the great depression he found himself riding a freight train in search of work. He arrived in Kelowna, British Columbia, during the 1937 grape harvest and found field work with a local grower, Peter Casorso. Frank did a great job in the vineyards and within a year Casorso gave him a house to live in and a contract to manage a vineyard.

It didn't take long for other growers to hear about the young guy from Unity. In 1942, J.W. Hughes offered Frank a substantial contract that included a house, a car, and $100 a month. With things going well and the business improving, it wasn't long before Hughes offered Frank and his colleagues an opportunity to earn ownership of the vineyards they managed.

In 1958 Frank Schmidt had earned his first vineyard property, then known as Lakeside Vineyards, at Okanagan Mission, south of Kelowna. In 1965 he sold the property to Growers' Wines of Victoria, who had been shipping fresh grapes from the valley since 1932. Growers' made the decision to begin crushing the grapes in the Okanagan then send the must to Victoria. The equipment was set up on the Schmidt property, and Frank was paid for operating it.

Allan (left) and Brian Schmidt

The relationship with Growers' only improved, and by 1960 they were giving a small number of class B voting shares to their dedicated grape growers. Frank and his son Lloyd became shareholders.

Lloyd Schmidt sometimes quips that he was born under a grapevine. After graduating from a two-year business college course, Lloyd ran the accounts for the Beau Sejour Vineyards, the new name Growers' had bestowed upon the property Lakeside Vineyards, which they had purchased from his father. For a young man in his early twenties, Lloyd was given a tremendous amount of responsibility and had to deal with as many as thirty-five contracted growers supplying grapes, supervise the harvest crush, and oversee the promotion of the wines throughout British Columbia. They were tasks he handled well.

In 1966 Lloyd signed a five-year contract with Growers, but the following months and years offered their share of unwelcome turbulence. New ownership, a dramatic change in mandate, and re-purposing of vineyard property for development and the resulting conflicts caused Lloyd much distress. By 1971 he had been through enough and decided not to renew his contract. It was time for a change.

Lloyd left the wine industry completely and ran a sporting goods store in Kelowna for a couple of years before joining the Provincial Agriculture Ministry as a viticulturist. By 1981 he partnered with Harry McWatters and opened Sumac Ridge Estate Winery at Summerland in the Okanagan Valley.

Lloyd's eldest son, Allan, had rented and operated his own small vineyard since the age of eleven and had an affinity for grape growing and winemaking. He had traveled to Germany where he worked in the vineyards and then to Heitz Vineyards in the Napa Valley, California, where he apprenticed. Allan Schmidt soon became the winemaker at Sumac.

In 1985 Lloyd left Sumac and moved to Ontario, where he became sales manager for Mori-Vin Inc., a Niagara-based nursery that also marketed grapevines. That same year, he and his wife, Noreen, spent time with the Weis family in Germany's Mosel Valley. They had known each other since the late 1960s. The Weis family owned an established winery and a nursery that developed vines for exporting. They also owned a young winery in Niagara, Vineland Estates. Lloyd had represented Weis in Canada and took this opportunity to learn more about the vines and German viticultural conditions.

Meanwhile, Lloyd's younger son, Brian, had an opportunity to spend his summer holidays working in the vineyards and cellars of the Nahe region in Germany. The following year (1986) Brian graduated from high school, and everyone thought he was destined to make his mark in the wine business, but he had other ideas.

Having enjoyed recreational diving for several years, Brian was drawn to Victoria on the West Coast, where he became a commercial diver. Everything was going well until the harsh realities of this dangerous career were brought home. With the death of a close friend in a diving accident and having barely escaped death himself, Brian had been given a "wakeup" call. After four years he decided to end his diving career.

During Brian's tenure in commercial diving, Allan Schmidt had left the Okanagan and moved to Ontario, where he had become the winemaker for Vineland Estates. When Brian ended his diving career, he joined Allan for the 1991 harvest at Vineland and stayed on to apprentice as a winemaker. In 1994 Brian took over as winemaker at Vineland as Allan had taken on increasing administrative responsibilities as general manager.

The Schmidt roots from western Canada are now firmly planted in Ontario, and the vine legacy that began with Frank Schmidt from Unity, Saskatchewan, and was handed down to Lloyd Schmidt, is being continued by Frank's grandsons. That's three generations and counting!

"Breathing" is the act of letting a wine stand open in the bottle or a decanter for several minutes, and sometimes for hours. It is believed that this prolonged exposure to air can improve the wine's character, especially with older reds.

"Bordeaux-style blend" is a term used to distinguish wines made with two or more of the traditional Bordeaux grape varieties such as Cabernet Sauvignon, Cabernet Franc, Merlot, Malbec, and Petite Verdot.

Chef Mark Picone: Simplicity as Beauty

On February 20, 1962, John Glenn orbited the earth and Mark Picone was born in Dundas, Ontario, fifty miles (eighty kilometers) west of Toronto.

Mark is from a family of food purveyors, with grandparents who immigrated from Italy in the early 1900s and established Picone's Foods in Dundas—a boutique shop that provided specialty goods and services to a discerning clientele.

Mark received his training at the University of Guelph, graduating in 1986 with his honors Bachelor of Commerce degree in hotel and food administration.

Chef Mark Picone (middle) flanked by his dedicated staff

Consistently working in the culinary world of Hamilton, Guelph, and Toronto, Mark covered many restaurants, including Maxwell's, Baker Street Bistro, Winston Group, and a variety of hotels including the Sheraton, Delta, and Marriott. Mark also worked in clubs such as the Dundas Valley Golf and Curling Club and had a catering business under the name of Picone's Catering from 1980 to 1990. With all of this behind him, eventually Mark left for Europe. The opportunity of working abroad was calling, and France was an obvious place to start: in Versailles at Trianon Palace, in Biarritz at Perraudin, and in Burgundy at Chez Camille.

The French word **merlot** *means "young blackbird," most likely suggesting the grape's beautiful dark-blue color. Merlot usually produces red wines that are regarded as soft and low in tannins.*

Upon arriving in Italy in the fall of 1992, at Ristorante Arnolfo in Colle val d'Elsa, Mark became sous chef under the direction of Chef Gaetano Trovato. Other experiences included "stages" at Sadler in Milan, Antica Dolceria Bonajuto in Modica, Sicily, Ristorante Tivoli in Cortina, and Agatha Romeo in Rome.

Returning to Canada in the spring of 1996, Mark accepted the position of executive chef at Vineland Estates Winery. Assembling a talented brigade of culinary professionals, apprentices, and stewards culminated in the successful completion of his certified Chef de Cuisine designation in the summer of 1999. Mark has been influenced by Mediterranean elements, by respect for the farmers who supply him with the product, and by

Canada itself. These conditions have led Mark to a clean, flavorful, and artistic style.

Mark has been featured in various publications including the *Organic Garden Cookbook*, *Food and Drink Magazine*, *The Toronto Star*, *Restaurateur Magazine*, *Where to Eat in Canada*, and *Air Canada's Top 100 Restaurants in Canada*. Most recently Mark was featured in *Gourmet Magazine* out of the United States, *Person Magazine* in Japan, and *Hamilton Magazine*.

Casual and fine dining at Vineland's summer terrace

As an ambassador of wine country and Canadian cuisine, Mark has participated in events in Toronto, Quebec, Hawaii, and Tuscany, Italy. He has recently been appointed to the Order of Professional Italian Restaurateurs, a designation that only three other Canadian chefs have received. This prestigious appointment is made to chefs around the world who demonstrate that they have brought Italian culinary standards to a new level outside of Italy. With stringent standards, there are only 100 members of this order worldwide.

Fundamentally, Mark sees "simplicity as beauty" and is energized with the purpose of making Niagara a true culinary region.

Whereas a "vintner" is one who makes or sells wine, a **negotiant** *(nay-goh-syahn)— the French term for merchant or seller—refers to a person or firm that sells and ships wine as a wholesaler.*

The Vineland complex houses the winery, offices, and a wine and gift boutique with tasting bar for visitors

Ball's Falls
Historical Park

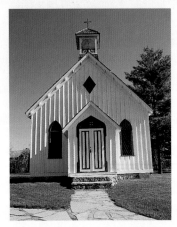

The rustic 1864 church relocated on the property is popular for weddings

Ball's Falls Historical Park is worth a stop when visiting the wine country. Located north of the village of Jordan and just above it on the escarpment, it fulfills all the ingredients for a super outing for the whole family. Scenic landscape and waterways and a cultural heritage superbly contained within a world-recognized natural environment point to a memorable stopover.

The history of Ball's Falls reflects the history of so many small villages and hamlets in the Niagara area. Originally, this area was part of a Crown land grant to Thomas Butler and family members in 1803. However, the "settlement duty" (improvement to the property) was never completed, and 1,200 acres were sold to George and John Ball of the Jacob Ball family, who were forced to flee their home in the Mohawk Valley near Albany, New York, in 1783.

The Ball brothers saw the enormous potential of land above the waters of Twenty Mile Creek. The cataracts of

One of two cataracts; this is the upper cataract

rushing water would provide a source of power for eventual industrial development as the tiny settlement grew. Over the years a saw mill, a flour and grist mill, and a five-story woolen mill were built nearby. G.P.M. Ball inherited this property and dreamed of calling his little settlement Glen Elgin, but the outside forces of economic and technological change were already at work to bypass this location. First the railroads then the major road builders chose more favorable locations below the escarpment and time-sealed this tiny hamlet.

The Ball's Falls lower cataract

The Ball's Falls bedrock gorge is recognized as part of a provincially significant earth science area of natural and scientific interest (ANSI). Trails start here and work their way down the Twenty Mile Valley past Jordan and on to Jordan Harbour. Some enjoyable hiking tracks start from these grounds. This is a charming spot, and events and festivals (especially the Thanksgiving Festival) throughout the year make it a valuable side trip.

Stoney Ridge Cellars

Barrel makers char the inside of barrels to various degrees. This process of "toasting" delivers the appealing smell of toasted bread, desirable in some Chardonnays and sparkling wines.

Stoney Ridge was originally established in 1985 on the Niagara Escarpment overlooking the city of Hamilton, Ontario, and winemaker Jim Warren quickly developed a strong demand for his unique style of winemaking.

By 1996 the winery was producing 20,000 cases annually and moved to its current location in Vineland. Jim Warren's skill as a winemaker created a loyal and dedicated following, which resulted in his selection by the industry as Winemaker of the Year in 1997. That year Jim sold the winery and agreed to stay on as winemaker. The new owners merged with a smaller winery known as Woods End.

In 1999 Liubomir Popovici joined the Stoney Ridge winemaking team. Liubomir had extensive experience in his native Romania as chief winemaker of the largest wine and spirits producers in the country. Since taking over as chief winemaker of Stoney Ridge in 2000, Liubomir has made his mark by producing a number of award-winning wines.

Stoney Ridge can boast state-of-the-art equipment, from its Bucher and Wilmes presses to a number of temperature-controlled fermentation tanks. The winery has always been an industry leader in the use of oak barrels for both barrel fermentation and aging of premium wines. It was also the first winery in Canada to produce a VQA port-style and VQA sherry-style product and an award-winning Cranberry wine.

Red and white wine production features both stainless steel and barrel fermentation. Some white wines, primarily the fruity and aromatic varieties, are fermented only in stainless steel. The more complex and age-worthy whites such as

Stoney Ridge Cellars in Vineland, Niagara Peninsula

Old oak barrels always set the tone for every wine tasting journey

Chardonnay are fermented in barrel and aged in barrel. All reds are fermented in stainless steel and aged in barrel up to fifteen months.

Stoney Ridge produces more than fifty different wines ranging from classic French varieties and hybrids to dessert and fruit wines. The introduction of a new premium series appears under the Cuesta Estates label while the winery also continues to sell VQA wines under the Stoney Ridge and Woods End labels.

The winery has won a large number of national and inter-national awards and continues to be at the cutting edge of the Canadian wine market. Visitors are invited to tour the winery and taste some of their VQA products.

This label boasts a Chardonnay grown on "bench" property

ROLLED GNOCCHI WITH BLACK TIGER SHRIMPS

—

from Allegro Ristorante

—

Serves 4 to 6

GNOCCHI
2 large Yukon potatoes, boiled and diced
1 egg yolk
$\frac{1}{2}$ cup (125 ml) flour
salt to taste
reserved flour for rolling

SAUCE
12 pieces of ¹⁶/₂₀ Black Tiger Shrimps, cleaned and butterflied
18 pieces of ³¹/₄₀ Black Tiger Shrimps, cleaned and butterflied
1 cup (250 ml) baby spinach
1 cup (250 ml) wedged Shitake mushrooms
1 tbsp (15 ml) garlic, minced
2 tbsp (30 ml) olive oil
$\frac{1}{2}$ cup (125 ml) basil leaves, torn
$\frac{1}{4}$ cup (60 ml) Cognac
juice of 1 orange
zest of 1 orange
2 cups (500 ml) reduced lobster or shrimp stock
1 tbsp (15 ml) butter

GNOCCHI PREPARATION
Mix potatoes, egg yolk, and flour, and allow dough to rest for 35 to 45 minutes before rolling. Cut pieces of dough and roll into $\frac{1}{2}$-inch (1.5-cm) diameter logs. Cut logs into $\frac{3}{4}$-inch (2-cm) long pieces. Boil in salted water.

SAUCE PREPARATION
In olive oil, add minced garlic and lightly brown. Add mushrooms and soften. Add shrimps and cook for 30 seconds. Deglaze with Cognac and orange juice. Add lobster or shrimp stock with orange zest. Add baby spinach and butter, and toss with gnocchi. The pasta sauce should nicely coat the gnocchi without any excess liquid. Serve immediately.

WINE MATCH
Stoney Ridge Bench Chardonnay

Thirty Bench Winery

FAST FACTS

4281 Mountainview Road
Beamsville, Ontario
LOR 1B0
Tel: 905-563-1698
Fax: 905-563-3921
E-mail: wine@thirtybench.com
Web: www.thirtybench.com

Blending is the centuries-old technique of assembling wines of the same or different variety in desired proportions to improve the quality, complexity, and consistency for a wine-maker's label from vintage to vintage.

Recognized as a boutique winery dedicated to producing small-scale locally crafted wines, Thirty Bench owners/ winemakers Tom Muckle, Yorgos Papageorgiou, and Franz Zeritsch are known for their various styles of Rieslings, premium Chardonnays, and Bordeaux reds.

Formerly a fruit orchard, Thirty Bench's main vineyard was established in 1980 with the initial plantings of Riesling vines. The winery now has over sixty acres planted with a variety of red and white vitis vinifera grapes and produces more than 8,000 cases of wine a year. Vineyard staff work to achieve the highest in grape quality from each harvest by bunch thinning, late harvesting, and tending the vines by hand. The grapes are also hand-harvested to preserve them until they are crushed.

Thirty Bench wines include (white and dessert wines) Chardonnay, Riesling, Vidal Riesling, Late Harvest Rieslings, Riesling Icewine, Vidal Icewine; (red wines) Cabernet/Merlot, Merlot, Cabernet Franc, Trillium Red, Meunier Red (Pinot Meunier blended with Riesling).

Visitors are welcome to visit the winery for a variety of educational tours and tastings of Thirty Bench wines. Wines can be ordered by telephone or fax.

Thirty Bench Winery in Beamsville, Niagara Peninsula

From left to right: Dr. Thomas Muckle, Franz Zeritsch, Yorgos Papageorgiou, and Marek Maniecki

The Three Vintners

Where wine at the table can bring people together, the three proprietors of Thirty Bench Winery—Tom, Yorgos, and Franz—are examples of people who have come together just *thinking* about wine at the table.

Back in 1970, Dr. Tom Muckle left England to settle in Hamilton, Ontario, where he would teach medicine at the new medical school at McMaster University. Several "Brits" settled in the area at the time and, having come from a heritage where fine wine was very much a part of everyday life, they were very disappointed by the local Ontario offerings.

Unsatisfied with the quality of Ontario wines, they formed a group of about twenty amateur winemakers who dedicated their efforts to maximizing the quality of wines made from Ontario grapes. In a relatively short period of time they were winning awards at several amateur winemaking events and knew they were on to something. Realizing that Niagara had much more potential than was being exhibited in the commercial wines of that time, Tom Muckle joined ranks with others to investigate the possibility of starting their own commercial wine operation.

Incidentally, Tom Muckle's interest in winemaking arose from a try-out of a recipe using Madeira in the famous Mrs. Beeton's (complete Victorian) cook book. In their teens, he and his brother made a batch. At the time the wine tasted indescribably foul, but some eight years later when the bottles were "rediscovered" in the basement, the Madeira was absolutely gorgeous. This marvelous transition left a lifelong impression.

FONDANT OF SALMON AND FENNEL HACHÉ WITH ROASTED TOMATO GASTRIQUE

from chefs Vincenza Smith and Jim McLean, Niagara Culinary Institute, Niagara Falls

Serves 6

6 fresh salmon fillets
olive oil as needed
½ cup (125 ml) safflower oil
1 fennel
1 apple
6 tomatoes
1 red onion, small
1 carrot, small
assorted fresh herbs (chives, parsley) to taste
salt and pepper to taste
½ cup (125 ml) sugar
½ cup (125 ml) red wine vinegar
½ cup (125 ml) apple cider vinegar
honey to taste

Julienne the fennel, apple, red onion, and carrot. Season with salt, pepper, chives, and parsley. Add a touch of honey, the cider vinegar, and safflower oil. Mix together and set in the fridge overnight.

Roast tomatoes in the oven with salt, pepper, and herbs. Caramelize sugar, add roasted tomatoes, and deglaze with vinegar. Puree and strain. Taste and adjust the seasoning. Reserve for later at room temperature.

Heat olive oil until it is tepid. Submerge the salmon and poach until medium to medium rare.

Serve with fennel haché, drizzle with roasted tomato gastrique and garnish.

WINE MATCH
Thirty Bench Chardonnay Reserve
Thirty Bench Cabernet-Merlot Tradition

The term "herbaceous," predominantly associated with Sauvignon Blanc, is also recognizable in some Merlot and Cabernet Sauvignon wines. When out of balance or over-powering, the unflattering descriptor "vegetal" is sometimes used.

Yorgos Papageorgiou, a geography and economics professor at McMaster University, shared Tom's love of winemaking. Through their winemaking ventures they came to know Franz Zeritsch, an Austrian amateur wine-maker who owned a winemaking shop in Hamilton. Franz was North America's second most celebrated amateur winemaker, hot on the heels of Jim Warren who established Stoney Ridge Winery.

In 1978 Tom, Yorgos, and Franz—each bolstered with several awards for their winemaking prowess—began to act on their shared wine passion. With three other col-leagues in their ranks, they began scouting and studying land in the Niagara Peninsula in their quest for ideal vine-yard property. They even enlisted the advice of renowned professor Hemut Becker from the famous Geisenheim Institute in Germany to assist in the site selection process. Producing wine commercially was a serious, expensive, and risky business, and they were determined to do their homework before taking the plunge.

By 1979 they had secured their first seventeen acres of Beamsville Bench property in the village of the Thirty (Mile Creek) in Lincoln County. In 1980 they planted their first 2.5 acres of Geisenheim Riesling vines on the advice of Helmut regarding terroir, microclimate, etc., and so began their endeavor entitled Heritage Vineyards. Several other varieties of premium vinifera vines were also planted experimentally.

Over the next three years, the partnership expanded, and in 1983 the name of the company was changed to French Oak Vineyards. International trade treaties a little later dictated another name change, and it wasn't until after many months of searching that a local newspaper proprietor sug-gested using the address on the Beamsville Bench.

Thirty Bench was ready to make wine commercially but, as it turned out, the then laws of the province made it virtually impossi-ble to obtain a winemaking license. With tonnes of grapes coming into production and no winemaking license, Thirty Bench was caught between a proverbial rock and a hard place. At that time, there was

Jonathan with Dr. Thomas Muckle and his daughter Fiona

little market for premium vinifera grapes, and production was far greater than they and all their amateur friends could use themselves.

The months of waiting for any sign of a license turned into years, and the years added up to over a decade—fourteen years after their first planting in 1980—before the license was finally granted in 1994. Talk about patience and perseverance!

Firmly committed to their belief in the Niagara Peninsula's excellent growing conditions, further vineyard expansions were still confined to only premium vinifera vines—the noble varieties from Europe that had historically produced the best-quality wines.

Vineyard practices were adapted to local conditions. For example, Cabernet Sauvignon does not ripen well in Niagara at a yield of four tonnes per acre and above, but ripens beautifully if the yield is reduced by crop thinning down to 2.5 tonnes per acre or less. As the yield drops, the quality rises. At Thirty Bench, the other varieties of vinifera are crop thinned as well, and some unusual treatments are used; for example, thinned Riesling is fermented in oak barrels, a practice considered verboten by most winemakers. Such Riesling develops flavor profiles similar to those from Alsace.

Niagara enjoys a similar climate to Bordeaux and Burgundy

At the same time, vineyard manager Marek Meniecki and the vineyard staff spare no effort in achieving the highest in grape quality from each harvest: Bunch thinning, leaf plucking, late harvesting, and hand tending are just a few of the costly methods employed. A complete aversion to insecticides and the utilization of more natural methods in the tending of the vineyard have also been key elements; a fungicidal spray is sometimes used to protect the vines from lethal diseases. The grapes are hand harvested to select them at their best condition until the moment of crushing. This devotion to the vines and attention to detail are the foundation of their winemaking philosophy.

Their approach to grape growing and winemaking is minimalist, close to "organic," and complemented with a flare for experimentation. In association with Professor Michael Risk of McMaster University, they are beginning to treat their barrels of Canadian oak, which grows slowly in the frigid north, and thus offers fine and tight-grained wood that is purported to be even more delicate than French oak, long considered the most prized oak for winemaking.

Canadian oak: Now there's a new world treat few would have expected!

Heralded as the most popular white wine in the world, Chardonnay is valued for its adaptability to different climates and its versatility in accommodating a winemaker's particular style, especially when treated with oak.

EastDell Estates

FAST FACTS

4041 Locust Lane
Beamsville, Ontario
L0R 1B2
Tel: 905-563-9463
E-mail: winery@eastdell.com
Web: www.eastdell.com

EastDell Estates on the bench in Beamsville

PROSCIUTTO AND FETA STUFFED EGGPLANT CANNELLONI WITH TOMATO CONFIT

——

from Chef de Cuisine
Mark Walpole, Bench Bistro,
EastDell Estates

——

Serves 8

2 large eggplants
4 medium-size tomatoes
16 slices of prosciutto
¼ lb (125 g) butter
16 oz (500 g) feta cheese
3 garlic cloves
½ cup (125 ml) basil leaves,
    tightly packed
2 oz (60 g) pine nuts
olive oil
black pepper

Preheat oven to 250°F (125°C).
continued on page 135

EastDell Estates is located on the Beamsville Bench in the heart of the Niagara Peninsula. Founded in 1999, the winery's goal is to produce premium wines that showcase the terroir of its vineyards.

Heading up the winemaking is Tatjana Cuk who emigrated from Europe where she grew up in a family steeped in viticulture. A traditionalist in her winemaking, she strives to make wine that features the purity of the varietal fruit. EastDell produces approximately 11,000 cases of wine annually, which includes innovations in winemaking such as a Black Cab, a Baco Noir, and Cabernet Franc blend. Wine production also includes sparkling wine, fruit wines such as pear, apple, and apricot, and fortified wines such as sherry.

EastDell varietals on its thirty-two acres of planted vines include Chardonnay, Riesling, Vidal, Pinot Gris, Cabernet Sauvignon, Cabernet Franc, Merlot, and Pinot Noir.

Among EastDell's many national and international awards are medals and honors from Intervin, VinItaly, the Air Ontario Awards, the All-Canadian Wine Championships, and the Fruit Wines of Canada Competition. The winery's Riesling was chosen by Ontario parliamentary members to be served in the dining room of the provincial parliament at Queen's Park, and its Unoaked Chardonnay was selected as the house white wine in Ottawa's House of Commons restaurant.

EastDell provides a unique experience for visitors. The winery is located on a migration path for a wide variety of birds, which are easily visible particularly in the spring and fall. Self-guided viticulture and nature tours are available on the fifty-acre property. In addition, cooking demonstrations, food and wine pairing seminars, and tutored wine tastings are other key components of the experience at the winery.

The winery features an on-site restaurant, the Bench Bistro, with Chef de Cuisine Mark Walpole—a pioneer of Niagara regional cuisine—at the helm. The menu changes every six weeks and focuses on simple but innovative dishes that highlight the area's bountiful products.

continued from page 134

TOMATO CONFIT
Quarter the tomatoes and remove the pulp. Rub lightly with oil and place skin-up on a lined baking sheet. Bake at 250°F (125°C) for 1½ hours. Remove from oven and peel off skin. Place in a pot and simmer with butter for 10 minutes. Set aside.

STUFFING
Prepare a pesto by combining the garlic, basil, and pine nuts in a food processor. Drizzle in 2 or 3 oz (60 to 90 ml) of olive oil while pureeing. Remove to a bowl and crumble in the feta cheese and mix thoroughly. Add black pepper to taste.

ASSEMBLING THE CANNELLONI
Slice eggplants as thinly as possible lengthwise for 16 slices of less than ⅛ inch in thickness. Heat ¼ inch of olive oil in a heavy-bottomed skillet. When hot, fry the eggplant slices for 2 minutes each side or until tender. Add oil as necessary throughout the frying process since the eggplant will absorb the oil. Lay fried eggplant on a flat working surface.

Place a slice of prosciutto lengthwise along the eggplant and 2 oz (60 g) of the cheese stuffing at one end. Roll the eggplant, beginning at the stuffing end, to form a log.

To serve, place 2 cannelloni (warmed, if necessary, in the oven) in the center of each plate, one leaning against the other. Ladle the tomato confit (heat it up, if necessary) on top of the cannelloni. Garnish with black pepper and a sprig of basil.

WINE MATCH
EastDell Estates Black Cab VQA

Great scenery, fine food, and wine are Niagara trademarks

Malivoire Wine Company

FAST FACTS

4260 King Street East, P.O. Box 475
Beamsville, Ontario
LOR 1B0
Tel: 905-563-9253
Fax: 905-563-9512
E-mail:
questions@malivoirewineco.com
Web: www.malivoirewineco.com

Malivoire has produced a blueprint for a world-class vineyard and winery operation. After studying the classic vineyards of the world, founder Martin Malivoire believed that the Beamsville Bench of the Niagara Peninsula offered many features similar to the great vineyards of Alsace and Burgundy. The soil, drainage, airflow, and other mesoclimatic factors have combined to produce uniqueness in Malivoire wines—*le goût de terroir*.

Currently totaling fifty acres, Malivoire vineyards comprise two properties approximately two-thirds of a mile (one kilometer) apart on the Beamsville Bench. The Moira vineyard, acquired first, produces Chardonnay, Gewurztraminer, Pinot Gris, and Pinot Noir. Gamay was added with the addition of a second vineyard in 1997. There is also a third vineyard with Marechal Foch "Old Vines," which was established in 1975. To augment Malivoire's own yields while waiting for the newest plantings to mature, the winery purchases grapes from other respected local growers.

Welcome to Malivoire's gravity-fed winery

The location of the winery itself is unique. In the center of the north side of the property, a large ravine provides superior air circulation and soil moisture drainage. The hillside drops thirty feet (ten meters), which is ideal for Malivoire's gravity-enhanced winemaking operation. The winery was designed to take advantage of the ravine, with winemaking activities carried out on seven levels. Wines can be made entirely without pumping. This gentle processing allows for precise oxygen management and minimum filtering during winemaking. The result is Malivoire's ability to produce first-class wines.

Malivoire produces the following VQA wines: (white wines) Chardonnay, Gewurztraminer, Pinot Gris; (red wines) Gamay, Pinot Noir, Cabernet Foch; (dessert wine) Riesling Icewine.

Although Malivoire does not offer regular public tours, visitors can taste the winery's premium wines seven days a week. In addition, Malivoire hosts by-invitation events during the year when visitors can tour this unique winery. E-mail the winery at invite@malivoirewineco.com to join the invitation list to events during the year.

Malivoire wines are available at the winery, occasionally through LCBO outlets, and through agents in British Columbia, Alberta, Manitoba, and Ontario.

Martin Malivoire: Birth of a Vintner

Martin Malivoire

Martin Malivoire was born in Eastchurch, Kent, England, and immigrated to Canada in 1952 at the age of three. Martin's father, a millwright, moved his family to Canada to find opportunities not available in pre- or post-war England.

Martin attended elementary and secondary school in Oakville, Ontario, before entering the University of Guelph at age seventeen. While majoring in agriculture, his diverse interests led him to courses from architecture to mycology, and included one course totally in French—the history of architecture—at the University of Laval in Quebec. Martin supported himself and financed his university studies working as a janitor, as a farm worker harvesting corn during the night, and as a private contractor.

After university, Martin returned to Oakville and became self-employed as a general contractor building custom homes and doing renovations. One of his clients recognized Martin's potential and arranged extensive

---

RACK OF LAMB WITH MUSHROOM RISOTTO

—

from Martin Malivoire

—

Serves 4

STOCK
2 tbsp (30 ml) grape seed oil
2 onions, chopped
3 garlic cloves, sliced
2 kg (4 lb) cremini mushrooms, sliced
3 thyme sprigs
1 bay leaf
water, to cover

RISOTTO
5 cups (1.25 L) mushroom stock
2 tsp (10 ml) olive oil
1 onion, finely chopped
1½ cups (375 ml) risotto rice
    (Arborio)
salt and pepper, to taste

RACK OF LAMB
1 rack of lamb
½ cup (125 ml) assorted herbs,
    chopped (rosemary, thyme,
    parsley)
2 large garlic cloves, minced
salt and pepper
2 tbsp (30 ml) olive oil

For the stock, in a large pot, heat oil over medium high heat. Add onions, garlic and, mushrooms. Sweat until the mushrooms are soft and are starting to brown.

Add thyme, bay leaf, and water to cover. Bring to a boil, reduce heat, and allow to simmer for 45 minutes. Remove from heat, strain, and press solids to extract as much liquid as possible. Reduce liquid to one-third after straining.

To make the risotto, in a medium saucepan, heat the stock, keeping at a gentle simmer. In a large saucepan, heat oil over medium heat. Add onions and sauté until transparent. Add Arborio rice and cook over medium heat for 2 to 3 minutes until well coated.

Slowly add ½ cup (125 ml) of hot stock; stir gently until it is absorbed. Continue this process,
continued on page 138

continued from page 137

adding ½ cup (125 ml) of stock at a time, until the risotto has been cooking for 10 to 12 minutes. Taste for doneness—a little resistance to the teeth.

Reduce remaining stock, approximately 2 cups (500 ml), until it is syrupy and dark brown. Season. Keep warm.

For the rack of lamb, preheat oven to 450°F (230°C).

Rub the herbs, garlic, and seasoning into the rack. Heat the oil in a large skillet over medium heat. Sear the rack until browned on all sides.

Pan roast lamb rack in the oven until internal temperature reaches 120°F (50°C). Remove from oven and let rest for 10 minutes.

Slice between the ribs. Arrange the ribs in pairs on a generous scoop of risotto and drizzle the reduction over them.

WINE MATCH
Malivoire 2000 Moira Vineyard Pinot Noir

A wine's "body" is often perceived in the mouth as a texture or weight and is determined by the balance of alcohol, glycerol, acid, and extract. A full-bodied wine feels rich and heavy in the mouth; a light-bodied wine feels thin.

aptitude testing for him. These tests showed that Martin had extremely high mechanical aptitude and the spatial perception necessary for design work. The summary accompanying the testing results recommended one career choice: special effects.

Martin, not knowing anything about special effects, contacted the CBC in Toronto and wangled an appointment to discuss employment opportunities. When he showed his aptitude tests to the head of special effects, they hired him on the spot. Thus, Martin started what would be the only salaried job he has ever held. He worked in live television and later in VTR (video tape recording) on venerable Canadian shows such as "Wayne and Schuster," "Reach for the Top," "Tommy Hunter," and "The Friendly Giant."

While at the CBC, Martin started moonlighting, doing special effects for commercials and small Canadian feature films. Demand was so great for his services that he took the plunge, left the CBC, and became the first full-time independent special effects practitioner in Toronto. In the beginning, Martin could not afford some of the equipment needed for special effects, so he designed and built his own. These fresh, innovative ideas became the standard for the industry, used and copied by many. Twenty-five years of special effects work and the development of several special effects companies followed. Martin's portfolio of work now includes over 150 feature films and 3,000 television commercials.

Along the way, Martin became a diver, a climber, a pilot, a chef, and everything else that interested and challenged him. These accomplishments were acquired for personal interest but Martin was also able to take advantage of them in his special effects work. His independent nature, complemented by an analytical and creative mind, eventually led him to the world of wine.

In the mid-1970s, Martin became interested in wine and began traveling in various wine regions to increase his knowledge and to add to his personal wine cellar. The change from wine enthusiast to more active involvement was spurred in 1994 when Martin was working on the film *Trapped in Paradise* in Niagara-on-the-Lake. He spent his free time taking a closer look at potential vineyard properties available and the wineries in existence in Niagara at that time. Although he had been looking on a casual basis much earlier than this, he decided then to become more diligent about acquiring a vineyard in Niagara.

With the encouragement of his partner, Moira, who was equally interested in purchasing a vineyard property,

Martin made a lifestyle decision to buy a vineyard in Beamsville and to build a weekend home. After acquiring this vineyard property in 1995 (now known as the Moira Vineyard), they oversaw their first harvest in 1996. By then, Martin and Moira were totally engaged by the challenges of growing grapes and making wine—and the Malivoire Wine Company was born.

   The prime motivation for Martin and Moira included the objective of incorporating a lifestyle choice with a love and respect of the outdoors, a life-long interest in wine, and the belief that they have the ability to build a meaningful vineyard and winery operation. It was also important for them to be able to actively participate, both physically and intellectually, in this new business venture. And as most vintners and winemakers will attest, the wine business offers all those challenges, and more.

While filtering wine before bottling removes yeast cells and other microorganisms, many winemakers argue that extreme, or sterile, filtering extracts too much flavor and character.

Our Path of Knowledge by Martin Malivoire

At Malivoire, we are very proud of the enviable reputation we have achieved for our fine wines and our gentle gravity-enhanced winemaking process. But there is more to Malivoire than that. At our heart, we value the harmonious integration of enological, environmental, social, and business goals. We are winegrowers in the holistic sense. We strive to be considerate neighbors, to lead by example in our industry and community, to be responsible citizens, and to share our knowledge and information with others.

   Our philosophy is ultimately expressed in the land we steward—it's the touchstone that keeps all of us "grounded," no matter whether our role is in growing, creating, or marketing. We believe that the earth is being thoughtlessly robbed of its vital energy and that our mandate is to aid its restoration. We study and respect the good efforts and sacrifices of past generations and intend to enrich the prospects of the future. Therefore, on our vineyard sites we are eliminating the unhealthy practices of conventional agriculture. This will provide a direct benefit to our vineyard workers, and will have a longer-term positive impact on our ecosystem.

   At Malivoire, we are learning how to succeed at organic farming. "Organic" refers to a group of methods that rely on the earth to care for the earth. Organic producers believe that the soil is the bedrock of fertility; therefore, it is vital to build the soil with natural nutrients

The Blossom Brunch at the Good Earth Cooking School features Malivoire's Ladybug Rosé matched with a special spring appetizer

rather than relying on chemical fertilizers. Healthy, living soil supports healthy, resilient vines. Our aim is to strengthen the vines in order to increase their natural resistance to stressors such as pests, disease, and climatic extremes. To this end, we compost our organic byproducts from winemaking for later use in the vineyard, and we plant a ground cover of soil-sustaining green crops that aid fertility and biodiversity.

"Veraison" marks the beginning of grape ripening, where the berries change color and soften, experiencing an increase in sugar and size, and a decrease in acidity.

Natural, organic biological and mechanical methods are employed as pest controls. We avoid the addictive quick fix of chemical herbicides, insecticides, and synthetic fungicides.

Beyond organic is a practice of farming called biodynamics, based on the teachings of Rudolf Steiner. Biodynamics is a science of life forces, and it appeals to us because it considers the totality of nature and views the vineyard as a system of interrelated organisms. It is about being synchronized with the rhythms of our vineyards—not just the vines, but also the soil, the microorganisms, the insects, the humans, the seasons, the planets: all the energy active in the vineyard. We have learned that it is not a prescription, but a way of thinking that demands attention to balance and healing. To quote the Biodynamic Farming and Gardening Association, "Biodynamics is an ongoing path of knowledge rather than an assemblage of methods and techniques."

Vineyard management is critical to growing great grapes

We do not need to make a choice between responsible, sustainable agriculture and high-quality wines. These ideals are not mutually exclusive. In fact, we believe that they are co-dependent. We have chosen to pursue excellence in our vineyards by integrating the principles of organic and biodynamic agriculture. As our winemaker, Ann Sperling, states, "My responsibility is to recognize and preserve every facet of the uniqueness that our vineyards communicate through our grapes." This focus is consistent with the old-world concept of "terroir": producing wines with a sense of place. Many of the world's great wine growers share the philosophy of pursuing a better environment in which to work, live, and grow while producing characteristic, high-quality that reflect the individual character of the vineyard that they come from—wines that are unique and expressive.

Methodically and respectfully, we nurture our vines to produce a high-quality, balanced yield, always conscious that we are a critical contributor to the legacy and pedigree of our appellation. We believe this attention, along with our exceptional vineyard sites and our judicious varietal selection, have already put us on equal footing with the top producers. Now, our responsible vineyard stewardship will secure our position among them.

At Malivoire, we recognize our responsibility to pursue sustainable agriculture, organic practices, and biodynamic farming on the continuum to improvement, not only for our grapes, our wines, our company, and ourselves, but for our customers, our neighbors, and, ultimately, our planet.

Vineyard manager Darryl Fields harvests the bounty

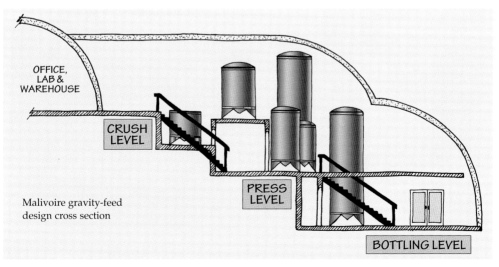

Malivoire gravity-feed design cross section

OFFICE, LAB & WAREHOUSE

CRUSH LEVEL

PRESS LEVEL

BOTTLING LEVEL

Magnotta Winery

FAST FACTS

Magnotta Beamsville
4701 Ontario Street
Beamsville, Ontario
L0R 1B4
Tel: 905-563-5313
E-mail: info@magnotta.com
Web: www.magnotta.com

Magnotta was the creator of the world's first sparkling champagne-style icewine and also produces Ice Grappa, the world's first grappa made entirely from icewine grape skins. Magnotta is widely recognized for its innovative and creative products and unique marketing.

Magnotta produces wines from its 180 acres in the Niagara Peninsula and another 351 acres in Maipo Valley, Chile. With 1,000 French and American oak barrels and capacity for three million liters in stainless steel cooperage, the winery produces more than 300,000 cases of wine annually.

Magnotta offers more than 150 products that include a wide range of VQA varietals and international blends, sparkling, aperitif, and dessert wines. The company also produces a selection of spirits.

Magnotta's main winery, boutique, and art gallery located in Vaughan just north of Toronto

Gabe and Rossana Magnotta

The winery's VQA varietals and varietal blends are produced exclusively from grapes grown in Magnotta's Ontario vineyards. The VQA wines include (white wines) Vidal-Seyval, Vidal, Riesling, Chardonnay, Viognier, Pinot Gris; (red wines) Marechal Foch, Gamay Noir, Zweigelt-Merlot, Pinot Noir, Cabernet Franc, Cabernet Sauvignon Merlot, Cabernet Franc Merlot, Merlot, Cabernet Sauvignon, Meritage Red.

Magnotta was awarded a large number of national and international awards at wine competitions around the world. Tours and tastings are offered at its Vaughan and Beamsville, Ontario, locations. Wine tastings are also available at all of its stores, which are open seven days a week.

The Magnottas: Love and Marriage, Pride and Passion

Gabe Magnotta once had aspirations to be a teacher, but his entrepreneurial instincts, his marriage to Rossana, and their drive to be unique led to the creation of Ontario's third largest winery. But it didn't happen overnight.

Having completed his degree at the Ontario Institute for Studies in Education in 1969, Gabe had second thoughts about the career he was now qualified to pursue. During his early entrepreneurial years, Gabe met and fell in love with Rossana when she was a student majoring in laboratory technologies. After four years of dating, they finally married and Rossana began her career working

---

MAGNOTTA POACHED PEARS
—
from Magnotta Winery
—
Serves 4

3 cups (750 ml) water
½ cup (125 ml) granulated sugar
1 tbsp (15 ml) lemon juice
4 almost-ripe pears (Bosc or others
  with stems on)
caramel sauce (optional)
1 tbsp (15 ml) icing sugar
1 tbsp (15 ml) ground cinnamon

In a large saucepan, combine the water, sugar, and lemon juice. Bring to a boil over medium high heat. Peel and core the pears, leaving the stems intact.

Add pears to the boiling syrup, and reduce heat to simmer gently. Cover the pot with a lid to help cook the pears. Simmer for 15 to 20 minutes until tender. Turn the pears halfway through cooking.

Pour hot caramel sauce over the pears and powder with a combination of the icing sugar and ground cinnamon.

WINE MATCH
Magnotta Vidal Limited Edition Icewine VQA

Vidal (vee-dahl)—bred from a French-American hybrid crossing of Ugni Blanc, from the Italian Trebbiano grape, and Seibel, another hybrid— is one of the most popular grapes for producing high-quality icewines.

Blending may involve combining two or more wine varieties, wine types, or different lots of wine, and is generally thought to produce wines that are more layered and complex than single varietal wines.

in a hospital as a laboratory technologist specializing in hematology.

One of Gabe's entrepreneurial goals was to acquire an entry-level business that was affordable and had potential—Humber Valley Live Bait was ripe for the picking. Hard work and specialization made it a profitable business venture that would last approximately fifteen years.

While running his live-bait business, Gabe was approached by a wine juice supplier who wanted to rent some of the large walk-in refrigeration space that Gabe used to keep his inventory fresh. Gabe accommodated the supplier and began to take an interest in winemaking. Rossana's laboratory skills proved beneficial in the analysis of wine chemistry, structure, and balance. It wasn't long before they were both enamored with the making of wine.

In 1985, Gabe and Rossana began Festa Juice, supplying amateur winemakers with a diverse variety of grape juices from all over the world. Part of their service to customers included personal advice on how to make better-quality wines. The couple were also making wine for themselves, and with glowing compliments from friends and family, wanted to take the next step and start their own winery!

In 1988, they discovered a small winery for sale in Blenheim, Ontario. They needed $250,000 to purchase the property ("Charal") that had just about everything they'd need. They mortgaged their house for the deposit and set out to secure the financing. At the same time, one of the larger wineries was in the process of liquidating some of its winemaking equipment. Gabe quickly negotiated a very favorable price. They acquired several 10,000-gallon stainless steel tanks along with various hoses and tubes.

Gabe and Rossana couldn't possibly use all of the tanks they'd purchased but saw an opportunity to resell them. This astute purchase and resale of the tanks netted Gabe and Rossana enough profit to purchase the Charal Winery. It was the beginning of what would soon become Magnotta Winery.

Building on their juice experiences with Festa and amateur winemakers, the pair began an innovative journey that enabled them to create a diverse series of international varietal and blended wines and some unique spirits. With over fifty VQA wines and a diverse selection of international blends they continue to develop new tasting adventures for their customers. Sparkling Ice and Ice Grappa are only two of their landmark creations.

Their love of art has also become a Magnotta signature. A piece of original art is purchased and rendered onto a label to match the taste and flavor profile of each wine. Touring Magnotta Vaughan is like venturing into a remarkable art gallery where paintings they've secured from all over the world adorn the retail shop, tasting room, and offices.

As Gabe and Rossana celebrate their love and marriage and the growing of their business, they share a pride and passion for the wines that bear their name.

A small sampling of the art used on Magnotta labels

Daniel Lenko Estate Winery

FAST FACTS

5246 King Street
Beamsville, Ontario
L0R 1B3
Tel: 905-563-7756
Fax: 905-563-3317
E-mail: oldvines@daniellenko.com
Web: www.daniellenko.com

The Lenko family has grown high-quality vinifera grapes for more than forty years and has some of the oldest Chardonnay and Merlot vines in Ontario. Daniel Lenko, who has taken over the operation of the farm from his father, Bill, is using his background of experience to grow the best possible grapes for his own estate wines.

Winemaker Jim Warren, a former owner and winemaker at Stoney Ridge, has a wealth of experience as one of Canada's most awarded and respected winemakers.

All Daniel Lenko wines are produced from the Lenko estate and are VQA. The Merlot and Chardonnay bear the designation "Old Vines" and, along with the other red wines, are barrel-aged in both French and American oak.

Thirty-year-old vines in early spring

Wines include (white wines) Chardonnay, Gewurztraminer, Riesling, Vidal, Viognier; (red wines) Cabernet Franc, Old Vines Merlot, Cabernet Sauvignon, Pinot Noir, Meritage; (rosé wine) a Cabernet Rosé; (dessert wines) Select Late Harvest Vidal, Vidal Icewine, and a Raspberry Reserve fruit wine.

Daniel Lenko has won a number of awards for both red and white wines at competitions including the All-Canadian Wine Championships and Intervin International Wine Competition.

Wines are only available at the winery. Wine tastings and tours are arranged by appointment.

Pickers' baskets await a new harvest

HELEN LENKO'S APPLE PIE

—

from Daniel Lenko Estates

—

Serves 4 to 6

½ cup (125 ml) butter, at room
    temperature
½ cup (125 ml) lard
2 cups (500 ml) flour
pinch of salt
½ cup (125 ml) cold water
Mutsu apples
white or brown sugar
cinnamon or nutmeg

Mix the flour, butter, lard, and salt quickly by hand. Add water a little at a time. Work the ball of dough quickly. Do not overmix. Dust with flour. Divide in half. Roll out bottom crust. Put on a large pie plate lightly greased.

Fill the bottom crust with sliced Mutsu apples. Sprinkle a few tea-spoons of white or brown sugar on top. Add some dabs of butter. Sprinkle with cinnamon or nutmeg.

Put on the top crust and prick holes into it with a fork. Press edges with fork.

Bake for 1 hour at 400°F (200°C).

WINE MATCH
Daniel Lenko Select Late Harvest Vidal

NOTES FROM THE CELLAR

THE TASTE TEST

When tasting, are there any rules to follow?
Memory and attention to detail are your best tools when tasting wines. Be aware of flavors and sensations, while logging them in your memory. This is where a journal comes in handy. It's a personal journey and you're it! Always consider whether it's the wine in the bottle or the experience that makes the first impression.

The one hard-and-fast rule is to share. You remember what you tasted, and each experience is personal and memorable, made more so by sharing the memory. So make an effort to recall and share; it's only natural. Begin by having some friends over for a simple tasting. Get some paper ready for note taking. Explain that everybody will learn as they share. It's not a contest. The wine is a simple matter. Start with the lightest or most fragile wine first. It doesn't have to be expensive. Choose a region, such as Chile, and explore its wines. Drink whites before rosés, before reds. Taste dry wines before sweeter wines. There's no mystery and no need to be intimidated. It's basic common sense. Light first and heavy last, just like food. Light food with the lightest wine. And that's your first step in hope-fully a long and enjoyable journey on the wine route, and you are your own guide!

When tasting wine, the mouth usually detects and assesses the dimensions of sweetness, acidity, bitter-ness, viscosity, and tannin levels, confirming the aroma characteristics already registered by the nose.

De Sousa Wine Cellars

FAST FACTS

3753 Quarry Road
Beamsville, Ontario
LOR 1B0
Tel: 905-563-7269
Fax: 905-338-9404
Web: desousawines.com

De Sousa Wine Cellars provides a glimpse into the old world with a taste of Portugal. The beautiful pink winery building, the surrounding gardens and groves of trees, the smell of fresh crusty bread in the wine boutique, the 270-year-old wine press display, and the full-bodied wine presented in clay bowls, all make visitors feel welcome and a part of that old world.

The antique press was built in 1820 in Portugal for the De Sousas, who were grape growers on the island of St. Michael's in the Azores. Four generations of growing grapes and making wine have been passed on to John De Sousa, Jr.

John's father purchased vineyards in Niagara in 1979, which he replanted with vinifera and French hybrid

De Sousa Wine Cellars located in Beamsville, Niagara Peninsula

vines. Three years later he opened the family's new winery. Today De Sousa has eighty-eight acres planted with a variety of vitis vinifera grapes including a unique varietal introduced from Portugal called Touriga Nacional for making Port. The winery produces more than 18,000 cases of wine each year.

Because 85% of De Sousa wine sales are to the Portuguese and Italian communities, the white and red wines are generally full bodied, robust, and dry. The wines are aged in massive 990-gallon oak puncheons and are sold in 1.5 liter and four liter bottles because the Portuguese and Italians like to purchase their wine that way.

VQA wines include (red wines) Cabernet Sauvignon, Cabernet Franc, Merlot, Merechal Foch, Baco Noir; (white wines) Chardonnay, Riesling, Vidal Blanc; (icewine) Vidal Icewine. De Sousa also offers a 1991 Port.

De Sousa opened a new winery located in the heart of Toronto in 1998. Visitors are invited to tour both wineries and taste their wines of exceptional character and quality.

Hot, sunny days produce the sugar while cool evenings help maintain the acid levels in grapes

DE SOUSA MAPLE BARBECUED CHICKEN

from the kitchen of
Dennis Bell,
Niagara-on-the-Lake

Serves 8

4 whole chicken breasts
¾ cup (180 ml) white wine
¾ cup (180 ml) olive oil
1 tbsp (15 ml) lemon juice
¼ tsp (1 ml) savory
¼ tsp (1 ml) thyme
salt and freshly ground pepper

MAPLE-BARBECUE SAUCE
1 large onion, finely chopped
2 tbsp (30 ml) olive oil
2 tbsp (30 ml) Worcestershire sauce
1 tbsp (15 ml) whole grain Dijon
    mustard
1½ cups (375 ml) chicken broth
1 cup (250 ml) ketchup
1 cup (250 ml) white wine
⅓ cup (75 ml) pure maple syrup

Lightly sprinkle the chicken breasts with salt, pepper, savory, and thyme. Place the chicken in a large zip-lock bag. Whisk together the white wine, olive oil, and lemon juice. Pour over the chicken, remove as much air as possible and seal the zip-lock bag. Let the chicken marinate for 6 to 12 hours.

Preheat the barbecue, then grill the chicken over medium heat for approximately 10 minutes per side, or until it is cooked through. Baste with the barbecue sauce and continue grilling for another 5 minutes (turning and basting). Serve with extra sauce on the side.

To prepare the maple-barbecue sauce, use a large, heavy saucepan and combine all of the ingredients. Bring the mixture to a boil and simmer for approximately 45 minutes, stirring occasionally. Reduce the sauce by at least 50% or until it reaches the consistency of a medium thick sauce. The sauce can be made a day or 2 in advance and kept covered in the refrigerator.

WINE MATCH
De Sousa Chardonnay

Niagara Peninsula Cuisine

Wine Country Cooking School

Wine Country Cooking School
students

Wine Country Cooking School, Niagara-on-the-Lake

Any visit to wine country should include one of the many cooking schools that are sprouting up throughout the Niagara Peninsula.

Joe Will and his wife and partner, Jane Langdon, have told me it wasn't so much a dream to open a winery and cooking school; in fact, they can't recall using the word "dream" to describe their achievement. It was just something they wanted to do!

I recommend Jane and Joe's Wine Country Cooking School for its hands-on demonstrations as a unique culinary experience for anyone interested in the pairing of food and wine. The focus is on Niagara regional cuisine, locally grown and raised products, recipes that change with the seasons and, of course, the successful pairing of local foodstuffs with local wine.

The school is located at the award-winning Strewn Winery, just five minutes from historic Niagara-on-the-Lake along Lakeshore Road (at Four Mile Creek Road). There are a variety of courses to choose from, including two- and three-hour cooking demonstration classes taught by regional food experts in the school's comfortable classroom. I know you'll have fun, and I personally love the sipping and tasting, especially since all the foods are matched with VQA wines. They also offer weekend and even week-long courses.

My connection to this space goes back to my Shaw Festival days in 1967. I had been hired as an apprentice during the festival's sixth year. One of my jobs was to prepare the canvas backdrops or scenery for three shows. The festival was still small then, and we were continually looking for locations in which to construct, paint, and store the completed scenery. One space I used was an abandoned canning factory on the Lakeshore Road. You guessed it! Thirty-five years ago, Joe and Jane's creation was my lonely workshop as I scraped and painted the sets for the Shaw Festival productions.

Michael Price (left) and Kevin Hamer of LIV

A Healthy Philosophy:
The LIV Restaurant in St. Catharines

Kevin Hamer and Michael Price are graduates of the Niagara Culinary Institute of Niagara College. These dynamic young chefs run the LIV Restaurant at the White Oaks Conference Resort and Spa in St. Catharines, smack in the middle of wine country.

They have set out to build a solid clientele, without fanfare and pizzazz. Their simple philosophy starts with a satisfied customer who has shared a simple meal of the finest produce available. Freshness is the key to fine dining, and these two strive to highlight the natural flavors of food. It's that simple!

This philosophy focuses on developing a healthy lifestyle, which will dictate its own rewards. LIV describes itself as a concept restaurant and follows the ancient path of Tao. They also use the Tao symbol for "above" as the restaurant signature. A horizontal line signifies the earth and a line above points upward. It suggests that we must be receptive to what is above and not only to the social swirl surrounding us. The simple theme for Michael and Kevin is to slow down and enjoy…it can

SPECK FARM
GRILLED QUAIL

—

from Pastry Chef
Mark Gerbrandt

—

Single serving

1 quail, deboned
3 oz (90 g) riblier (ripened goat
   cheese)
1 Granny Smith apple
1 handful of mesculin mix (baby
   greens)
1 oz (30 g) clarified butter
2 oz (60 ml) apple cider vinegar
2 oz (60 ml) apple cider
4 oz (125 ml) grape seed oil
chopped garlic, cloves, thyme, flour,
   salt, pepper, to taste

To make the vinaigrette, whisk together the apple cider vinegar, apple cider, and grape seed oil until incorporated. Add garlic, cloves, thyme, salt, and pepper.

Marinate the quail with 4 oz (125 ml) of the vinaigrette for at least 2 hours, and save the remaining. While grilling the quail, cut the apple into thirds and place the top and bottom pieces on the grill as well.

Dredge the riblier in seasoned flour, and pan sear until golden on both sides.

In a sauté pan, heat the remaining vinaigrette, then add the greens and heat until wilted.

On a plate, place the bottom third of the apple, then riblier, quail, greens, and the top third of the apple. Use the remaining vinaigrette from the greens to garnish the plate around the apple.

WINE MATCH
Malivoire Gamay

HARVEST PEAR MOUSSE

from Pastry Chef
Mark Gerbrandt

Serves 6

PEAR BUTTER
6 pears, peelings and core
½ cup (125 ml) sugar
1 lemon, squeezed
½ cup (125 ml) Late Harvest wine

SAUTÉED PEARS
6 pears, sliced
½ cup (125 ml) Late Harvest wine
2 tbsp (30 ml) sugar
2 tbsp (30 ml) butter
⅛ tsp (0.5 ml) cinnamon

PEAR MOUSSE
4 egg yolks
¼ cup (60 ml) sugar
2 tsp (10 ml) gelatin powder
1 cup (250 ml) whipping cream

MERINGUE BASE
4 egg whites
¼ cup (60 ml) sugar

For the butter, peel, core, and slice
6 pears and squeeze half a lemon
on the pears. In a saucepan, combine the peels, cores, sugar, half
a lemon, and the Late Harvest
wine. Bring to a boil and turn
down the heat to a simmer. Cook
for 2 hours. Force through a fine
screen and let cool.

For the sautéed pears, melt the
butter, and add the sugar, cinnamon, and pear slices. Sauté until
softened. Add the Late Harvest and
remove from heat.

For the pear mousse, over a
double boiler with the water at a
simmer, cook the egg yolks and
sugar. Whisk until hot and at ribbon
state. Add softened gelatin powder
and the pear butter. Whip up the
cream and add it into the egg and
pear mixture.

For the meringue base, whip the
egg whites with sugar until they
are thick and white and there is no

continued on page 153

Jonathan with Niagara College Culinary Institute students

make a difference. It starts with a good, relaxing meal
and grows from there.

Kevin and Michael are a real tag team with youthful
energy and élan, and judging by the contented faces of
departing diners, the combination works for them. Their
philosophy fits in with the management's intent on
reestablishing St. Catharines to its former glory as a spa
center celebrated across North America. It was the destination of choice for most of the second half of the nineteenth century, eclipsing even the storied Saratoga Springs
of New York State. The White Oaks Conference Resort
and Spa has its share of converts intent on experiencing
an age-old philosophy of renewal of both spirit and body.

Kevin and Michael describe their cooking theory: "We
work with local produce as a base, and try to enhance
whenever possible. For example, we take beef tenderloin
and smoke it over some oak chips soaked in Cabernet—
adding but not smothering—to achieve a marriage of flavors designed to excite rather than overwhelm."

And Kevin and Michael don't think twice about taking
advantage of local produce whenever it is offered. Once,
a waitress happened to mention that she had two acres of
wild rhubarb available. The chefs jumped at the offer,
harvested the crop, and canned it for future use. Another
time, a waiter said that he noticed a sumac tree while he

was fishing in a stream. The boys saw a golden opportunity to experiment. The sumac's red cone reveals fuzzy seeds that, when pressed, give off a strong citrus flavor, perfect for their evolving kitchen.

Michael and Kevin seek to transform the basics to create an inspired menu that will excite and renew. And they will gladly share their recipes! Their philosophy also extends to the dining room area, where Kevin often mingles with the diners, who are treated as honored guests, almost part of an extended family.

Our motto—Think Globally, Drink Locally—has special application here at LIV. A completely Ontario wine list designed to complement any choice of food is always a plus when in wine country. Exploration is the key and knowledgeable help is at hand.

continued from page 152
gritty feeling when rubbed between 2 fingers. Spoon 4 equal portions of the meringue on a baking sheet with parchment paper. Make a well in the center of each one with the back of a spoon. Bake at 300°F (150°C) until dry, approximately 2 to 2.5 hours.

To assemble, put the meringue in the center of a plate. Spoon mousse on top and pour hot pears over the mousse, letting it run down the side of the meringue. Garnish with fresh fruit and serve.

WINE MATCH
Late Harvest Vidal

Good Earth Cooking School

One of the joys of traveling wine country is discovering treasures right under our noses. In the case of the Good Earth Cooking School this was literally true. The Good Earth Cooking School is nestled in an enchanting setting smack in the middle of a fifty-five-acre fruit farm in Beamsville. A pond filled with fowl and majestic old trees skirting the simple buildings convey a rustic charm that is hard to resist. And everywhere there is the heavenly perfume of fruit swirling about the colorful flower and herb gardens. I was captivated! And I hadn't even entered the kitchens.

Classes are conducted inside the renovated cottage and former garage in a newly minted cosy kitchen. Classes in summer are conducted outside under an awning and with a full-brick open oven.

Niagara wine country is developing its peculiar tastebuds and the word is out: Come for a sip of wine and you're sure to stay for supper. The enjoyment of local bounty will be a memorable experience. Fruits and vegetables harvested at the height of their ripeness and availability is the focal point of the school's

The Good Earth Cooking School's enchanting setting, smack in the middle of a fruit orchard

Elizabetta Di Iorio culling from the on-site herb garden

Just the place to savor a local wine!

experiment in sharing. Small classes offer hands-on application and an intimacy of fun and laughter.

The special attraction offered by the school is the ability to draw from Niagara's most talented chefs. Niagara is gaining recognition internationally, with acclaim for such chefs as Michael Olson of On the Twenty fame, Stephen Treadwell of Queen's Landing Inn, and Antonio deLuca of Hillebrand Vineyard Café, to name just a few. Working with the best produce available they create magical interpretations. The school is determined to share the simple joys and pleasures of cooking in a friendly and engaging style in their unique setting.

For me, the "al fresco" kitchen is the most rewarding part of the experience. Outside, surrounded by pear trees, in my green apron, I felt more in touch with the "good earth" than ever before.

I recommend that you take a class and feel it for yourself. They have an assortment of weekend demonstrations and hands-on cooking classes, and you can learn tips to try out at home with renewed confidence. Be sure to check the spring and summer schedule for a menu of choices. The catchy titles of the spring weekend demos should pique your interest. Classes such as "Of Moose and Men" are designed to celebrate some truly Canadian dishes without resorting to clichés. Or how about "Flash in the Pan" with hilarious Chef Chuck Eller, where you'll learn to flambé with flair? Or you could try "Claws for Celebration" (lobster), "Meat and Greet" (getting the most out of barbecue season), or "Rolling in Dough" (pasta to pasta) classes. In the "Pucker Up" class, Executive Chef Roberto Fracchioni from On the Twenty reveals the secrets of balsamic vinegar, trying to smile throughout! My favorite is "Clueless in the Kitchen," which guided me from a simple appetizer through to dessert. I made it, and it made me feel great. If I can do it, anyone can!

Of course, wine is never far from the groaning tables and you will have a chance to mix and match and make new discoveries all in this magical setting in wine country. Always a trip worth taking.

Chef Roberto Fracchioni prepares the timbalo, places it in the oven, and voilà!

Peninsula Ridge Estates Winery

FAST FACTS

5600 King Street West, P.O. Box 550
Beamsville, Ontario
L0R 1B0
Tel: 905-563-0900
Fax: 905-563-0995
E-mail: info@peninsularidge.com
Web: www.peninsularidge.com

The views from Peninsula Ridge Estates on the Niagara Escarpment are some of the most spectacular in the area. Sampling outstanding wines in the retail shop or enjoying a gourmet meal in the restaurant, a visitor can savor the views of the Escarpment, the beautiful rolling vineyards, and Lake Ontario far below.

Officially opened in August 2000, the winery is located on eighty acres of premier grape-growing land on the Beamsville Bench—an area designated by UNESCO as a World Biosphere Reserve. The forty acres of estate vineyards include twenty-five acres of vinifera grapes including Cabernet Sauvignon, Merlot, Cabernet Franc, and Chardonnay. Another fifteen acres are devoted to Merlot, Chardonnay, and Syrah varietals. In addition, the winery controls and manages another neighboring twenty-acre vineyard with varietals that include Sauvignon Blanc, Viognier, Chardonnay, Cabernet Franc, Merlot, and Syrah. Peninsula Ridge also has long-term contracts with some of the best growers in Niagara to ensure the finest quality fruit for its wines.

Head winemaker Jean-Pierre Colas is focused on finding the best expression of Niagara—its soils, climate, and geography—in producing wines of supreme quality and character. He joined Peninsula Ridge after a decade of distinction as head winemaker at Domaine Laroche in Chablis, France. While there, he was awarded the prestigious 1998 Wine Spectator White Wine of the Year for his 1996 Les Clos Grand Cru Chablis.

State-of-the-art equipment is used at Peninsula Ridge. Fermentation is regulated using high-tech, dual-batch, temperature-controlled tanks imported from France. In the barrel cellar, wines age in 265 French oak

Peninsula Ridge Estates Winery and Restaurant in Beamsville, Niagara Peninsual

barrels to develop sublime depth and complexity. Peninsula Ridge utilizes the combination of New Age technology with old-world tradition to reveal the distinction of Niagara's terroir in wines of world-class quality.

Peninsula Ridge offers visitors a number of features, which make it a must-see destination in Niagara. A Queen Anne revival Victorian manor, a landmark in the area since its construction in 1885, has been meticulously restored and is now The Restaurant at Peninsula Ridge, one of the finest restaurants in the area. In an intimate environment, diners are offered a culinary adventure with such enticing entrées as Pan Seared Arctic Char, Roasted Rack of Venison, or Grilled Atlantic Salmon. The cuisine is rooted in classical French techniques using the finest quality ingredients from neighboring Niagara farms and orchards. The restaurant brings in farmhouse cheeses from Quebec and the freshest seafood from British Columbia and the Maritimes.

The winery retail shop is located in an 1885 restored post-and-beam barn, where knowledgeable staff lead visitors through a tasting of VQA wines and a guided tour of modern winery facilities and a traditional barrel cellar. The adjacent Coach House, a reconstruction of the farm's original coach house, is perfect for corporate and private functions.

Peninsula Ridge wines are available at LCBO stores, the local winery store and restaurant at Peninsula Ridge, and at fine restaurants throughout Ontario.

Norman Beal: From Oil Patch to Vineyard

Norman Beal's mom loved music and often suggested that playing in a philharmonic orchestra would be a wonderful career for her son. Norman seemed to be destined to fulfill his mother's dream by majoring in music. That was until he struck oil—or conversely, it struck him.

Like several young men at the time, Norman was drawn to the oil boom of the late 1970s in Alberta. Oil patch work was physically demanding and high paying. Over a relatively short period of time a young hard-working guy could earn some extremely serious dollars. It was always Norman's intention to save his oil field earnings so that he could return to his academic pursuit with greater financial security. Destiny had other plans.

Norman worked his way through the ranks, from the oil sands of Fort McMurray in northern Alberta to the

CHARDONNAY BRAISED RABBIT

—

from Raymond Poitras, Chef de Cuisine, The Restaurant at Peninsula Ridge

—

Serves 4

BRAISING LIQUID
1½ cup (375 ml) Chardonnay
2¼ cup (550 ml) chicken stock
2 large carrots, coarsely chopped
2 medium-size onions, chopped
4½ stocks of celery, chopped
5 whole cloves of garlic, cut in half
3 tbsp (45 ml) olive oil

RABBIT
1 whole rabbit, portioned (butcher will portion; portions should include 4 legs, 2 half breasts and thigh section)
4 sprigs fresh rosemary
7 sprigs fresh thyme
2 tbsp (30 ml) olive oil
salt and pepper to taste

Place all the vegetables in a mixing bowl and toss with 3 tbsp (45 ml) of olive oil. Place them in a roasting pan in a 400°F (200°C) oven for 25 minutes. Stir every 10 minutes.

In a stockpot, bring the chicken stock to a boil and reduce to a soft simmer.

Brown the rabbit portions in a frying pan with the remaining oil.

Place the rabbit in with the browned vegetables that have now been removed from the oven. Add fresh herbs, Chardonnay, and simmering chicken stock. Cover with foil and place in a 350°F (175°C) oven for approximately 3 hours.

Check after 2½ hours and then every few minutes until the meat can be gently pulled from the bone with a fork.

When completed, remove the rabbit from the roasting pan and strain the liquid.

Place the liquid in a sauce pot and reduce to a thickened consistency to be served as a sauce.

WINE MATCH
Peninsula Ridge 2000 Chardonnay
Peninsula Ridge 1999 Chardonnay Reserve

Norman Beal (left) and winemaker Jean-Pierre Colas

corporate offices of Shell Canada in Calgary. In 1981 Shell Canada recognized Norman's accomplishments and offered him a job in lubricants marketing just at the same time he'd been accepted at the University of Calgary where he was primed to pursue a degree in business. The challenge and opportunity with Shell prevailed.

From 1985 to 1989, Norman implemented a successful export marketing initiative on behalf of Shell. In 1990 he accepted a position at Glencore as an oil products trader. In 1997 he joined British Petroleum to head up their Americas Clean Product Trading Division. The demands of international marketing meant he had to travel frequently, and this gave Norman the opportunity to explore several wine regions.

Discovering the remarkable diversity of wines was a well-appreciated break from the hectic business itinerary

The Peninsula Ridge Barrel Cellars

that kept him virtually living on airplanes and traveling up to forty-two weeks of the year. Side trips to the vineyards and wineries of California, Chile, and Australia soon excited his interest in the wine business.

By the late 1990s his growing fascination with the making of fine wine led him to seriously consider changing his career. He had accomplished his goals in the oil business and was now determined to strike out on a new pursuit. Now all he needed was a winery.

Securing vineyard property proved more daunting than Norman had first anticipated. Buying property in the old world, where winemaking was entrenched in centuries of tradition, was out of the question. Vineyard prices throughout the new world had escalated dramatically. Fortunately, Norman's sister Teresa encouraged him to explore the Niagara region. His memories of Niagara wine from the 1970s coupled with his passion for finer wines made him reluctant to even consider Niagara, but as he was about to discover, a lot of exciting changes had taken place with Ontario wines in twenty years.

Norman was taken by surprise when he toured Niagara and noted the remarkable changes in quality and flavor profiles. The days of Baby Duck were relegated to the past. Norman quickly realized that the opportunity he was looking for was in his own boyhood backyard. What he didn't realize was how desirable vineyard properties had become in Niagara.

True to the adage that "nothing gets accomplished when you're sitting down," Norman's search ended when he almost stumbled across a historic property in Beamsville. The rundown fruit orchard, house, and barn were on the property that the Crown had granted W.H. Kitchen, a United Empire Loyalist, in 1790. In those days Kitchen partnered with Jacob Beam (the namesake of the town of Beamsville) and operated a successful sawmill and gristmill. In the late 1880s Kitchen's grandson built a grand Victorian home perched on the elevated ridge of the property.

The buildings were in need of serious repair but Norman didn't hesitate in his decision to buy the land, which sits on the prized Escarpment Bench. He immediately set out to restore the original post-and-beam barn and renovate the Victorian house into a fine-dining restaurant. Norman had recruited winemaker Jean-Pierre Colas from a top winery in Chablis, France, and by August of 2000 Peninsula Ridge released its first vintage with 4,200 cases of wine. The formal birth of The Restaurant at Peninsula Ridge was launched in July 2001.

With an extensive background in export marketing and a firm grasp of where he wants to take Peninsula Ridge Estates Winery, Norman realizes that one of the first challenges in establishing a fine wine label is to excite the local population about the quality. He intuitively knows and appreciates the role that wine can play in defining a unique and rare place like Niagara. This environment is blessed with all the attributes required to produce exceptional wines. But one of his toughest challenges will be to convince Canadians that Ontario wines have come of age and will only get better.

Canadians tend to undervalue indigenous success stories until they've made it on the world stage. As the "new kid on the block" and heavily involved with wine industry organizations, Norman takes on this task with great relish.

Because of the oak used in the vinification process, Chardonnay often imparts smells or tastes that are described as toasty, smoky, nutty, spicy, or vanilla-like, masking the Chardonnay fruit characteristics.

The Peninsula Ridge wine boutique

Traditionally, the term "aroma" indicated the fruity smell of the grape variety. Today's broader meaning combines that simple smell with other complexities developed during vinification or aging.

Kittling Ridge Estate Wine and Spirits

FAST FACTS

297 South Service Road
Grimsby, Ontario
L3M 1Y6
Tel: 905-945-9225
Fax: 905-945-4330
E-mail: admin@kittlingridge.com
Web: www.kittlingridge.com

Cooler temperatures are desired for the storage and aging of wine. While serving temperature is a personal preference, it's important to remember that if the wine is too cold, its aromas and flavors will be muted.

As the last remaining privately owned Canadian distillery in Ontario, Kittling Ridge is set apart by a special blend of tradition and innovation. Guests have an opportunity to see both a winery and a distillery, and the visit includes a tour of the fruit-processing area, fermentation cellars, distilling columns and copper pot stills, and a 50,000 square foot barrel aging cellar. And the seventy-nine-room Kittling Ridge Winery Inn and Suites opened in May 2000.

Many of the company's products are unique. Kittling Ridge Icewine & Brandy, the company's signature brand, was launched in 1992. The only product of its kind in the world, it has half the sweetness of traditional icewine and is a delicate blend of Vidal Icewine and seven-year barrel-aged brandy. This product alone has won more than twenty international awards. Inferno Pepper Pot Vodka is bottled with its own pair of hydroponically grown fresh flaming-red peppers and is tailor-made for the perfect Bloody Caesar. Forty Creek whiskies are handcrafted premium whiskeys that bring the art and passion back into making Canadian whiskey. During the past eight years, Kittling Ridge has won more than 100 awards at international competitions for these and other products.

This success has translated into a dramatic increase in size from fifteen employees eight years ago to its current 120 employees and exports to the United States, Taiwan, Japan, Hong Kong, England, Mexico, and South America. Kittling Ridge has been recognized by the Ontario government as an Innovative Growth Firm, the only beverage alcohol company selected for this honor.

Kittling Ridge Estate Wines and Spirits located in Grimsby

Kittling Ridge products can be purchased at their seven stores in Ontario, through the LCBO, and at the winery and distillery. The company's portfolio includes the following products: (table wines) VQA wines, Proprietor's Cuvée varietals and blends; (dessert wines) Icewine & Brandy, Vidal Icewine, Cabernet Franc Icewine, Kingsgate Sherry; (distilled spirits) Prince Igor Vodka, Inferno Pepper Pot Vodka, Pure Gold Canadian Whiskey, Forty Creek Barrel Select Whiskey, Forty Creek Three Grain Whiskey, Black Stripe White Rum, Small Cask Brandy; (liqueurs) Bolivar Coffee Liqueur, Oh Canada Maple Liqueur, Oh Canada Maple Cream Whiskey; (refreshments) Loaded Soda vodka and rum coolers, Shakers Ready-to-Drink Piña Colada, Shakers Strawberry Daiquiri; (cocktails) Shakers Piña Colada, Shakers Strawberry Daiquiri, Shakers Singapore Sling.

John Hall: A Taste for Adventure

Confucius once noted that if you find a job you love, you'll never work a day in your life. This blessing has graced winemaker and distiller John Hall, proprietor of Kittling Ridge Estate Wines and Spirits. With over thirty years of winemaking experience, John finds every moment of every day an exciting and enjoyable taste adventure.

With a formal education in microbiology, one of his first jobs was as a chemist for an international soup company, and one of his duties was to taste and approve hundreds of herbs and spices used for making soup. After a year of being an "official soup taster," John's palate was a finely honed tasting machine. Little did he know that this experience would be the key to opening a new world of opportunity. John's microbiology background and scholarly palate were about to lead him into his first winemaking venture.

John joined the ranks of Chateau Cartier, a relatively large Canadian winery, owned by Labatt Brewers in the late 1960s. Cartier owned 250 acres of experimental vineyards on the Niagara Bench. They were growing Chardonnay, Riesling, Gamay, and Cabernet Sauvignon. It was his work with these noble grape varieties from which John developed his winemaking style. But it was a far different market in those days. Canadians were drinking sweeter wines. A dry Chardonnay would not have pleased the consumer palate of the 1970s. With the increase in higher-quality restaurants and more exciting food choices being offered, Canadians' tastes evolved and consumers began demanding drier, higher-quality wines.

MAPLE LIQUEUR GLAZED APPLE TART

from Karen McGillivray,
Pastry Chef,
Kittling Ridge Winery Inn

FRUIT TOP
5 large Granny Smith apples, peeled, cored and cut into eighths
pinch of cinnamon
2 tbsp (30 ml) unsalted butter
1 cup (250 ml) sugar

BASE
4 large eggs, separated
½ cup (125 ml) sugar
⅓ cup (75 ml) Kittling Ridge Oh Canada Maple Liqueur
½ cup (125 ml) all-purpose flour, sifted
¼ tsp (1 ml) salt

GLAZE
¼ cup (60 ml) Kittling Ridge Oh Canada Maple Liqueur
¼ cup (60 ml) sugar

To make the caramelized fruit, melt the sugar in a frying pan until golden. Add the apples, cinnamon, and butter. Gently shake pan to coat apples, and cook until slightly tender. Remove from heat and strain apples through colander to remove excess caramel. Arrange apple wedges in circle on bottom of buttered frying pan.

To make the base, in a bowl combine the sugar and egg yolks. Whisk until fluffy. Slowly pour in the maple liqueur and continue whisking. Fold in the sifted flour. In a second bowl, beat egg whites with salt until peaks form. Gently fold whites into the yolk mixture. Pour the batter onto the caramelized apples in the frying pan. Bake for 13 to 15 minutes. Invert warm tart onto plate and brush with glaze.

For the glaze, combine the sugar and maple liqueur. Bring to a boil and melt the sugar. Brush top of apple tart with all of glaze.

WINE MATCH
Kittling Ridge Icewine & Brandy

In the early 1990s John left Cartier to start his own wine business. After three decades in the wine industry, John was ready to embrace a new challenge. Always looking at new ways to excite his own creative thirst, John was intrigued with the thought of expanding his winemaking repertoire. It didn't take long to discover Rieder Distillery in the town of Grimsby.

John purchased the distillery and added a winery. Now he had the added opportunity to explore the craft of distilling spirits, a process that had always fascinated him.

"Blush" is an American generic term that came about in the late 1970s for wines that vary in color from pale pink to salmon. Called **blanc de noir** *or* **rosé** *in France, they range from somewhat sweet to very dry.*

He changed the name to Kittling Ridge, a name based on the migrating hawks and eagles that soar on the spring air thermals (a breathtaking sight known as "kittling") above the Niagara Escarpment. The combination of the escarpment and the moderating effects of the lake that create the air thermals provides ideal growing conditions for tender grape varieties within the Niagara Peninsula.

Where an artist has several canvases on which to paint, the winemaker is limited to one "canvas" a year: a harvest; one vintage upon which to produce wines. While every winemaker appreciates the patience required to make wine, John soon realized that distilling fine spirits such as whiskey and brandy requires even greater patience and equal passion. While some wines might age in oak for two or three years before release, his whiskies and brandies are in oak for six, eight, twelve years or more.

With the ability to ferment wines and distill spirits all under one roof, John's first product combined his winemaker's art with his newly discovered still master's craft—a unique blend of icewine and seven-year barrel-aged brandy. Icewine & Brandy now boasts over twenty international awards and is John's own signature brand—the culmination of what a winery and distillery can be. One more taste adventure for his portfolio.

John started making his first whiskey in 1992, and it wasn't ready for release until 2000. Under the brand name Forty Creek, these handcrafted, copper pot distilled whiskies—Barrel Select and Three Grain—won gold and silver medals at the Brussels World Selection competitions in 2001. Not bad for a first-generation whiskey maker.

The Kittling Ridge facility was once the home of Rieder Distillery

With a penchant for fine whiskey and a knack for innovation, John translated his winemaking experience through to the art of distilling. Where distillers traditionally ferment, distill, and blend a variety of grains together, John treats each grain separately, as though it was a varietal wine. The rye, barley, and maize are prepared and aged individually to bring out their own unique character. The barrels are toasted to various degrees depending on the taste profiles of each grain. Where rye is lighter, fruitier, and more delicate, he uses a lightly toasted American oak barrel. In contrast, the more aggressive maize needs to be smoothed out, so he uses a heavier charred American oak barrel. Only when he is pleased with the taste profiles of each grain does he begin the blending process.

Proprietor, winemaker, and still master, John Hall

John's creative passion translates into a drive for innovation. The diverse Kittling Ridge product line satisfies his goal to provide products that can't be found anywhere else. With a third of his beverage production devoted to wine and two-thirds to spirits, you'll find a range of single varietal and blended wines and a host of unique spirits such as Inferno Vodka—with red peppers suspended inside the bottle for the Bloody Caesar fan. He's even created a Maple Cream liqueur labeled Oh Canada!

John's taste adventure has recently taken him to China, an old-world country embracing new-world fermenting and distilling methods. John has established a winery and distillery that is making vodka, whiskey, brandy, and wine from locally grown grains and varietal grapes in northwest China.

John firmly believes that innovation is his duty to consumers and that there are unlimited taste sensations awaiting discovery. John's taste adventure is a never-ending story and one that is still succeeding beyond even his wildest dreams.

Detected on the very tip of the tongue, sweetness in a wine usually comes from the residual sugar that is not turned into alcohol during fermentation. The term "sweet" is used to identify both flavor and bouquet.

Puddicombe Estate Winery

Although Puddicombe Estate Winery is relatively new, Puddicombe Farms has been growing vinifera and hybrid grapes since the 1960s, including Gamay, Chardonnay, Riesling, and Pinot Noir. Puddicombe grows 155 acres of grapes for both the juice and wine markets.

The winery produces a variety of wines from grapes selected from its estate vineyards. They include (white wines) Chardonnay, Sauvignon Blanc, Riesling, French

Well suited to cooler climates, the early ripening Cabernet Franc has been used by the French in their blends to salvage the effects of a poorer-quality Cabernet Sauvignon crop.

Pumpkins on Puddicombe Farm and Winery signal the arrival of harvest

Colombard, Viognier, Vidal, Seyval, Muscat; (red wines) Cabernet Franc, Foch, Gamay Noir, Pinot Noir, Meritage, Cabernet Sauvignon, Merlot; (icewines) Vidal, Riesling, Cabernet Franc; (fruit wines) Iced Apple, Peach, Cranberry, Strawberry, Raspberry, Pear.

Winemaker Lindsay Puddicombe has won awards at the All-Canadian Wine Championships and the North American Wine Competition.

Visiting Puddicombe Estate Winery is a unique experience. After touring the winery and sampling fine wines, visitors can take a train-ride tour of the farm, enjoy lunch or dinner in the Tea Room Restaurant, and purchase homemade baked goods, preserves, and other items from the general store. The farm also has a petting zoo and children's playground.

A Serious Family Tree

Puddicombe Estate Farms and Winery is well rooted with vines, fruit trees, and over 350 years of family history in North America.

Back in 1634 a fellow by the name of Edmund Lewis and his wife, Mary, left Devonshire, England, for America. Their passage was aboard the Ipswich, which took them to Lynn, Massachusetts, where they settled as cattle farmers. The Lewis family continued farming in Massachusetts for five generations until 1797 when Levi Lewis III, a staunch United Empire Loyalist, left to settle in Saltfleet Township in Ontario.

King George III granted Levi a land deed that included 800 acres stretching from Lake Ontario to Ridge Road, near the Niagara Escarpment. Levi established a new cattle farm, which the family managed throughout the early 1800s. By the 1850s Levi's son, James Lewis, took over the farm operations. With the help of his son-in-law, Isaac Brock Henry, they began planting fruit orchards. (Stick with us for the Puddicombe connection.) Isaac's son, James Edgar Henry, eventually married Ada Belle Carpenter in 1883.

(And here's the connection.) James Edgar's daughter, Clara, fell in love with J.B. Puddicombe and they were married in 1922. Puddicombe took over the farm when James Edgar passed away in 1938. Thirteen years later J.B. Puddicombe passed away and his son, Lewis, who had a diploma in agriculture from Guelph University, inherited the property.

In 1976 Lewis retired and his two sons, Murray and William Puddicombe, took over the farming operations.

STRAWBERRIES WITH WINE CREAM
—
from Puddicombe Estate Winery
—
Serves 4

2 tbsp (30 ml) Puddicombe Viognier White Wine, chilled
2 tbsp (30 ml) sugar
½ tsp (2 ml) vanilla
½ cup (125 ml) whipping cream
4 cups (1 L) fresh strawberries

Combine the wine, sugar, and vanilla in a chilled mixing bowl. Add the whipping cream and beat until soft peaks form. Serve immediately or cover and chill. Wash and hull the strawberries, and slice as desired. Spoon into dessert dishes and top with wine cream.

WINE MATCH
Puddicombe Estate Winery Iced Apple or Vidal Icewine

Sparkling wines are usually labeled according to their sweetness levels, with **brut** *or* **extra brut** *being the driest, and* **demi-sec** *or* **doux** *being the sweetest.*

Both boys were also graduates of Guelph University. In 1985 Murray purchased William's share, which now incorporates both a farm and a winery.

Following are some interesting and little-known facts about the family and property.

The original homestead built by Levi Lewis III in the 1800s burned to the ground in 1929 and was rebuilt the next year. Murray and his family still live in the rebuilt home.

Cattle farming ended in 1956 and fruit farming (which had started in the 1850s) became the agricultural mainstay for Puddicombe. Workhorses were slowly phased out as machinery was introduced and the last workhorse retired in 1966. Fruit from the farm was traditionally used by canning factories and wineries and was often shipped by train to Montreal and Winnipeg.

Over 20 fruit wineries are located throughout Ontario. To find out more about fruit wines and winery locations, call 1-877-839-6447 or visit FWO (Fruit Wines of Ontario) website at www. fruitwinesofontario.com

The five tenant houses on the property were built to house seasonal workers and are still in use. During World War II help came from Hamilton and environs, and students were recruited from the government Farm Service Force. If students worked the farm for thirteen consecutive weeks they were excused from writing final exams.

In 1989 Puddicombe Farms became the new home for Stoney Ridge Cellars, which had been started in 1985 with a partnership between Murray Puddicombe and winemaker Jim Warren. Several years later in 1998 Stoney Ridge Cellars was sold and moved to another Niagara location, and Jim went on to consult and advise new and upcoming wineries. Murray's wife, Carol, opened a retail store with baked goods and fruit sales. The farm grows a wide range of fruit and the main crop is now grapes for juice and wine production. Peaches, pears, cherries, apples, and strawberries are also grown for juice production and fruit wines.

In 1999 Lindsay Puddicombe (Murray and Carol's daughter) graduated from Guelph University and is now winemaker for the Puddicombe Estate Farms and Winery.

There has to be a movie in there somewhere! After such an illustrious family ancestry you can bet cattle to grapes this story's going to be continued. (No pressure on Lindsay implied!)

Other Niagara Peninsula Wineries

Sunnybrook Farm Estate Winery

Gerald and Vivien Goertz opened Sunnybrook in 1993 as the first winery in Canada to specialize in making wine from tree fruit and berries. Sunnybrook Winery produces wines from peaches, cherries, plums, apples, apricots, pears, strawberries, blueberries, and blackberries, most of which are grown on the Sunnybrook farm.

The wines made from 100% Ontario fruit include 4 Poire Sec, Empire Apple, Damson Plum, Golden Plum, Bosc Pear, Wild Blueberry, Fantasia Nectarine, Black Raspberry, Cherry, Strawberry, Golden Peach, Blackberry, Spiced Apple, and Iced Cherry.

Fruit wines were produced in Niagara as early as the 1700s when locally made apple wine was very popular. Gerald grew up in the fruit-growing industry, working in his father's fruit processing plant. His expertise is being passed on to his daughter Rebecca who now assists with the winemaking.

Visitors are welcome to enjoy the fine fruit wines of Sunnybrook.

FAST FACTS

1425 Lakeshore Road
Niagara-on-the-Lake, Ontario
L0S 1J0
Tel: 905-468-1122
Web:
www.sunnybrookfarmwinery.com

The terms "oaky" and "oakiness" are used to describe the desirable toasty, vanilla flavor and fragrance of wines that are in proper balance.

Fruit farm wineries are becoming increasingly popular

Thomas and Vaughan Vintners

A family estate winery, Thomas and Vaughan is owned and operated by Thomas Kocsis and Barbara Vaughan. Both have a viticultural background and Thomas is a second-generation grape grower.

On their seventy-five acres, Thomas and Vaughan produce vinifera and hybrid varietals, with many vines that are more than twenty-five years old. Varietals include (white wines) Vidal, Pinot Gris, Riesling, Chardonnay; (red wines) Dechaunac, Baco Noir, Marechal Foch, Cabernet Franc, Cabernet Sauvignon, Merlot; (dessert wines) Vidal Icewine and Late Harvest Vidal.

The winery offers guided tours of the vineyard and winery with wine tastings. Reservations are required for large groups. Special events are also held throughout the year.

"Microclimate," or **terroir** *in French, is the term used by winemakers to describe environmental factors affecting the quality and taste profile of grapes.*

Thomas and Vaughan Winery and boutique

Lakeview Cellars Estate Winery

Founded in 1991 by Eddie and Lorraine Gurinskas and set on thirteen acres, Lakeview Cellars is one of Niagara's first boutique wineries. Winemaker Eddie has won many national and international awards for his outstanding wines.

Lakeview produces a large variety of wines. They include (white wines) Chardonnay, Pinot Gris, Riesling, Gewurztraminer, Chardonnay Musque, Vidal; (red wines) Gamay Noir, Gamay Zweigelt, Pinot Noir, Zweigelt, Baco Noir, Marechal Foch, Merlot, Cabernet Sauvignon, Cabernet Franc, Meritage; (dessert wines) Late Harvest

Vidal, Riesling Icewine, Gewurztraminer Icewine, Vidal Icewine, Late Harvest Riesling.

A unique aspect about Lakeview is a public tour that is conducted in the vineyard rather than the production area of the winery. Visitors are led through the vines by one of Lakeview's experienced wine consultants who provides an informative and in-depth discussion on topics that include the winery's history, terroir, canopy management, and other vineyard practices that affect the flavors and style of the wines produced. Visitors then have an opportunity to sample four of Lakeview's outstanding wines in the middle of the vineyard.

Zweigelt, developed in 1922 by Dr. Zweigelt, is a cross-breeding of the Blau-Frankisch and St.-Laurent varietals and is one of Austria's most popular dark-berried grapes.

In addition to the vineyard tours, Lakeview has a fully licensed event room, which seats between sixty and seventy-five and overlooks Lake Ontario and the lush vineyards below.

Harbour Estates Winery

Located on one of the most unique properties in the Niagara Peninsula, Harbour Estates Winery has 1,800 feet of frontage on Jordan Harbour—part of Lake Ontario—and has developed trail systems through their woods and will soon have a boardwalk on the harbor.

Harbour Estates is dedicated to the production of fine VQA wines with an emphasis on red viniferas. Thirty acres of red vinifera varietals include Cabernet Sauvignon, Cabernet Franc, and Merlot. VQA wines include (white wines) Chardonnay, Sauvignon Blanc, Riesling,

FAST FACTS

4362 Jordan Road
Jordan Station, Ontario
L0R 1S0
Tel: 905-562-6279
Fax: 905-562-3829
E-mail: info@hewwine.com
Web: www.hewwine.com

Sometimes referred to as "Traminer," Gewurztraminer (guh-vurts-trah-mee-ner)— cultivated for over a thousand years—is thought to have originated in Tramin or Temeno in Italy's Alto Adige region.

Gewurztraminer, Vidal; (red wines) Cabernet, Gamay Noir, Gamay Zweigelt. The winery also produces icewines and a fruit wine called Fragole, a wine produced from strawberries grown on the winery property.

Visitors are welcome to enjoy Harbour Estate wines in the wine boutique and special barbecue and other events during the year.

Royal DeMaria Wines

Royal DeMaria Wines is unique in focusing exclusively on the production of icewines. Winemaker Joseph DeMaria started producing icewine in Niagara in 1993. Since then the family estate winery has grown significantly and now specializes in producing twelve varieties of icewine. These include Vidal, Riesling, Gewurztraminer, Pinot Gris, Pinot Blanc, Chenin Blanc, Cabernet Franc, Chardonnay, Muscat Ottonel, Gamay, Sauvignon Blanc, and Merlot. Current markets for their icewines include Canada, the United States, and Europe. Visitors are welcome by appointment only.

Harvest Estate Wines

A vaulted ceiling and floor-to-roof stone fireplace create a warm chalet feeling to Harvest Estate winery, which specializes in fruit wines in addition to producing VQA wines.

Wines include (white wines) Riesling, Pinot Gris, Chardonnay; (red wines) Baco Noir, Zweigelt, Cabernet Franc, Marechal Foch, Merlot, Cabernet Sauvignon, Cabernet Merlot. The winery also produces Riesling Icewine and Late Harvest Vidal. Harvest Estate produces a variety of exotic fruit wines including rhubarb, iced blueberry, cranberry, and iced peach.

Visitors can get free tastings in the wine boutique and enjoy the adjoining fruit market, bakery, and deli in a country atmosphere.

Birchwood Estate Wines

Birchwood is a small, charming winery set on approximately ten acres of planted vinifera vines near the town of Beamsville.

The winery produces a variety of wines, including VQA wines (white wines) Gewurztraminer/Riesling, Auxerrois, Pinot Gris, Chardonnay; (red wines) Cabernet Franc, Baco Noir, Cabernet Franc/Merlot; (icewine) Vidal Icewine.

Traditional negotiants bought, matured, often blended, bottled, and then shipped wine. The term négociant éleveur is sometimes noted on a label and suggests that the merchant played a role in actually making the wine.

The winery is open daily to visitors. Wine orders can be placed by contacting the winery directly.

Crown Bench Estates Winery

Situated in one of the most scenic and natural areas of the Niagara Peninsula, Crown Bench produces a variety of white, red, and dessert wines.

FAST FACTS

3850 Aberdeen Road
Beamsville, Ontario
L0R 1B7
Tel: 905-563-3959
E-mail:
winery@crownbenchestates.com
Web: www.crownbenchestates.com

On the southern border of the winery is the Niagara Escarpment, a World Biosphere Reserve. The Bruce Trail is only about 110 yards (100 meters) behind the winery. Spectacular views from the winery include Lake Ontario far below and the Toronto skyline in the distance. The natural features of the Crown Bench property include streams, waterfalls, ponds with nesting Canada geese and ducks, and bordering forests.The winery produces VQA red wines that include Cabernet Franc, Merlot, Gamay Noir, Pinot Noir, and Crown Bench's flagship blend red of Cabernet Sauvignon, Cabernet Franc, and Merlot. White wines include Chardonnay and Vidal; dessert wines Vidal Icewine, Winter Harvest, and Livia's Gold VQA, a Crown Bench innovation in the style of a Sauterne that is an early harvest botrytis-affected Chardonnay. Visitors are welcome to tour the winery and taste some of their fine wines.

Kacaba Vineyards

FAST FACTS

3550 King Street
Vineland, Ontario
Tel: 905-562-5625
Web: www.kacabavineyards.com

Kacaba Vineyards is a truly family affair with Michael Kacaba, his wife, Joanne, and three daughters involved in the business. The opening of Kacaba has been a dream come true for Michael, the descendant of two European families.

A silver bridge, acquired from the St. Lawrence Seaway, leads to Kacaba Vineyards off the Highway 8 wine route in Vineland. The bridge crosses a ravine, which has been terraced for the planting of Syrah vines. Across the bridge is a 1998 planting of Cabernet Sauvignon, Cabernet Franc, and Merlot. The winery and vineyard is part of the com-

Kacaba Vineyards Winery

munity with local residents walking and jogging through the property.

Kacaba wines include (white wines) Riesling, Chardonnay, Chardonnay on Oak; (red wines) Cabernet Franc, Merlot, Pinot Noir, Rose; (dessert wines) Late Harvest Vidal and Icewine. Wines can be purchased at the winery store or through a distributor.

Angels Gate Winery

With a new winery facility opening in the summer of 2002, founders David and Catharine Burr with winemaker Natalie Spytkowsky are producing a variety of excellent white, red, and dessert wines.

The wines include (white wines) Chardonnay, Riesling, Gewurztraminer; (red wines) Pinot Noir, Merlot, Cabernet Sauvignon, Cabernet Franc. Angels Gate also produces Riesling Icewine and Cabernet Franc Icewine.

FAST FACTS

4260 Mountainview Road
Beamsville, Ontario
L0R 1B2
Tel: 905-563-3942
Fax: 905-563-4127
Web: www.angelsgatewinery.com

The new Angels Gate Winery

Greater Toronto Area

Southbrook Winery

FAST FACTS

1061 Major MacKenzie Drive
Maple, Ontario
L6A 3P2
Tel: 905-832-2548
Fax: 905-832-9811
E-mail: office@southbrook.com
Web: www.southbrook.com

The history of Southbrook Winery can be traced back to Southbrook Farms, a successful market garden in Richmond Hill, Ontario. The market, owned by Bill and Marilyn Redelmeier, had its humble beginnings selling corn from a roadside picnic table in 1984.

Southbrook Farms was known for its top-quality produce, which led to a very successful market garden. That success translated into the opening of Southbrook Winery, which began producing wines in 1991 with Derek Barnett as winemaker. A year later, during a rainy picking season at the farm's self-picking raspberry fields, an over-abundance of fruit led to the production of the winery's first fruit wine, Canadian Framboise. In 1996 Framboise became the first Ontario wine in history to be carried by Harrods department store in England. Southbrook Winery has never looked back, and they have won over fifty international fruit wine awards. Bill has played an important role in the development of the industry as the founder and chair of the Fruit Wines of Canada.

Proprietors Bill and Marilyn Redelmeier

Winemaker Derek Barnett

Traditional bottle shapes and colours can be indicative of the type of wine inside

Southbrook sources grapes from Niagara-region growers for its VQA products and produces approximately 7,000 cases a year. Now headed by winemaker Colin Campbell, Southbrook produces wines that include (white wines) Chardonnay, Pinot Gris, Sauvignon Blanc, and Vidal; (red wines) Pinot Noir, Merlot, Cabernet Franc, Cabernet Merlot, and Cabernet Sauvignon; (dessert wines) Late Harvest Vidal, Vidal Icewine, Gewurztraminer Icewine, and Riesling Icewine.

Berries for Southbrook's fruit wines are grown on the Southbrook estate and sourced from Ontario growers. Annual production of 7,000 cases includes Framboise, Cassis, Blueberry, and Blackberry.

Southbrook Winery has earned more than 150 international awards at competitions including the All-Canadian Wine Championships, the World Wine Championships in the U.S., and wine competitions in the U.K.

Southbrook wines are available in the provinces of British Columbia, Alberta, Manitoba, Ontario, and Quebec and in the United States, the U.K., Germany, France, Taiwan, and Hong Kong. Wines can also be purchased seven days a week at the Southbrook Winery store.

SAUTÉED CHICKEN BREAST WITH FRAMBOISE AND CREAM

Serves 4

4 chicken breasts
3 tbsp (45 ml) clarified butter or
   olive oil
1 tbsp (5 ml) fresh rosemary
juice of ½ a lemon
2 oz (60 ml) brandy
4 oz (125 ml) Southbrook Winery
   Framboise
4 oz (125 g) whipping cream
salt and freshly ground black pepper

Heat the butter or oil in a skillet or frying pan until very hot. Add the chicken breasts and sauté until golden brown and cooked through. Add rosemary, salt, and pepper while cooking.

When the meat is cooked, add brandy, and flame or boil off the alcohol. Scrape any bits of meat from the bottom of the pan, reduce heat, and add Framboise.

After approximately 30 seconds, remove the meat to a heated or covered platter. Add the lemon juice.

Put the heat up to medium high and reduce the liquid until quite thick (about ⅓ of the original quantity). Remove from heat and slowly add cream while whisking the mixture. Pour in any juices accumulated on the platter and mix into the sauce. Add meat for about 2 to 3 minutes on very low heat. Do not bring to boil again.

Serve the chicken breasts with the sauce poured on top and with boiled new potatoes and sweet corn.

WINE MATCH
Southbrook Winery Chardonnay

The McMichael Canadian Art Collection

Wine country in and around Toronto has a treat that will delight any visitor. Cilento, Magnotta, and Southbrook wineries are all within a short distance of this national treasure.

The McMichael Canadian Art Collection is situated in a dream house in the woods—a log cabin—and its location is idyllic! Signe and Robert McMichael carefully built their country retreat and wanted others to share the beauty of the surrounding nature. Their imaginations were captured by a hardy band of artists who attempted to lay bare the Canadian landscape. They wanted to share this vision, and building the log cabin was only the first of many steps taken to realize their dream in the rolling country just north of Toronto in the village of Kleinberg. And the McMichael Trail is situated on over 100 acres of woodland that showcases wildlife, natural beauty, artwork, and historic sites that will enchant any visitors who give their spirit over to the beckoning wilderness.

View of Inukshuk at the McMichael Collection

Starting with 194 paintings, the McMichael Collection has grown into a major international gallery housing almost 6,000 works of art. Canadian artworks by Inuit and First Nations artists are displayed along with pieces by the renowned Group of Seven and their contemporaries. Tom Thomson, one of the Group of Seven, has helped to represent the adventurous spirit of Canadians bent on taming the landscape. He drew nature, glimmering and sparkling, on tiny pieces of canvas. His colorful and emotional paintings now inspire many to question the confines of modern space.

Robert and Signe sought to showcase the infant steps of the artists towards artistic maturity and to celebrate the Canadian identity. Their determination to do this led to a much wider recognition of Canadian art than they ever dreamed. The art of Canada found a loving home and the beginning of a large extended family that continues to grow with each new visitor.

For an exciting preview of the gallery and its breathtaking location, visit the comprehensive website at www.mcmichael.com. It features a showcase of current exhibitions and virtual tours of their extensive collection. Anyone, young or old, with an interest in art will be treated to a memorable visit and will resolve to return again and again. When in wine country this is a surefire stopover that no one will regret.

Enjoying the setting overlooking the valley

OAK RIDGES MISO DUCK

—

from EDO Chef/Owner
Barry Chaim

—

Appetizer—Serves 4

12 oz (350 g) duck breasts, boneless with skin
16 oz (500 g) white miso paste
2 oz (60 ml) sake
2 oz (60 ml) mirin
1 tsp (5 ml) fresh ginger, finely grated
snow peas, for garnish
5, 20-in (50-cm) metal skewers

Trim excess fat from the breast of duck. Insert one end of each skewer into the breast about 4 inches (50 cm). Holding the other end of the skewer, roast the duck skin-side down about 3 inches (8 cm) over the grill, allowing fat to drip off and skin to tighten. Turn over and roast the other side until meat just begins to change color. Put the duck into a bowl of ice water to stop the cooking process.

Combine the miso, sake, mirin, and ginger to form a marinade. When the duck is cold, remove from the water and pat dry with paper towels. Put the duck into the marinade and let sit in the refrigerator for 2 days.

Wash excess marinade from duck. Grill on medium high heat until golden brown on one side (cooked medium).

Slice the meat into diagonal strips. Pour boiling water over the snow peas in a small bowl and let sit for about 2 minutes until cooked. Arrange the duck slices on four small plates. Garnish with snow peas.

WINE MATCH
Puddicombe Pinot Noir

"Nose" is a general wine term that refers to the olfactory sense of smelling wine, and is commonly used to note the intensity of wine aroma and bouquet, and to detect any defects or imbalances.

Corks showing labels of Greater Toronto Area wineries

Cilento Wines

In 1997 Angelo and Grace Locilento opened their dream winery, a new 36,000 square foot California mission-style building housing a wine boutique and barrel aging cellar. Since then they have not looked back. Recognized internationally as a success story with gold medals at prestigious international competitions in their short time in the wine business, they have continued to produce a variety of quality VQA wines.

They include (white wines) Seyval Blanc, Riesling, Chardonnay, Auxerrois, Sauvignon Blanc; (red wines) Baco Foch, Marechal Foch, Cabernet, Baco Noir, Cabernet Sauvignon, Merlot, and Pinot Noir. Dessert wines include Select Late Harvest, Vidal Icewine, Riesling Icewine, Gewurztraminer Icewine; and sparkling wines Cilento Spumante (pink) and Riesling Brut.

The winery features special events, wine seminars, and cooking demonstrations. Visitors interested in touring the winery are encouraged to call 888-245-WINE to arrange for individual or group tours.

Vinoteca Winery

Vinoteca was founded in 1989 as the first winery in the Greater Toronto Area. Giovanni and Rosanna Follegot coined the name of the winery from "vino" (wine) and "teca" (a chest for special treasures). The Follegots believe that the name conveys the spirit and sincerity with which the family runs their business.

FAST FACTS

672 Chrislea Road
Woodbridge, Ontario
L4L 8K9
Tel: 905-264-9463
Fax: 905-264-8671
E-mail: cilento@ica.net
Web: www.cilento.com

FAST FACTS

527 Jevlan Drive
Woodbridge, Ontario
L4L 8W1
Tel: 905-856-5700
Fax: 905-856-8208
Web: www.toronto.com/vinoteca

In 1992 the family purchased vineyards in the Vineland area of Niagara to establish a sustainable production of vinifera grapes for their VQA wines supplemented by imported grapes from Giovanni's own Italian vineyard.

Vinoteca wines include (white wines) Pinot Grigio, Sauvignon Blanc, Riesling, Chardonnay; (red wines) Cabernet Sauvignon, Merlot, Pinot Noir, Cabernet Merlot. The winery also produces a variety of icewines.

Vinoteca has won a number of awards at international wine competitions in Italy, France, and England. The winery is open daily to visitors for winery tours and tastings.

"Maceration" is the period of time the grape juice spends in contact with the skins and seeds, and an extended maceration will increase the wine's depth of color and intensify its aroma characteristics.

Magnotta Winery (Vaughan)

We said "Mag-notta" and Gabe said "Mun-yotta". No matter how you pronounce it, Gabe and Rossana Magnotta have built one of Ontario's most prolific winery and beverage companies. Their Niagara winery, located in Beamsville is one of seven locations featuring the diverse and eclectic Magnotta product line. It is however worth taking the trip to their Head Office located in Vaughan just north of Toronto. In Vaughan you'll find an expansive winery and boutique that is graced with original art from all over the world; art that has been chosen for labels to reflect the essence found in each bottled product.

Magnotta has become one of Ontario's leaders in beverage innovation. Their lengthy list of Ontario-produced VQA wines is augmented by a wide range of single varietal and blended wines in their International Series, for which they have sourced grapes and juices from all over the world.

Gabe and Rossana have adopted a philosophy that strives to please almost every taste. Visitors to any of their seven locations will find their ingenious sparkling icewines (made from Vidal and Cabernet Franc) a range of sparkling wines, dessert wines and just about any varietal or blended wine you might think of. Magnotta has also experienced notable success with their bag-in-the-box wines.

As a one-stop beverage shop, Magnotta offers various beers, a wide selection of fortified wines (ports, vermouth and sherries) a sacramental white wine, and several distilled spirits from their Still Master. By the time you visit, we're confident they will have added something new to their list.

FAST FACTS

Head Office, Gallery and Boutique
271 Chrislea Road
Vaughan, Ontario
L4L 8N6
Tel: 905-738-9463
or 1-800-461-9463
Fax: 905-738-5551
E-mail: info@magnotta.com
Web: www.magnotta.com

The Fellowship of Wine

We had the pleasure of meeting a delightful wine connoisseur on one of our shoots. He didn't have any pretensions about the enjoyment of wine. He only knew that a wine had to be good to be appreciated, and it was good if the person drinking it liked it! A story he told reminded us that the fellowship of wine is a rare and beautiful thing. The story goes something like this…

For many years our man had worked in the hospitality business in Europe and Canada. In order to keep a remarkable wine cellar for the owners of the hotel he served, he would be sent on a trek each year to secure the best wines he could find from various regions.

On a particular venture to Italy, one of his goals was to acquire the best Barolo he could find. Somewhere along the line an acquaintance had told him about two brothers who lived in the hills near a quaint village and made a limited number of Barolo wines. However, the brothers did not take kindly to strangers, and so the acquaintance provided a label with his signature on it. The signed label, coupled with his ability to speak some Italian, would guarantee the traveler an opportunity to sample the wines and procure them for the hotel.

After hours of driving and getting lost several times, he finally came upon the small house on the hill where the brothers made their wines. There were no signs or billboards announcing that he had arrived at the place where one of the world's best (if not *the* best) Barolo wines were made. It was all very understated. With the signed label in hand, the visitor approached the gate to the yard. An older man was already making his way down the pathway from the house. They met at the gate and when he handed over the signed label, the man, who was the winemaker, welcomed him onto the property.

There was no formal tasting room or retail shop. The wine was made in the basement in a variety of large glass carboys, which were lined up from wall to wall. They sat on some crates, and the man's wife brought some cheeses and bread, then disappeared as quickly as she had arrived. While some introductory remarks were exchanged, the winemaker shuffled about and siphoned some wine from a carboy into two glasses. This was the first sampling of many to follow.

They had a most enjoyable time talking, and the wine was without doubt the best, most incredible Barolo our man had ever tasted. It was in a class by itself and was a remarkable find. After a few hours, many wine samples, and several servings of food, the visitor brought up the subject of cost. The winemaker looked up and shook his head. The wine was not for sale!

This was a shock. The winemaker spoke of his brother, who had always grown the grapes and had died almost a year earlier. Since the wines were grown in the vineyard and the brothers had made them together, the surviving brother felt that selling the wine would betray his love and respect for his brother. His brother's death had brought their business to an end.

Despite the visitor's pleadings and offerings of substantial amounts of money, there was no deal to be had. The winemaker was vehement. The wine was not for sale—not to anyone, at any price.

The sun began setting and there was no way the winemaker could be swayed. The meeting had to come to an end. The winemaker was complimented on the wines he made and thanked for sharing such a remarkable experience. One that would never be forgotten. As they walked out from the basement and down the hill, they saw the winemaker's wife at the back of the visitor's car with the trunk open.

When they reached the car she had just finished loading a third case of Barolo wines. Our man turned to the winemaker in disbelief, noting that it was clear the wines were not for sale. The winemaker patted the traveler on the shoulder and offered a humble smile. The wines were not for sale. They were for him to enjoy.

Perhaps this is one of the reasons they say "you'll find the winemaker's heart in the bottle."

Pelee Island and Lake Erie North Shore

Lake Erie North Shore and Pelee Island is the oldest commercial grape-growing area in Canada. Situated in the western part of Lake Erie and at Canada's southernmost point of inhabited land, Pelee Island is a unique microclimate.

On the same latitude as some of the prestigious wine regions of the world—including California, Portugal, Spain, Italy, Germany, and France—the fertile soil, summer heat, and warm, shallow waters of Lake Erie combine to create a perfect climate to grow grapes.

Pelee Island is home to the rarest natural habitat in the province of Ontario. Honey Locust, Hop Trees, Prickly Pear Cactus and Sassafras are

Carlo Negri instructs Jonathan in the use of a refractometer

Erie Shore vineyard in Harrow

examples of plants that thrive in the unique geological conditions on the island. The soils on the island are shallow glacial deposits of clay over a limestone bedrock, since Pelee Island was once a coral reef. While the island is ideal for grape growing, dedicated bird watchers visit to witness the seasonal bird migration of hundreds of species.

The island also offers a number of other attractions including fishing, hiking, biking, and charming bed and breakfasts.

Pelee Island Winery

FAST FACTS

455 Seacliff Drive, County Road #20
Kingsville, Ontario
N9Y 2K5
Tel: 519-733-6551
Fax: 519-733-6553
E-mail: inquiries@peleeisland.com
Web: www.peleeisland.com

"Wine was created from the beginning to make men joyful, and not to make men drunk. Wine used in moderation is the joy of the soul and the heart."

Ecclesiastes 31: 35–36

Pelee Island Winery is Canada's largest estate-owned winery with approximately 600 acres of vineyards planted with mainly European vitis vinifera varietals including Chardonnay, Pinot Noir, Cabernet, and Merlot. The vineyards are located on Pelee Island, Canada's southernmost point of inhabited land and the largest of the Lake Erie islands. The vineyards are on the same latitude as many of the prestigious wine regions of the world including Napa Valley, California, Portugal, Spain, Italy, Germany, and France.

During the harvest, grapes are shipped to the winery on the mainland for processing. The winery production facilities are located in Kingsville, only thirty minutes from the Ambassador Bridge between Windsor, Ontario, and Detroit, Michigan. The winery has a fermentation and storage capacity of 2.4 million liters and a barrel aging cellar with 150 French, Hungarian, and American barriques. Capacity can reach 2,800 bottles a day.

Over the last decade, Pelee Island Winery has won dozens of domestic and international awards for their outstanding wines. For example, in 1999 the winery won a gold medal at one of the world's most prestigious competitions—VinItaly in Verona—for its 1997 Cabernet Sauvignon, VQA. In 2001 it won a gold medal for its 1999 Vidal Icewine at Intervin International.

Visitors can take a detailed tour through the winery cellars and watch an informational video. After the tour there is an opportunity to taste some of their fine wines while learning about wine tasting techniques and etiquette. On Pelee Island, visitors can tour the vineyards, taste some of the outstanding wines, and enjoy a barbecue lunch in the wine garden at the Wine Pavilion, with beautiful views overlooking Lake Erie.

Pelee Island Winery in Kingsville

Pelee Island Winery products can be purchased at their local winery store, at LCBO stores, across Canada, and through distributors in the U.S. and internationally.

Some of their VQA products include (red wines) Cabernet Merlot, Cabernet Franc, Baco Noir, Pinot Noir, Zweigelt-Gamay Noir; (white wines) Chardonnay, Sauvignon Blanc, Gewurztraminer, Monarch Vidal, Pinot Gris, Riesling; (dessert wines) Late Harvest Vidal, Vidal Icewine.

Walter Schmoranz: Home Is Where the Heart Is

Walter Schmoranz is not one for pretentious wine talk. While he can—if he wants to—muster an array of impressive descriptors about any wine, Walter prefers to enjoy drinking it at the table with good food, good company, and hearty conversation. In most European families wine is a staple at the dinner table to be enjoyed with food and good conversation. Isn't that what wine's all about?

Walter Schmoranz is patient with Jonathan

Raised in the heart of German wine country, Walter grew up in Ruedesheim (*heim* translates as "home") along the famous Rhine River and just north of Mittelheim (loosely translates as "middle home").

As a young man living in the renowned Rheingau wine region of Germany, it wasn't difficult to find part-time work in vineyards and wineries. This was a great hands-on opportunity but Walter's real interest in wine sprang from his father, who taught winemaking at the distinguished Geisenheim College and University. His winemaking apprenticeship began in 1976, and he also pursued academic credentials in Weinsberg from 1980 to 1982.

After receiving his degree in viticulture and enology he worked as a winemaker and vineyard manager in Eltville,

RABBIT À LA CACCIATORE
—
from Chef Anthony DelBrocco, Kingsville Golf and Country Club
—
Serves 4

½ cup (125 ml) all-purpose flour
salt and pepper
1 rabbit cut into 8 pieces
4 tbsp (60 ml) extra virgin olive oil
4 cloves garlic, finely chopped
1 medium Spanish onion, chopped
   ½-inch (15-mm) dice
2 red bell peppers, chopped
   ½-inch dice
1 green bell pepper, chopped
   ½-inch dice
1 cup (250 ml) mushrooms, cut
   into halves
1 tbsp (15 ml) of rosemary, chopped
zest of 1 orange
1 cup (250 ml) dry white wine
2 cups (500 ml) plum tomatoes,
   pureed
2 tbsp (30 ml) Italian parsley,
   chopped

Season the flour with salt and pepper. Rinse and pat dry the rabbit pieces, dredge in flour, and shake off excess.
In a heavy bottom saucepan, heat the olive oil and cook the pieces of rabbit until golden brown, about 20 minutes, remove, and set aside.
   To the pot add garlic, onions, peppers, and mushrooms and cook until softened, about 8 to 10 minutes. Add the rosemary, orange zest, and half the parsley.
   Deglaze with white wine, add tomatoes, and bring to a boil.
   Add rabbit pieces, lower the temperature to a simmer, and cook until the meat is tender and the sauce has reduced by two-thirds, about 35 to 40 minutes.
   Check for seasoning and place on a serving platter. Garnish with a sprig of rosemary and sprinkled chopped parsley and serve.

WINE MATCH
Pelee Island Zweigelt Reserve

Vintner Walter Schmoranz (left)
and winemaker Martin Janz

*Lemberger, commonly
known as Blaufrankisch
(blouw-frahn-keesh), is a
grape that produces lighter-
style reds with good acidity
and is most widely planted
in Austria, Hungary, and
Germany.*

*Sauvignon Blanc is the
vine variety responsible for
some of the world's most
distinctive popular dry
white French wines such as
Sancerre. When used as a
blending wine for both dry
and sweet wines, it adds a
desired zest.*

a Rheingau region winery. However, limitations imposed
by regulations and agricultural laws were strictly rooted
in centuries of winemaking traditions, which made it
difficult if not impossible for the young winemaker to
strike out on his own and influence change. Vineyards
and wineries had been in families since the 1600s. Land
practices, varietals grown, and vinification techniques
were rigidly established. Young winemakers were
trained to carry on these practices, not to alter them.
Walter became increasingly interested in "new world"
winemaking opportunities. He applied for work with a
winery in New York.

In September of 1983 Walter was invited by the
Gehringer brothers—two college friends from the
Geisenheim—to spend his vacation in British Columbia.
The brothers were part of a second-generation Canadian
winemaking family and had already established a winery
in the Okanagan Valley. It was Walter's first trip to
Canada and he was immediately taken by the expansive,
pristine beauty of the valley.

Shortly after his return to Germany Walter read an
unusual advertisement in a wine trade magazine. He
remembers it clearly because it read more like a placement
for an executive of an automotive company than a winery.
A winery in Canada needed a "manager" with winemaking experience. Walter had already accepted a job as
a winemaker in Long Island, New York, but the paper-
work to get his Green Card was taking forever. Hungry
for a new-world winemaking opportunity, Walter applied
for the position and within weeks was accepted. He and
his wife had to move to Canada without delay. He was
excited at the prospect of seeing mountains again, but as
he soon discovered, Ontario was very different from
British Columbia. Welcome to Pelee Island.

Walter quickly came to appreciate the remarkable natural flora and fauna history of the region. Pelee Island is
well known by bird watchers, who gather there by the
thousands every year, and the area also has a substantial
history in Canadian winemaking folklore. American businessmen from Ohio had established Canada's first commercial winery, Vin Villa, on the island in the 1860s. It
went on to win a medal in a Paris wine competition in
the early 1900s. (Wine in those days was heavily fortified
and wouldn't appeal to most contemporary palates.) Vin
Villa also had a lucrative business in providing sacramental wines.

Impressed by the region's unique wildlife and rare
flora, Walter drew on his love of nature and instituted a

new label design for Pelee Island wines. With the new world emphasizing single varietal wines, Walter sensed the need to establish an easy way for consumers to identify and remember Pelee's wines. In 1988 the first nature label premiered with a red-winged blackbird signifying a Pelee Island Pinot Noir.

The subsequent releases of other nature labels that were selected to reflect the essence of the wines were well received by consumers. The vivid yellow Prickly Pear Cactus dressed the label of Pelee Island Gewurztraminer. To this day some consumers still buy their selection by asking for the "yellow flowered" wine. Simple, straightforward, and easy for consumers to remember—a customer service that also promoted the environment in which Pelee Island thrives.

The host samples yet another fabulous wine

Walter's approach to winemaking reinforces the need for improving quality through every means at his disposal. Site selection, row planting orientation, canopy management, rootstock selection, drainage, etc.—all the critical elements that add up to the definition of the final product are on his radar. Walter shrugs at his more formal title of wine master, and in his straightforward, candid fashion suggests that the best way to assure the highest quality wine is to continue learning from each step and to minimize the number of mistakes that can be made. Winemaking is definitely a team approach.

While awards and critical acclaim warm Walter's heart, the greatest honor bestowed upon Pelee Island wines continues to be by their loyal customers. Establishing enduring relationships with people and the environment is second nature to Walter. Wine is his calling card and, like the old saying, "the winemaker's heart is in the bottle," you'll find Walter's on the label.

A table setting inside a wine barrel

Winemaker's Matches
Walter Schmoranz, Pelee Island

White Wine: Sauvignon Blanc
Food: Lake Erie perch or pickerel lightly seasoned with lemon and pepper, served with a side dish of cold asparagus that's been lightly steamed (still crunchy) and marinated in the refrigerator for a couple of hours in some olive oil, chopped fresh garlic, and onions to taste
Comment: Simple and sensational.

Red Wine: Zweigelt Reserve
Food: Moose (or substitute rabbit) prepared in a ragout with red peppers, a bit of hot pepper, and simmered in some Zweigelt wine and broth
Comment: Try it!

Point Pelee and Pelee Island

Pelee Island Winery has two sites, one on the mainland and the other, Pelee Island Pavilion, on the island proper. The area of Pelee Island and Point Pelee is a unique environment and a wonderful place to stop in wine country.

For the curious traveler, Point Pelee is a pure delight at harvest time. You won't want to miss the butterfly tree. It's an annual event, produced by hundreds of roosting Monarchs. It delights the senses with its sheer beauty. And it'll make you think: How and why? It was only recently that we discovered where the Monarchs spend the winter months, when the colony was discovered 10,000 feet (3,000 meters) above sea level in the Sierra Madre Mountains of Mexico.

Monarchs belong to a family of butterflies whose origins are tropical. They are unable to stand freezing temperatures during their lifecycle. Mother Nature has allowed them over millennia to expand their breeding territory into the extensive milkweed fields of the U.S.A. and Canada.

Pelee Island is a 12-mile (20-kilometer) ferry ride from the mainland. It feels like time has been suspended somewhere in the 1950s or thereabouts. It's a quiet haven for simple souls who cherish the rustic country style of a relaxed pace. That is, it is quiet most of the time except when the island hosts the annual pheasant hunt in October and November. The island is literally overrun by hunters after the game birds. Hundreds of hunters throng the tiny countryside, blasting away at everything that moves. It is tolerated as the influx of much-needed tourist dollars compensates for the racket and disruption. Every available surface is given over to sleeping arrangements for tired hunters: hallways, broom

The Pavilion on Pelee Island

A bird's-eye view of Pelee Island

closets, garages, anywhere. The din during the long weekend is said to be ear-shattering.

The word "hunt" is really a misnomer. A flock of
captured birds are transported to the island a day or so
before the marathon hunt begins. This gives the pheasants
time to find cover. The birds are so disoriented that they
tend to cluster together and so prove to be simple targets.
Well, just think of the boon to the economy and try to
avoid visiting on that weekend.

The Art of Labels

Baron Philippe de Rothschild is often credited with developing the concept of artists' wine labels, and he has established one of the finest international collections of wine-related works of art.

PELEE ISLAND WINERY

1999

Pelee Rouge

1 Litre   Red Wine / Vin Rouge   12.4% alc./vol.
Product of Canada / Produit du Canada

PELEE ISLAND WINERY

2000
Gewürztraminer
VQA Ontario VQA

12.5% alc./vol.   750 ml
White Wine / Vin Blanc
Product of Canada / Produit du Canada

Price can often indicate the quality of a wine but labels are usually the winemaker's first opportunity to make an impression on consumers. Vintners put a great deal of time, thought, and money into the design of their labels. An attractive label can seduce the shopper into making the purchase. Labels are created to deliver information and, more important, to convey a positive first impression. A label is a signature for the winemaker and a memory bank, good or bad, for the consumer.

Early labels indicated the name of the negotiant (merchant or dealer), sometimes the name of the chateau or winery, the contents, and, in some instances, an address. When we were filming in Bordeaux we were shown one of the first bottle-labeled wines from Chateau Kirwan in the Margaux region. At the bottom of the label were the name, address, and phone number of the wine negotiant in Amsterdam. The phone number was "3"! Needless to say, they don't do that anymore.

Labels have moved from being mundane to highly creative and artistic. Baron Philippe de Rothschild has been credited as one of the first vintners to feature the work of an artist on wine labels. Over the years vintners have increasingly used art to reflect the essence of the wine in the bottle. While there are many winemakers doing this, Magnotta Winery seems to be the most prolific. Virtually all of their wine labels and even their beer labels are decorated with original works of art. The walls in their main winery are akin to a mini art gallery.

Walter Schmoranz at Pelee Island Winery adopts various flora and fauna from the region to adorn the labels of his wines. His Gewurztraminer is signified by a yellow Prickly Pear Cactus, and it is not unusual for his repeat customers to ask for the wine "with the yellow flower on it," as opposed to asking for it by its varietal name. They know the wine. They enjoy the wine, but they don't want to fuss with trying to pronounce Gewurztraminer (guh-VURTS-trah-mee-ner). An impressionable label can make the world of difference for vintners and consumers.

Unfortunately, a label is no guarantee of what you will find in the bottle. It provides the basic information you need in making your decision. It will help you to remember the wine if you want to buy it again or recommend it to your friends. The label will often be your visual reference, and that's important to everyone concerned, for better or worse.

The laws of the region where the wine is made or the laws of the land in which it's being sold often guide basic front-label information. The back labels are used to give the consumer some indication of the wine's flavor attributes and possible suggestions on matching with foods. Assuming the label will tell you the volume and alcohol content, what else might a label tell you?

What kind of wine it is.

The center of a label's attention is usually dedicated to the contents and the producer. In new-world wines the varietal (e.g., a Merlot, Chardonnay, Pinot Grigio, Gamay) is one of the first things you'll note. If you are a lover of a particular varietal wine, your search is made easy by the label. That would be more difficult in old-world wines that are identified under a chateau or villa name, although even old-world wineries are beginning to identify their wines by the varietal.

It will also be indicated if it's a blend of some kind. You can assume that a Cabernet-Merlot blend will deliver something less aggressive than a Cabernet Sauvignon but a little more aggressive than the softer Merlot. If you aren't fond of tannins—that dry puckering, astringent feel—you'll probably lean towards Merlot. However, if your mate likes the big, full-bodied tannic Cabernet Sauvignon, a Cabernet-Merlot blend can offer both of you an enjoyable compromise.

The producer.

The name of the producer is usually front and center. It could be a family name or a winery name. Inniskillin is a heritage name from a military brigade. Jackson-Triggs is the name of the two men (Allan Jackson and Donald Triggs) who founded the winery. Reif reflects thirteen generations of winemaking, while the Kittling Ridge location is a viewpoint from which to observe migrating hawks that "kittle" or float on thermal air currents. Some names can be dedicated to the land from which they get their grapes or to the view from the winery doorstep.

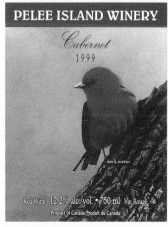

Increasingly you will find Ontario wineries also noting a specific vineyard designation on some of their premium quality wines. Where growers have provided a winery with exceptional grapes year after year, a winemaker may celebrate this quality by attributing the contents to the specific vineyard. Vineyard designation can be an important footnote, implying consistent or higher quality, good grower/winemaker relationships, and unique flavors and taste characteristics found only in that particular vineyard.

The place of origin.

Most wine regions in the world have their own quality standard associations, some legislated by law, others managed by regional representatives. Near the bottom of every label you should find a reference to the region or appellation where the grapes were grown and the wine was made. Identifying the region and the authority under which the wine was produced is the consumer's assurance of quality and certain standards.

For the purist, it is important to note that not all Ontario wines are made exclusively from Ontario-grown grapes. Ontario doesn't grow enough grapes to satisfy the wine market. Government regulations allow winemakers to blend up to 75% of their wines with foreign grapes or juice. Magnotta was one of the earliest wineries to promote its international series of wines, made by blending grapes and juices sourced from all over the world.

Ontario's appellation control is handled by the Vintners Quality Alliance. The VQA symbol on the wine indicates strict standards and an assurance that the grapes for the wine were grown and processed in Ontario. Any Ontario wine that doesn't have the VQA symbol can contain up to 75% of its juice from anywhere in the world.

The date of harvest, or vintage.

A generic or brand-name wine may not have a vintage designation because these types of ordinary table wines are made to taste the same year after year. They are made with various grapes from any number of locations, and are produced as inexpensive and consistently flavored wines.

Vintage wines are simply those that indicate the year the grapes were harvested. Winemaking standards are so refined that it is difficult to find a truly bad vintage wine, although there are lesser years or better years in which winemakers define a good, better, and best vintage. Cork-dorks and wine enthusiasts are guided by the declaration of a good or poor vintage year.

Special descriptors.

You will eventually come to those wines graced with more honorable adjectives, such as "Family Reserve," "Proprietor's Reserve," "Select Harvest," and "Limited Release"—these phrases and words suggest superior quality and are often accompanied by a higher price tag. This can be a mug's game. Honorable vintners will use these special terms when they truly have something exciting and limited that is worthy of a higher price. However, there are also those who exploit the term for its marketing values.

When Klaus Reif introduced the term "Reserve" to table guest and comedian Red Green, he implied that the wine was special and held back for unique attention. Red immediately jumped in and asked, "Reserved for a higher price?" There is some truth to Red's observation.

Grapes that express some unique and exceptional characteristics but are limited in volume offer winemakers an opportunity to create something special. Whenever the vintner or winemaker has such an opportunity they "reserve" this limited batch and treat it accordingly. It could involve special fermentation or extended oak treatment or longer barrel aging before bottling, all of which could enhance the quality and usually elevate the price.

Wine shop personnel can offer help when you are attempting to translate price and value relationship between the label and the contents. Our only advice is to take some initiative in trying new wines as frequently as possible, even if you buy a specific bottle because of a sexy label. Sticking with the same old wine all the time limits the opportunity to experience new tastes and discover new finds. One method is to experiment in the price range, first trying a range of wines under $10. When you've meddled with this formula, splurge on a $15 or $20 bottle once in a while. Your palate will signal the wisdom of your purchase!

PELEE ISLAND WINERY

2000

MERLOT

12.2% alc./vol.   750 ml
Red Wine / Vin Rouge
Cellared by Pelee Island Winery, Kingsville, On., Canada
from imported and domestic wines

PELEE ISLAND WINERY

1999

TRIO BLANC
VQA Ontario VQA

12.3% alc./vol.   750 ml
White Wine / Vin Blanc
Product of Canada / Produit du Canada

The Cabernet Brothers

Cabernet Franc—KA-behr-nay Frahn (Frahngk)

This is a wine to watch out for. It likes Ontario, and winemakers are producing some wonderfully luscious Cabernet Franc wines.

Most of the international wine talk is directed at the well-known and well-respected Cabernet Sauvignon—often referred to as the "king" of the red grapes. The Cab-Sauvignon has long been the predominant grape in the famous chateau-labeled Bordeaux blended wines. Little brother "Franc" is used to a lesser degree in those blends to soften the body and help enhance the flavor profile where needed. The Bordeaux winemakers have traditionally used the earlier-ripening Franc to salvage vintages that have been unkind to the later-ripening Cabernet Sauvignon.

Cabernet Franc is not as aggressive or herbaceous as big brother Sauvignon but can be more aromatic. While similar in flavor and structure, the Franc has less tannin, less acid, and, theoretically, less ageability. In the Medoc and Graves region of Bordeaux, Franc is the minor player in the blend. It is, however, more prominent in the blends from the Pomerol and St. Emilion regions, which ironically tend to produce some of the most expensive Bordeaux wines.

Cabernet Franc does quite well in cooler climates, and Ontario seems to favor it as a single varietal wine, although it can also be blended with other varietals. Where Cabernet Franc is viewed as the lighter-weight, less flavorful brother to the Cabernet Sauvignon, Ontario has been producing some noteworthy Francs with considerable body, flavor profiles, and complexities achieved through oak influences. Some have dared to call it *the* up-and-coming red wine of the region.

"They" say all wine drinkers eventually move to red wines because reds are more complex than whites

A near-perfect cluster of the early-ripening Cabernet Franc grapes

Depending on the vintage a Cabernet Franc can offer profiles of blackberries, currants, cranberry, and green pepper—to name a few. The Loire valley turns Cabernet Franc into a specialty wine and in some French Cabernet Francs you might hear about a desired scent of potato peelings! Cabernet Franc is widely planted and has several aliases, including Bordo, Bouchet, Brenton, Carmenet, and Trouchet Noir. It is certainly a grape to watch for in Ontario and well worth exploring on its own terms.

Cabernet Sauvignon—Ka-behr-nay Soh-vihn-YOHN (soh-vee-NYAWN)

What can you say about the king that hasn't already been said? It's bigger than Franc on all fronts and is possibly the most popular planted red grape in the world. However, things change, and other reds are gaining favor with the public, especially Shiraz, Merlot, and some remarkable Zinfandels coming out of California.

Cabernet Sauvignon's solid flavor structure, complexity, and ageability have made it popular and very much the standard upon which other reds are judged. When grown in hot growing conditions it produces big jammy flavors. It has big tannins and acids, which are imperative in the making of top-quality wines that will age well and develop even more complexities in the bottle.

Cabernet Sauvignon is often described as having a taste of black and red fruits, cherry, black cherry, cassis, raspberry, bell pepper, and, in the older vintages, the desirable traits of tobacco and leather. Other names for Cabernet Sauvignon include Bouche, Bouchet, Petit-Cabernet, Sauvignon Rouge, and Vidure.

New-world wines are usually released by their varietal names but new-world winemakers are also drawn to the art of blending. Blending—or *assemblage,* as the French call it (they have a lovely name for everything)—has its most notable roots in Bordeaux, where the famous chateaux-labeled wines sell for exorbitant amounts of money. Some vineyards are actually planted with the various varietals in proportion to how they will eventually be blended together. In North America, Bordeaux-style blended wines are usually identified as "meritage" (meri-tidge, not meri-taj). Blending is considered a serious art and is done primarily to improve the quality of finished wine. It can produce remarkable results, and you can even try it at home.

Cabernet Sauvignon grapes take longer to ripen than Cabernet Franc

Take two or three different red wines (you could probably do it with whites too) and taste them individually. Identify the attributes of each—lighter, fruitier, drier, fuller, more tannic and astringent, etc.—and mix them in various proportions, working towards the profile you prefer. It's surprising how you can create your own blend. This can be a valuable exercise when you have one wine that's lacking and another that's well endowed. However, it can also diminish the excellent values of a better wine so don't get too carried away. We suggest doing it in small measures until you find the best ratio.

While you can try blending any red wine, the most commonly used in a blend are Cabernet Sauvignon, Cabernet Franc, Merlot, Petit Verdot, and Malbec. In Ontario, you'll find all kinds of blends, including Cabernet and Merlot, and unusual ones like Gamay and Zweigelt. It's the new world!

Colio Estate Wines

Colio Estate Wines

The Pride of Lake Erie North Shore

Carbon dioxide is created naturally when yeast converts sugar into alcohol. Wine becomes sparkling when fermented in a closed container, such as a tank or bottle, trapping the carbon dioxide.

Colio Estates is located in Essex County in Ontario, a viticultural area designated as Lake Erie North Shore. With a southern exposure to Lake Erie, the area offers the longest growing season in Canada with optimum microclimatic and soil conditions for growing premium vinifera and hybrid grapes.

In the late nineteenth century Essex County was the sight of the largest commercial vineyards in the country. Established in 1980, Colio became the first winery to reestablish in Essex County after prohibition. When it opened with a 600,000 liter capacity in the town of Harrow, the winery initially had twelve employees.

Today, the 34,000 square foot operation produces VQA wines from its own 240 acres and from growers in other designated VQA regions in Ontario. The winery has a current capacity of 2,100,000 liters with a crushing facility, a unique barrel cellar aging room, a full-service lab, tasting suite, a retail boutique, and an outside pavilion for local events. Colio now employs more than 100 and produces 198,000 cases annually.

Colio welcomes visitors who can take a twenty-minute tour of the production process in the winery followed by a wine tasting.

The winery produces VQA wines from vinifera varietals that include (white wines) Chardonnay, Riesling, Gewurztraminer, Sauvignon Blanc; (red wines) Cabernet Franc, Merlot, Pinot Noir, Cabernet Sauvignon.

The winery produces a selection of products—including Colio's internationally recognized icewine—under the following brands: Colio Estate Vineyards—estate-grown prestige VQA varietals; Harrow Estates—premium vinifera and hybrid VQA varietals; Oak Aged Classic—varietal blends of superior character and value; Colio Estate Wines—popular premium house blends.

As one of the largest boutique wineries, Colio has enjoyed significant success while accumulating more than 200 awards for its products, including Winery of the Year Award, VQA Award of Excellence, and LCBO Supplier of the Year Award.

Colio wines can be purchased at thirteen stores across the province of Ontario, at their local winery shop, in LCBO stores, and in other provinces including Alberta, Saskatchewan, Manitoba, New Brunswick, and Nova Scotia. Products are exported to the United States, China, Taiwan, Korea, Germany, Great Britain, Switzerland, Greenland, and Trinidad.

Carlo Negri: The Man from Trentino

Like many of his peers, master winemaker Carlo Negri uses the cumulative experience of thousands of years of winemaking. Born in the Trentino/Alto-Adige region in Northern Italy, Carlo was never far from historic vineyards and the traditions of winemaking. As a young man he decided that enology was a career he passionately wanted to pursue.

Wanting a formal education, Carlo was determined to overcome the financial hurdles imposed by coming from a poor family. With the support of scholarships from the province of Trento, Carlo attended the Instituto Agrario Provinciale di San Michele a/A. He made the right career choice.

Winemaker Carlo Negri in Colio Estate vineyards, Lake Erie North Shore

ASPARAGUS RISOTTO

from Carlo Negri,
Colio Estate Wines

Serves 4

1 medium onion, finely chopped
4 tbsp (60 ml) butter or olive oil
1 lb (500 g) asparagus
1½ cups (375 ml) Arborio rice
2 cups (500 ml) broth
½ cup (125 ml) dry white wine
1 tsp (5 ml) salt
½ cup (125 ml) grated parmigiano reggiano or grana padano cheese
water to cover asparagus

Cut asparagus into 1-in (2.5-cm) pieces. Boil asparagus for 5 minutes in salted water.

Sauté onions in butter or olive oil until golden color. Add dry rice to sautéed onions, stirring with a wooden spoon for approximately 2 minutes.

Add the asparagus with boiling water to the rice. As soon as the rice has absorbed the liquid, add the wine and gradually add hot broth while continuing to stir. Do not let the rice become too dry. Cook until al dente (approximately 12 to 15 minutes at medium heat). Do not overcook.

At the very end of cooking time, add grated cheese and stir well. After tasting, season with additional salt if required.

Serve immediately (best enjoyed hot). Cheese lovers, feel free to add more cheese.

Note: One beef bouillon cube with boiling water can substitute for homemade broth.

WINE MATCH
Colio Chardonnay

Grapes are best when their sugar and acid levels are in balance

Upon graduating from the Institute as a winemaker, Carlo worked for two years in his native province of Trento before becoming a master winemaker for a major winery, Collavini, located in Friuli. Over the next fifteen years Carlo gained a reputation for his quality wines at Collavini. He soon became a member of the distinguished wine-testing organization Ordine Nazionale degli Assaggiatori di Vino in Asti, Italy.

By the late 1970s Carlo was well established in the wine industry in Friuli, but he had no inkling that he was about to be courted for a new posting. Fantinel, a Friuli winery owner who had co-partnered with some Canadian businessmen, was in charge of providing equipment and technical expertise for the establishment of a new winery. Under the recommendation of Fantinel, they asked Carlo if he would start a new tradition of winemaking in the southwestern Ontario region now known as Lake Erie North Shore. Carlo's knowledge of North American wine regions was limited to California. He had no idea that Canada even had a winemaking region. It was a big decision.

In 1980, at the age of 38, after fifteen years with Collavini and unable to speak any English, Carlo left for Canada to establish what would become known as Colio Estate Winery in Harrow, Ontario.

Jonathan in the vineyard with winemaker Carlo Negri...

...and in the barrel room with Carlo Negri

Carlo became a vital member of the wine industry in its efforts to raise the bar of quality and excellence for Ontario wines. With over twenty years of dedication to Colio and an impressive list of international awards, Carlo has helped to establish the designated viticultural area of Lake Erie North Shore as a world-class wine-producing region. Salute!

Spumante, the Italian word for sparkling wine, comes from the verb **spumare,** *which means to foam or froth. The most famous Spumante, Asti Spumante, produces 80 million bottles in an average year.*

Other Wineries in the Pelee/Erie North Shore Area

LeBlanc Estate Winery

North of the small farming community of Harrow, LeBlanc Estate Winery is located in a picturesque setting near the shores of Lake Erie. Winemaker Lyse LeBlanc provides individual care and attention in producing small quantities of award-winning wines. Wines include (white wines) Vidal, Pinot Blanc, Chardonnay, and Pinot Gris; (red wines) Pinot Noir, Cabernet Franc. Individual tours and tastings are available from Tuesday through Sunday. Tours for groups of ten or more may be booked in advance. LeBlanc Estate Winery also holds a number of special events "under the tent" in the summer.

D'Angelo Estate Winery

In 1979 Salvatore D'Angelo began his search for land on which to plant his vineyard. He settled on fifty acres in the heart of Essex County—in an area designated as Lake Erie North Shore—and located just south of Windsor, Ontario. The first year he planted one acre. Today he has forty-two acres of planted vines, which include such varietals as Cabernet Franc, Marechal Foch, Pinot Noir, Vidal, Chardonnay, Sangiovese, and Merlot.

On the tenth anniversary of D'Angelo's Estates, Sal won the prestigious award of Grape King, signifying his expert skills in the vineyard. He is particularly proud of his Vidal Icewine and Old Vines Foch Reserve.

D'Angelo Winery produces 100% estate-grown red, white, and dessert wines. The winery produces up to 5,000 cases of wine per year. Using both French and American oak barrels, D'Angelo has forty-six barrels with almost 10,000 liters of wine in oak at one time.

Sal D'Angelo has won about sixty awards for his wines, including a double gold medal at the Great Lakes Wine Competition. His Marechal Foch has been rated in the top 100 wines in Canada.

The winery is open year round for tours and tastings of fine wines. Groups are asked to call ahead. Every summer the winery hosts events including an annual open house featuring Art in the Vineyard and a barbecue.

Meadow Lane Winery

FAST FACTS

R.R. #3, St. Thomas, Ontario
Tel: 519-633-1993
E-mail:
wines@meadowlanewinery.com
Web: www.meadowlanewinery.com

Meadow Lane Winery, located near St. Thomas, produces mainly fruit wines

Quai Du Vin Winery

FAST FACTS

45811 Fruitridge Line
R.R. #5, St. Thomas, Ontario
N5P 3S9
Tel: 519-775-2216
E-mail: info@quaiduvin.com
Web: www.quaiduvin.com

Quai Du Vin Winery, located near St. Thomas, opened its doors in 1990

Bellamere Country Winery

FAST FACTS

1260 Gainsborough Road
London, Ontario
N6H 5K8
Tel: 519-473-2273
E-mail: farm@bellamere.com
Web: www.bellamere.com

Established in 1998, the Bellamere Winery is an impressive timber-frame structure built of Douglas fir and pine. Ceilings reach thirty-eight feet, and streams of light pass through the skylight to cast warm shadows against the thick winery walls graced with real sheaves of grain.

The winery houses the production facilities, a retail shop, and a banquet hall. Bellamere winemaker Jim Patience is in charge of producing wines from classic varietals including Baco Noir and Chardonnay and fruit wines that range dramatically in style and sweetness, from the depth and complexity of full-bodied Blackberry Wine to the sweetness of icewines.

Bellamere has won more than twenty national and international awards for its innovative wines, including medals for its Apple and Raspberry Ice, Baco Noir, Baked Apple, Blueberry, Strawberry Champagne, and Kindred Spirit Port.

Visitors to the winery can tour the production facilities then taste their award-winning wines complemented with a selection of cheeses, fresh fruit, and crackers. During the summer and fall seasons they can also ride on the Fruit

Bellamere Winery located in London, Ontario

Blossom Express, a replica of an 1865 steam engine train that makes several daily trips around the farm and vineyard. Visitors can also shop at the Bellamere Country Market, a full-scale farm market store with a butcher shop, bakery, tearoom, farm fresh produce area, and gift shop.

Stainless steel vats are inert and won't influence the wine in any way

PASTA WITH SCALLOPS AND SWEET PEPPERS IN CREAM SAUCE

from Bellamere Winery

—

Serves 4

1 lb (500 g) linguine or fettuccini
2 tbsp (30 ml) olive oil
2 garlic cloves, crushed
1 lb (500 g) scallops, halved
    horizontally
1 medium red or yellow pepper,
    julienned
salt and pepper
2 tbsp (30 ml) fresh basil, chopped
½ cup (125 ml) Bellamere Winery
    Saveur Blanc

SAUCE
⅓ cup (75 ml) butter
⅔ cup (150 ml) 35% cream
4 tbsp (60 ml) parmesan, grated

Combine the olive oil and garlic in a nonstick frying pan and cook until just sizzling or about 30 seconds. Add the scallops and ½ tsp (2ml) of salt and cook over high heat, tossing until the scallops are just cooked through, about 3 minutes. Remove scallops and set aside.

Cook pepper over medium heat until just tender, adding more oil if necessary. Salt and pepper to taste. Add the wine and half of the basil and bring to a boil over high heat. Whisk in butter. When melted add cream and parmesan. Simmer until sauce bubbles and thickens.

Return scallops to pan and add remaining basil. Simmer for additional 1½ to 2 minutes.

Add sauce to drained al dente pasta and toss. Sprinkle with additional cheese and serve immediately.

WINE MATCH
Bellamere Winery Saveur Blanc

Contact Information

Ball's Falls and Conservation Area
c/o Niagara Peninsula Conservation
Authority
250 Thorold Road West, 3rd Floor
Welland, Ontario L3C 3W2
Tel: 905-788-3135
Web: www.conservation-niagara.on.ca

**The Good Earth Cooking School and Food
Co.**
4556 Lincoln Avenue
Beamsville, Ontario L0R 1B3
Tel: 905-563-7856; 800-308-5124
Fax: 905-563-9143
Web: www.goodearthcooking.com

Jordan Historical Museum
3802 Main Street
Jordan, Ontario L0R 1S0
Tel: 905-562-5242
Fax: 905-562-7786
E-mail: jhmtchin@vaxxine.com
Web: www.tourismniagara.com/
jordanmuseum

Kurtz Orchards
16006 Niagara Parkway
Niagara-on-the-Lake, Ontario L0S 1J0
Tel: 905-468-2937
Fax: 905-468-7479
Web: www.kurtzorchards.com

Mackenzie Heritage Printery Museum
1 Queenston Street
Queenston, Ontario L0S 1J0
Tel: 905-262-5676
Web: www.niagaraparks.com
(under Attractions, Heritage Sites)

The McMichael Gallery
10365 Islington Avenue
Kleinburg, Ontario L0J 1C0
Tel: 905-893-1121; 888-213-1121
Fax: 905-893-0692
Web: www.mcmichael.com

Niagara Culinary Institute
5881 Dunn Street
Niagara Falls, Ontario L2G 2N9
Tel: 905-735-2211

Niagara Grape and Wine Festival
8 Church Street, Suite 100
St. Catharines, Ontario L2R 3B3
Tel: 905-688-0212
Fax: 905-688-2570
Web: www.grapeandwine.com

Niagara Parks Butterfly Conservatory
Niagara Parkway
Niagara Falls, Ontario
Tel: 905-371-0254 or 1-877-642-7275
Web: www.niagaraparks.com
(under Attractions, Horticulture)

Niagara Parks Commission
7400 Portage Road South
Niagara Falls, Ontario L2E 6X8
Tel: 905-356-2241
Fax: 905-356-9237
Web: www.niagaraparks.com

Old Fort Erie
350 Lakeshore Road
Fort Erie, Ontario
Tel: 905-371-0245; 877-642-7275
Web: www.niagaraparks.com

Pelee Island Pheasant Hunt
See Web: www.pelee.com

Point Pelee National Park
R.R. #1
Leamington, Ontario N8H 3V4
Tel: 519-322-2365
Fax: 519-322-1277
Web: http://parkscanada.pch.gc.ca/parks/
ontario/point_pelee/point_pelee_e.htm

St. Catharines Museum
1932 Government Road at Lock 3 of
Welland Canal
P.O. Box 3012
St. Catharines, Ontario L2R 7C2
Tel: 905-984-8880; 800-305-5134
Fax: 905-984-6910
E-mail: muslk3@niagara.com

Laura Secord Homestead
P.O. Box 1812
29 Queenston Street
Queenston, Ontario L0S 1L0
Tel: 905-468-3322
Book tours in advance by calling 905-684-1227

Recipe Index

TAKE YOUR
Time

...*Savour*

ONTARIO'S FINEST INNS

Taste the wines and cuisine of Ontario
at twenty-eight outstanding properties

Innkeepers
OF ONTARIO

ontariosfinestinns.com
800-340-INNS (4667)

We invite you to Visit our Estate Winery and Experience our Award-Winning VQA Icewines, Premium & Fruit Wines.

OPEN DAILY - Free Winery Tours
May - October 10 am to 7 pm
November - April 10 am to 6 pm
Friendly Hospitality Awaits You!

JOSEPH'S ESTATE WINES
1811 Niagara Stone Rd., Hwy. 55, Niagara-on-the-Lake
Tel: **905-468-1259** Fax **905-468-9242**
Toll Free **1-866-468-1259**

www.josephsestatewines.com

the heart of niagara wine country

From early spring to late fall, St. Catharines is surrounded by blossoming orchards, stately vineyards, rose gardens, nurseries, century-old farms, farmers' markets and roadside fruit stands.

St. Catharines was the home of the oldest winery in Canada, Barnes Wines, founded in 1873. Today, the city lies at the heart of Niagara wine country. Visit St. Catharines' own wineries as you make your way along the Ontario Wine Route for a hands-on experience, vineyard tours and special tastings and events throughout the year.

To receive visitor information on St. Catharines, please call 905-688-5601 ext. 1722 or e-mail tourism@city.stcatharines.on.ca

www.st.catharines.com

Niagara Grape & Wine Festival

Join our Wine Country Celebration of Niagara's internationally acclaimed grape and wine industry the last two weeks of September. Over 100 events including fine wine tastings, winery tours and tastings, concerts, regional cuisine, artisan shows, wine seminars, family entertainment and one of Canada's largest parades. Selected as Ontario's Cultural Event of the Year

NIAGARA GRAPE & WINE FESTIVAL and One of North America's Top 100 Events.

Call 905-688-0212 or visit www.grapeandwine.com.